W9-DHU-110

Adirondack Community College Library

DISCARDED

Prehistoric BRITAIN and IRELAND

In Memoriam
Terence Powell

J. Forde-Johnston

Prehistoric BRITAIN and IRELAND

W. W. Norton & Company Inc.

New York

First American Edition 1976

Copyright © J. Forde-Johnston, 1976

35693

Printed in Great Britain

ISBN 0-393-05605-8   76-20287

Contents

	Acknowledgments	6
	List of Illustrations in the text	7
	List of Plates	9
1	Man the Builder	11
2	Ancient Houses and Settlements	29
3	The Windmill Hill People	61
4	Megalithic Tombs	81
5	Ceremonial Sites	105
6	Barrows and Graves	131
7	Circles and Standing Stones	149
8	Hillforts and Ramparts	164
9	Fortifications of the Far North	187
	Bibliography	201
	Index	205

Acknowledgments

The author wishes to thank the following for permission to use their photographs: Trustees of British Museum, Plate 1; National Museum of Antiquities of Scotland, Plate 2; Stanley Thomas, University of Leicester, Plates 3, 4; Department of the Environment, Plates 5, 6, 11, 13, 14, 15, 17, 18, 21, 23, 24, 25, 42, 43, 44, 45, 46, 47; Professor M. J. O'Kelly, University College, Cork, Plate 7; Cambridge University Collection: copyright reserved, Plates 8, 12, 16, 35, 36, 37; Denis Harding, University of Durham, Plate 9; London Museum, Plates 10, 29; Office of Public Works, Dublin, Plates 19, 20; Society of Antiquaries, London, Plate 22; Professor R. J. C. Atkinson, University College, Cardiff, and Hamish Hamilton Ltd, Plate 26; Ashmolean Museum, Plate 27; National Museum of Wales, Plates 28, 38; Plates 30, 31, 32 reproduced from *Prehistoric Dartmoor* by Paul Pettit.

The author also wishes to thank the following for permission to use their line illustrations: Cambridge University Press, Figs. 2, 21, 26, 29; Trustees of British Museum, Figs. 3, 4, 5, 6, 7; Leicester University Press (from D. D. A. Simpson (ed.) *Economy and Settlement in Neolithic and Early Bronze Age Britain and Europe*) and The Irish Academy, Figs. 8, 12; Thomas Nelson & Sons Ltd, Figs. 9, 10, 11; Brighton and Hove Archaeological Society and the Prehistoric Society, Fig. 13; Department of the Environment, Figs. 14, 18, 69, 71, 72; Prehistoric Society, Figs. 15, 19; Society of Antiquaries, Fig. 16; Fig. 20 after S. Piggott, *Neolithic Cultures of the British Isles* (Cambridge University Press, 1954) Fig. 1; Figs. 22, 23, 24 reproduced from *The Earthen Long Barrow in Britain* by Paul Ashbee (J. M. Dent & Sons Ltd); Methuen & Co. Ltd, Figs. 25, 46, 47, 55; Liverpool University Press, Figs. 27, 28; Audrey Henshall and Edinburgh University Press, Figs. 30, 31; B. T. Batsford Ltd, Figs. 32, 34, 35, 36; Mrs Claire O'Kelley (from *Illustrated Guide to New Grange*, 1971 ed.), Fig. 33; Professor J. G. D. Clark and the Prehistoric Society, Figs. 37, 38, 39, 40; Fig. 41 reproduced from *Windmill Hill and Avebury: Excavations by Alexander Keiller* by Isobel Smith (Clarendon Press, Oxford, 1965); Dr G. J. Wainwright and the Society of Antiquaries, London, Figs. 42, 43, 44; Dr G. J. Wainwright and the editor, *Current Archaeology*, Fig. 45; Figs. 48, 49, 52, 53 reproduced from *The Bronze Age Round Barrow in Britain* by Paul Ashbee (J. M. Dent & Sons Ltd); Fig. 51 reproduced from *Life and Death in the Bronze Age* by Sir Cyril Fox (Routledge & Kegan Paul Ltd, 1959); Scottish Archaeological Forum, Glasgow, Fig. 54; Figs. 56, 57, 59 reproduced from *Megalithic Sites in Britain* by Alexander Thom (Clarendon Press, Oxford, 1967); Royal Commission on Ancient Monuments, Scotland, Fig. 58; R. W. Feachem and Edinburgh University Press, Figs. 63, 64; G. Jobey and Edinburgh University Press, Fig. 65; Edinburgh University Press, Fig. 70.

List of Illustrations in the text

Fig. 1 Map showing the two major routes along which influence was diffused from the ancient Near East through prehistoric Europe.

Fig. 2 Stone and flint axes, arrowheads, etc. and pottery of the Windmill Hill people.

Fig. 3 Tanged-and-barbed flint arrowheads and stone battle-axes of the Early Bronze Age.

Fig. 4 Bronze Age axes.

Fig. 5 Bronze rapiers and bronze leaf-shaped swords, bronze chapes (for scabbards) and bronze shields.

Fig. 6 Late Bronze Age equipment.

Fig. 7 Iron Age swords and scabbards decorated in La Tène style.

Fig. 8 Neolithic houses: A, Mount Pleasant, Glamorganshire; B, Ronaldsway, Isle of Man; C, Site A, Lough Gur, Ireland.

Fig. 9 Plan of Skara Brae, Orkneys.

Fig. 10 Plan of the Benie Hoose, Shetland.

Fig. 11 Neolithic houses in the Shetlands.

Fig. 12 Early Bronze Age houses: A, Gwithian, Cornwall; B, Northton, Outer Hebrides.

Fig. 13 Reconstruction drawing of the Itford settlement, Sussex.

Fig. 14 Late Bronze Age (black) and Iron Age (black & white) settlements at Jarlshof, Shetlands.

Fig. 15 Plan and elevation of the Iron Age house at Little Woodbury, Wiltshire.

Fig. 16 Plan of Glastonbury settlement; plan and section of hut 74.

Fig. 17 Plan of the Iron Age village of Chysauster, Cornwall.

Fig. 18 Plan of the broch courtyard, the aisled house (A), and the wheelhouses (W1–3) at Jarlshof, Shetlands.

Fig. 19 Plan of the aisled round house at Clettraval, Outer Hebrides.

Fig. 20 Map of southern Britain showing the area occupied by the Windmill Hill people.

Fig. 21 Plans of causewayed enclosures in Wessex.

Fig. 22 Plans of earthen long barrows in the north.

Fig. 23 Isometric reconstruction of the mortuary house of the Fussell's Lodge long barrow, Wiltshire.

Fig. 24 Reconstruction drawing of the Fussell's Lodge long barrow, Wiltshire.

Fig. 25 Plan of the Dorset cursus.

Fig. 26 Plan of a flint mine (Pit No. 2), Grime's Graves, Norfolk.

Fig. 27 Plans and elevations of two Passage Graves in Anglesey.

Fig. 28 Plans of Cotswold-Severn megalithic tombs.

Fig. 29 Plan and sections of the Clyde-type megalithic tomb at Carn Ban, Arran.

Fig. 30 Plans of megalithic tombs in N.E. Scotland: A, Camster Round; B, Balnuaran of Clava; C, Camster Long.

Fig. 31 Plans and sections of megalithic tombs in the Orkneys.

Fig. 32 Plan and section of the cruciform internal structure at the Passage Grave of New Grange, Ireland.

Fig. 33 Passage Graves of the Boyne culture (plans): A, Loughcrew; B, Carrowkeel; C, Carrowmore.

Fig. 34 Plans of Court cairns in Ireland.

Fig. 35   Plans of Wedge-shaped tombs and Portal Dolmens in Ireland.

Fig. 36   Reconstruction drawing of a Wedge-shaped tomb in Ireland.

Fig. 37   Plan of the henge monument at Arbor Low, Derbyshire.

Fig. 38   Plan of the henge monument at Mayburgh, Westmorland.

Fig. 39   Plans of henge monuments in the Orkneys.

Fig. 40   Plan of the Arminghall henge monument, Norfolk.

Fig. 41   Map of the Avebury area, showing the Avebury henge monument, the West Kennet Avenue and The Sanctuary.

Fig. 42   Plans of the four large henge monuments in Wessex.

Fig. 43   Plan, section and drawn reconstruction of the Southern Circle at Durrington Walls, Wiltshire.

Fig. 44   Plan of Woodhenge, Wiltshire.

Fig. 45   Plan of the timber structure at Mount Pleasant henge monument, Dorset.

Fig. 46   Plan of the stone structures at Stonehenge, Wiltshire.

Fig. 47   Types of Bronze Age barrow.

Fig. 48   Map of the Stonehenge area showing the principal Bronze Age barrow cemeteries.

Fig. 49   Plans of two Beaker barrows, with flexed inhumation burials.

Fig. 50   Plan and sections of the Bronze Age burial mound at Dudsbury, Dorset.

Fig. 51   Stone cist in the Bronze Age burial mound at Corston Beacon, Pembrokeshire.

Fig. 52   Plan and section of the mortuary house in a Bronze Age barrow at Beaulieu, Hampshire.

Fig. 53   Plans of timber circles under Bronze Age burial mounds.

Fig. 54   Plans of ring-cairns.

Fig. 55   Plan of the stone circles at Stanton Drew, Somerset.

Fig. 56   Plan of the Stannon (flattened) circle at Dinnever Hill, Cornwall.

Fig. 57   Plan of Long Meg and her Daughters, Cumberland.

Fig. 58   Plan and oblique view of the stone circle and alignments at Callanish, Outer Hebrides.

Fig. 59   Recumbent stone circle and ring-cairn at Aquorthies, Kingausie, Kincardineshire.

Fig. 60   Diagrammatic plans of the eleven types of Iron Age fort.

Fig. 61   Plan of the Iron Age fort of Caer Caradoc, Clun, Shropshire.

Fig. 62   Plan of the Iron Age concentric fort of Tregeare Rounds, Cornwall.

Fig. 63   Plan of the Iron Age fort at Carman, Dumbartonshire.

Fig. 64   Plan and sections of the Iron Age fort on Eildon Hill North, Roxburghshire.

Fig. 65   Plan and section of the Iron Age fort at Yevering Bell, Northumberland.

Fig. 66   Iron Age ramparts: (a) simple glacis; (b) glacis with back revetment; (c) hybrid glacis/revetted rampart.

Fig. 67   Iron Age ramparts: (a) timber-revetted, wedge-shaped; (b) stone-revetted, wedge-shaped; (c) stepped rampart; (d) timber-revetted box rampart; (e) stone-revetted box rampart.

Fig. 68   Iron Age fort entrances.

Fig. 69   Plan of the Iron Age fort and broch at Clickhimin, Shetlands.

Fig. 70   Drawn reconstruction of the Iron Age fort and blockhouse at Clickhimin, Shetlands.

Fig. 71   Plan, sections and elevations of the blockhouse at Clickhimin, Shetlands.

Fig. 72   Suggested structural relationship between Iron Age forts, duns and brochs.

List of Plates

1 Early Bronze Age Beaker pottery.

2 Late Bronze Age cauldron.

3 Iron Age pottery.

4 Iron Age weaving equipment: loom-weights, spindle-whorls, bobbins and weaving combs.

5 General view of the Neolithic settlement at Skara Brae, Orkneys.

6 Hut No. 7, Skara Brae, Orkneys.

7 Model of the Early Bronze Age farmstead at Carrigillihy, Co. Cork.

8 Enclosed settlement of Rider's Rings, Dartmoor, Devon.

9 Post-holes of the Iron Age house at Pimperne, Dorset.

10 Reconstruction drawing of the Iron Age settlement at Heathrow, Middlesex, by Alan Sorrell.

11 Oblique aerial view of the Iron Age village at Chysauster, Cornwall.

12 Oblique aerial view of the bank barrow at Long Bredy, Dorset.

13 Neolithic flint mine at Grime's Graves, Norfolk: entrance to galleries in Pit 1.

14 Entrance to the circular Passage Grave of Bryn Celli Ddu, Anglesey.

15 Interior view of the West Kennet long barrow.

16 Oblique aerial view of the Maes Howe megalithic tomb, Orkneys.

17 Maes Howe megalithic tomb, view along entrance passage towards exterior.

18 Interior of the Midhowe stalled cairn, Orkneys.

19 General view of the Knowth Passage Grave, Co. Meath, during excavation.

20 Decorated stone basin in the Knowth Passage Grave, Co. Meath.

21 Trethevy Quoit dolmen, Cornwall.

22 The ditch at Avebury henge monument, Wiltshire, during excavation.

23 Oblique aerial view of the Arbor Low henge monument, Derbyshire.

24 Ring of Brodgar henge monument, Orkneys.

25 Oblique aerial view of Avebury henge monument, Wiltshire.

26 The Sarsen Circle and a trilithon at Stonehenge, Wiltshire.

27 Oblique aerial view of part of the Normanton Down cemetery, near Stonehenge, Wiltshire.

28 Stone cist in the Simonstown barrow, Glamorganshire.

29 Wooden coffin made from a single length of tree trunk.

30 Stone circle at Scorhill, Dartmoor, Devon.

31 The Longstone on Shovel Down, Dartmoor, Devon.

32 Stone row on Stalldon Down, Devon.

33 The Iron Age promontory fort at Helsby, Cheshire: univallate defences.

34 The Iron Age fort of Eggardon, Dorset: multivallate defences.

35 The multivallate Iron Age fort of Badbury Rings, Dorset.

36 The multivallate Iron Age fort of Bratton Castle, Wiltshire.

37   The Iron Age fort of Uley Bury, Gloucestershire.

38   Reconstruction drawing of the inturned entrance at Llanmelin Iron Age fort, Monmouthshire, by Alan Sorrell.

39   The Iron Age promontory fort at Linney Head, Pembrokeshire.

40   The southern multivallate enclosure at Pen Dinas, Aberystwyth, Cardiganshire, viewed from the northern enclosure.

41   The stone revetment of the wedge-shaped rampart at Carl Wark Iron Age fort, Yorkshire.

42   The broch and blockhouse at Clickhimin, Shetlands.

43   Reconstruction view of Clickhimin, Shetlands, during the broch period, by Alan Sorrell.

44   General view of the Broch of Mousa, Shetlands.

45   The Broch of Mousa, Shetlands, interior view.

46   The Broch of Gurness.

47   The Broch of Midhowe.

1 Man the Builder

In the long history of civilisation one of the most familiar concepts is that of man the tool-maker, a role which he has occupied now for something like a million years. Less familiar, and of much shorter duration, is the concept of man as a builder, during only the last 10,000 years or so. In spite of the difference in date, however, man the tool-maker and man the builder are essentially the same concept. The end products of both roles are artefacts, in the widest sense of the word, things made by man (Latin, *arte*, by skill, *facto*, made) for his own purposes, regardless of size. The term artefact is more frequently applied to those products (tools, weapons, pottery, ornaments, etc.) which are small enough to be carried or moved around (portable antiquities), and these constitute one great body of archaeological evidence. But the non-portable antiquities, the buildings which man erected for his accommodation, his worship, his defence, etc., constitute a second body of evidence which is at least as important as the first, and in some ways more important. By their very nature the monuments, unlike the smaller antiquities, are immovable and therefore focus our attention on the actual locations where man carried on his existence. In looking at buildings of any type we are looking at the physical framework within which much of human life is carried on, and this applies to all periods, right up to the present day. There are very few human activities which are not in some way associated with buildings. Hunting, for example, so essentially a matter of movement in the open, none the less has its hunting lodges, medieval and later, which, apart from their architecture, are surely important social documents of the period. It is this sort of evidence, in the social, economic, political and many other fields, which monuments can so eloquently supply.

As defined here an Old Stone Age hand-axe on the one hand and a medieval cathedral on the other are both artefacts, even though one is of extreme simplicity and the other of very great complexity. Production of the hand-axe requires no more than a lump of flint, a certain manual dexterity and, it has been estimated, a few minutes' work; nevertheless, it is an artefact and therefore a piece of evidence relating to the past. By contrast, the erection of a medieval cathedral such as Notre Dame, Canterbury or Cologne is an enormously complex, long-term undertaking, involving people, resources, planning and organisation on a huge scale. It is not something that can be lightly or quickly undertaken, or quickly completed. It can be called into being only in very particular circumstances. Because it involves so much in religious, social, economic and even political terms, it is thereby a much more valuable and informative document about the period in which it was built. Its plan, its size, its decoration, its state of completion, etc., must reflect to a considerable degree the resources, attitudes and conditions which went into its construction. Few types of man-made structure are admittedly as complex as medieval cathedrals, and the comparison with the Old Stone Age hand-axe has been a deliberately extreme one, but the broad principle outlined above holds true. What we can perceive in archaeological remains is, in a large measure, dictated by what has gone into their manufacture; and since buildings as a class demand more effort and resources than more portable artefacts, they are that much more likely to provide the evidence for those wider considerations of a social, religious, economic and political nature without which any study of the past becomes meaningless.

For about a million years the pace of human progress was infinitely slow, with the same relatively simple types of stone tools remaining in use for tens of thousands of years at a time. During this Palaeolithic or Old Stone Age period man lived mainly by hunting (supplemented by food-gathering), so that he was almost entirely dependent for his existence on the herds of wild animals which, from season to season, moved around a wide territory, perhaps several thousand square miles in extent, seeking new grazing grounds to ensure their survival. To ensure his own survival man was compelled to move with them, so that settlements were of short duration and inevitably of fairly flimsy construction. Even if he had had sufficient knowledge of building, there was little point in perma-nent houses and settlements since there was no prospect of long occupation. When the herds moved on, so did man; and because he needed to move as part of his perma-nent way of life, not only did he not need permanent settlements, he also had little or no interest in heavy domestic equipment. What he possessed he needed to be able to carry without too much diffi-culty, and this must have consisted largely of tools, weapons, clothing and some sort of rudimentary shelter, probably a skin tent or windbreak. This is a very broad picture and there are inevitably some variations; we know that caves were occupied, par-ticularly in the Upper Palaeolithic period, and these suggest a greater degree of per-manence than indicated above. There is also some evidence from South Russia, in the same period, of actual built dwellings. None the less, the essential characteristic of the Old Stone Age is man's almost complete dependence on hunting for his survival; his existence must at most times have been precarious.

The remedy for this very long-standing state of affairs was the discovery of agri-culture and stock breeding, the growing of crops and the raising of domestic animals. This took place in the Near East shortly after 10,000 B.C. Just how the discovery was achieved, and why at this particular time, are matters beyond the scope of this brief outline of events, but a couple of relevant points can be made. From 10,000 B.C., and linked with the retreat of the glaciers at the end of the Ice Age, there was a climatic change which in the Near East took the form of increasingly dry conditions. In the same area there were wild species of both animals and plants which at the onset of such conditions would have begun gradually to disappear. Since these formed the main, indeed the only, food supply of the population it is likely that they would have taken steps to ensure their own survival by capturing groups of animals and keeping them under their control until, very gradually, they became domesticated; similarly, by nurturing patches of wild cereals they would gradually achieve a control over the growth of plants which would enable them to produce supplies at will. These two processes are sometimes designated the Neolithic Revolution, but this is misleading on two counts. The revolution was no sudden, overnight happening; it probably occupied something like 3,000 years to achieve, from c. 10,000 to c. 7000 B.C. Nor did it, in fact, take place in the Neolithic

(New Stone Age) period but in the preceding Mesolithic (Middle Stone Age) period (c. 10,000–7000 B.C.) which followed the end of the Old Stone Age.

However long and complex the processes involved, by c. 7000 B.C. man in the Near East had achieved a mastery of stock breeding and plant cultivation which has remained the basis of human existence down to the present day. The implications of this newly acquired control over his food supply were profound, particularly with regard to the pattern of his existence. Most particularly the need for a nomadic way of life, following the wild game, had gone. Within limits, food could be produced at will so that man could now contemplate living in one place, and feel justified in building something a little more substantial than the light shelter of the nomad. Moreover, where plant cultivation was involved, it was indeed necessary to stay in one place, at least for a part of the year. Once crops have been planted they need attention, and if the farmer is not around eventually to harvest them, then the whole effort has been wasted and there is a food shortage in the following winter. The net result of all this was that from shortly after 9000 B.C. the signs of a more settled pattern of life began to appear, in the form of buildings, rudimentary at first, but none the less the unmistakable beginning of a long tradition of building which has continued in unbroken line until the present day. In spite of one or two earlier efforts mentioned above in South Russia, the real story of man as a builder begins at the same time as that of man the food producer, some 10,000 years ago in the ancient Near East.

The earliest efforts take the form of simple agricultural villages, and these must always have remained the basis of life and economy even when the great cities had developed. With increasing productivity and prosperity some settlements grew in size to become towns (Jericho, for example), and later again other settlements developed into the great cities of Mesopotamia and adjacent areas, with a wide range of build-ings for different purposes, far removed in scale and style from the simple round huts of the earliest villages. Already by 4500 B.C. many of the great cities were taking shape in the Tigris/Euphrates valleys; and by 3000 B.C. and the beginning of the dynastic period and written history, many of these cities were already of great size and complexity with elaborate temples and palaces and great encircling walls.

Inevitably these profound developments in the Near East had their effects on surrounding areas, including Europe. By c. 6000 B.C. the knowledge of agriculture and stock breeding had spread into the south-east, into Greece and the Balkans, leading again to the development of agricultural village communities. From there, via the river valleys, there was a spread over much of central Europe in the form of the Danubian civilisation which lasted from c. 5000 to c. 2000 B.C. (Fig. 1). Western Europe was affected by a different route, westwards through the Mediterranean to Italy, France, Spain and the adjacent islands. Eventually the whole of Europe was a Neolithic province, including, by shortly after 4000 B.C., the British Isles. The first arrivals seem to have had a relatively low level of civilisation, with little to show in the way of buildings, but before 3000 B.C. there is clear evidence of a range of structures which presumably met the main needs of the Neolithic communities. There is thus a 5,000-year history of building, even in these islands, and it is the first 3,000 years or so of this history, from the earliest Neolithic structures until the Roman conquest of A.D. 43, which form the subject of this book.

As will be seen chapter by chapter, the various types of monument have very different patterns of distribution, and among the factors producing this result are the geography and the geology of the British Isles. Geography is always a basic fact of human settlement, at any period and in any region, but is particularly relevant in a prehistoric context and in an island situation. The British Isles stand off the north-west corner of Europe, more or less at the opposite end of the two major routes (the Danube and the Mediterranean) through which influence was diffused from the Near East. Britain itself (i.e. England, Scotland and Wales) is roughly triangular in shape, with the three sides of the triangle facing, or related to, very different parts of Europe. Much of the southern and eastern coasts face Scandinavia, north Germany, the Low Countries and northern France, with attention focused, although not exclusively, on the narrow crossing between Dover and Calais. The consequences are many triangular distributions (defined roughly by Dover, the Wash and Portland Bill), which presumably originated in the facing parts of Europe (Fig. 20, for example). The long western coast of Britain, however, faces away from the continent and is therefore unlikely to be affected from the same source. Its links are, by sea, with the Atlantic coastlands of Europe, and ultimately the west Mediterranean region. Judging by distribution

Fig. 1 Map showing the two major routes along which influence was diffused from the ancient Near East through prehistoric Europe. The stipple shows the distribution of megalithic tombs.

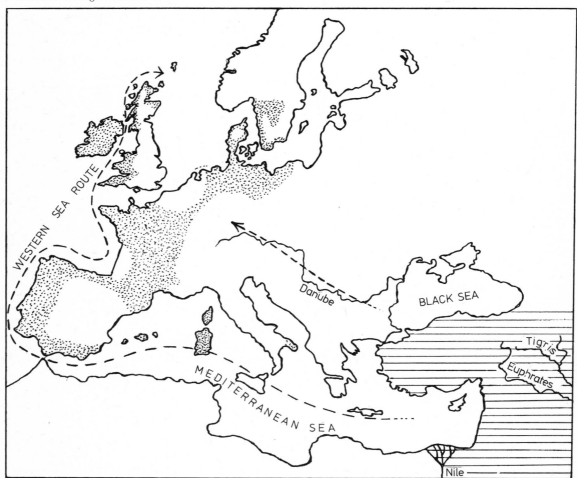

patterns, what is known as the Western sea route embraces the Atlantic coasts of Spain, Portugal and France and thence passes up the western side of Britain, affecting in particular the western and northern extremities and islands: Cornwall, Pembrokeshire, Caernarvonshire, Anglesey, Man, south-west Scotland, the Hebrides, the northern and north-eastern coasts, the Orkneys and Shetlands (Fig. 1). The same route, of course, provides access to Ireland, particularly to its southern and eastern coasts.

This necessarily brief look at the geographical background is quite clearly a simplification of a much more complex situation. Internal events within the British Isles inevitably played their part in the distribution patterns now observable so that not everything is to be explained in terms of European origins. Nevertheless, an awareness of this basic geographical relationship is essential to any understanding of the prehistory of the British Isles. Equally essential, and closely linked, is some understanding of the basic geology of these islands.

To some extent, the geological pattern follows the geographical one, the south and east supporting a different pattern of existence from that in the north and west. Broadly speaking, the south and east (from Dorset to Kent and northwards as far as Yorkshire) consists of chalk and limestone, producing stretches of relatively open country with only light vegetation; these have been designated 'areas of easy settlement' meaning that in prehistoric times clearance for agriculture would not have been difficult. This is the territory of the Windmill Hill culture and its monuments (see Chapter 3 and Fig. 20). To the west of this region and between it and the Welsh Marches is the area of the Midland clay supporting, in prehistoric times, a dense, heavy oak type of vegetation which must have been largely impenetrable and very difficult to clear. For this reason the Midlands are largely a blank in prehistoric times.

The remainder of the British Isles, to the north and west, is composed of older and harder rocks, with greater elevations than the relatively low south-eastern territories. Mountain and moorland, island and promontory are dominant features of the region. The landscape is more rugged, less hospitable and less easy of settlement, or at least settlement similar to that on the chalk and limestone. Except by sea, communication is more difficult. Settlement tends to be fragmented in small units. Inevitably, therefore, modes of life and food production develop which arise out of the structure of the region, and because this is basically different from the chalk/limestone territories, so inevitably are the cultures which arise out of it. To understand this fundamental geological pattern is to understand, indeed to anticipate, that an Iron Age settlement in, say, Wiltshire will be very different from one in north-west Scotland. Once again the brief geological statement is a simplification of a very complex pattern, but at least an awareness of this aspect is essential to any study of the prehistoric past.

Human existence calls also for a chronological setting, a broad sequence of dates, periods and events against which the monuments can be set, the more so since the overall treatment here is by types rather than by dates. The chronological survey which follows is again necessarily brief but will enable the whole range of prehistoric monuments in the British Isles to be seen in their time relationship not only to each other but also to the major cultural divisions of prehistory during the last 3,000 years.

As in the ancient Near East, it is necessary to go back to the end of the Old Stone Age (Palaeolithic) period and the beginning of the Mesolithic. In the British Isles, however, the Mesolithic period lasted until after 4000 B.C., when the first Neolithic settlers arrived from the continent, and it is with them that the story of monuments begins. In fact, the very earliest Neolithic settlers seem to have lived at a fairly primitive level and it is only several

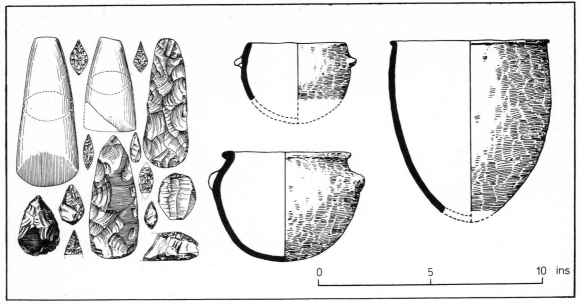

Fig. 2 Stone and flint axes, arrowheads, etc. and pottery of the Windmill Hill people.

centuries later that the first monuments begin to appear, perhaps c. 3300 B.C. The Neolithic culture of southern England is known as the Windmill Hill culture, after a famous site in Wiltshire, and occupies the area south and east of a line from the Severn to the Wash, with a northward extension into Lincolnshire and Yorkshire. Such scanty information as there is on houses and settlements will be considered in Chapter 2. The principal structures of the Windmill Hill culture were causewayed enclosures, earthen long barrows, cursus earthworks and flint mines, and these will be described and discussed in Chapter 3.

The non-structural remains of the Windmill Hill people consist of pottery, tools, weapons, etc., together with evidence of their diet and economy (Fig. 2). Windmill Hill pottery, generally dark brown in colour, is usually described as bag-shaped. It is round bottomed (as opposed to flat), and is often quite plain; where decoration does occur it is usually around the rim. Handles are in the form of lugs, sometimes

perforated. A slightly more sophisticated shape is represented by a carinated type, i.e. one with a horizontal ridge running around it, dividing the pot into two zones. Perhaps the most vital piece of equipment was the stone or flint axe, flaked and/or polished. The flint axes were presumably the products of local flint mines, but axes made of stone must have come from outside the region, from the axe-factories of the north and west. Flint arrowheads, of leaf-shaped form, were another common type, indicating that hunting still had an important role in the economy. Other equipment included flint scrapers (for treating skins), flint knives, bone and antler combs and points (for skins again), chalk cups (for blubber lamps?) and objects for personal adornment such as perforated chalk pendants. Actual grain, in carbonised form, or grain impressions on pottery, indicate that the Windmill Hill people grew wheat and barley. Bone remains show that cattle, sheep, goats and pigs were kept, as well as the dog. There is no evidence of the domestic horse, such few remains as are found being presumably wild species. These remains indicate a mixed farming economy, supplemented by hunting and presumably food gathering, the animals providing not only food but also skins, bone, horn and sinew for other needs as well.

Not surprisingly, in view of what was said earlier, the Neolithic of the west and north took a different form, at least in its monuments. In the western regions of England and Wales, in northern and western Scotland and in much of Ireland, large numbers of tombs built of very large stones and covered by long and round mounds, are clear evidence of a considerable Neolithic population closely linked in its origins to the Western sea route (Fig. 1). These burial monuments, the earliest stone architecture in the British Isles, will be dealt with in Chapter 4. In the remoter parts of Scotland, in the Orkneys and Shetlands, there are remains of stone-built settlements which provide an all too rare glimpse of Neolithic domestic life and these are described in Chapter 2. Megalithic tombs are divided into a number of clearly defined groups, both large and small. Among the larger groups, and distinguished by outstanding architecture, are the Cotswold-Severn Group of England and Wales, the Boyne Group of Ireland and the Orkney-Cromarty Group of north-east Scotland.

In its portable equipment, however, the culture of the megalith-building groups was broadly similar to that of the Windmill Hill people. Bag-shaped and carinated pottery are common, although sometimes now with more decoration. Stone and flint axes, leaf-shaped arrowheads, bone and horn tools, etc., match those of the Windmill Hill culture. The economy also is in many cases broadly similar, with mixed farming supplemented by hunting. In remoter regions, however, in northern Scotland and in more rugged terrain, the emphasis shifts to stock raising rather than cultivation of crops, with perhaps more emphasis on purely local resources such as fishing and fowling.

The Neolithic cultures considered so far, both in the south and east (Windmill Hill) and in the north and west, are often described as Primary Neolithic, implying that they represent a more or less direct migration from the continent, although clearly from different regions thereof. Alongside the Primary Neolithic groups, however, are what have in the past been termed Secondary Neolithic cultures. These are (or were) deemed to be the result of the adoption of Neolithic ideas and practices by the surviving Mesolithic population. The main distinguishing feature of these groups is their pottery and its close association with the ritual monuments which form the subject of Chapter 5. However, more recently it has been suggested that these so-called Secondary Neolithic groups, or at least some of them, were simply other, later immigrant groups from the continent, bringing with them a version of Neolithic culture different from either the Windmill Hill or megalithic groups. The main culture involved is known as the Rinyo-Clacton (indicating its wide geographical spread from Rinyo in Orkney to Clacton in Essex), and belongs to the latter part of the Neolithic period from c. 2500 B.C. to c. 2000 B.C. Rinyo-Clacton pottery is noticeably different from types considered so far. It is flat bottomed, heavily decorated and shaped either like a cylinder or a flowerpot.

Whatever their precise status in the Neolithic period, the Rinyo-Clacton and allied groups seem to have been heavily involved in a very important industrial and trading activity, that of the so-called stone axe-factories. In the chalk regions of the south and east the main raw material was flint and this was exploited by means of flint mines. Outside the flint-bearing regions, however, in the north and west, stone was used. Suitable, smooth-grained stone which flakes easily and regularly was, in fact, available in only a few places and these are the so-called axe-factories. Although no buildings were involved the term 'factory' is fully justified by the fact that a great part of the production work was carried out on the spot. The sites were scree slopes in mountainous regions where large quantities of stone were easily available on the surface. The technique was to rough-out the axes on the spot to very nearly their final shape but to do the finishing work elsewhere. Thus all the worker had to carry away were rough-outs rather than quantities of the basic raw material, which would have been impossibly heavy. There is no doubt that these were important manufacturing centres. The major axe-factories are Tievebulliagh in Antrim, Northern Ireland, Great Langdale in the Lake District, Craig Llwyd in North Wales and a site in Cornwall which has not been precisely identified. Equally interesting is the extent of the trade in such stone axes throughout the British Isles. By petrological examination it is possible to establish which factory an axe found on an archaeological site came from, and by plotting these locations on a map it is possible to see how far the products of a particular factory were traded. Craig Llwyd axes, for example, were traded as far south as the Hampshire coast, while the Great Langdale axes were even more widely spread, extending both to the south and to the north, over much of Scotland. Quite clearly the stone axe trade was an important economic aspect of the Neolithic period.

The Neolithic period as a whole lasted for something like 2,000 years and was brought to a gradual end by the arrival, principally along the south and east coasts, of the Beaker people from the continent, c. 1900–1800 B.C., bringing with them the first signs of bronze metal working. Although there are certain definite changes there are also clear signs of continuity from the Neolithic period. Beaker pottery appears in collective tombs, although these were very different from their own burial practice, and the Beaker people seem to have adopted the existing henge monuments, their principal contribution being the addition of stone circles to some of them. Simple stone circles (i.e. circles not

associated with henge monuments) which are numerous in the Bronze Age, form the subject of Chapter 7. The principal, and most numerous, Bronze Age monuments, however, are the round barrows or cairns (involving single burial, as opposed to the Neolithic practice of collective burial), and these begin in the Beaker period and form the subject of Chapter 6.

The Beaker people take their name from their very characteristic pottery, the so-called beakers, thus labelled because they were presumed to be drinking vessels (Pl. 1). Beakers, usually 6–8 in. high and 5–6 in. in diameter, are normally decorated all over, often in horizontal bands, and have an S-shaped profile, sometimes evenly curved, sometimes more angular. These are found most frequently accompanying inhumation (as opposed to cremation) burials under round barrows. Other notable changes include tanged-and-barbed flint arrowheads instead of the Neolithic leaf-shaped type, flint daggers, stone battle-axes (Fig. 3), and occasional simple triangular-bladed bronze daggers, attached to a handle by means of rivets. Metal tools and weapons were, however, still quite rare and probably acquired by trade rather than manufactured; stone and flint continued to be the main raw materials.

The Beaker people mark only the very beginning of the Bronze Age. The full Early Bronze Age is represented by two very largely separate geographical groups, the Wessex culture and the Food-vessel culture. As its name implies, the Wessex culture flourished in the area known as Wessex (roughly Dorset, Wiltshire, Hampshire and Berkshire). Judging by the rich contents of many of their graves, often under bell and disc barrows, the Wessex people were fairly prosperous and terms such as 'warrior aristocrats' and 'chieftains' have been applied to them. However, rich grave goods do not necessarily imply powerful warriors, and the graves are just as likely to be those of wealthy merchants or landowners or successful farmers as anything else. This implied wealth would

1   Early Bronze Age Beaker pottery.

appear to have enabled the Wessex people to make the final structural addition to Stonehenge which transformed it into the form in which we recognise it now. The material equipment of the Wessex people included large bronze daggers with riveted handles and ribbed blades, bronze axes strengthened by flanges, bronze spear heads with tangs and/or sockets, stone battle-axes, ornaments of sheet-gold and much else besides, eloquently demonstrating the wealth and long-range trade contacts of the Wessex civilisation which flourished from c. 1600 to c. 1400 B.C.

In the north and west there was a different pattern of events. There the full Early Bronze Age is represented by the so-called Food-vessel culture, again named after a very characteristic form of pottery. Two major types of food-vessel are distinguished, the Yorkshire type and the Irish

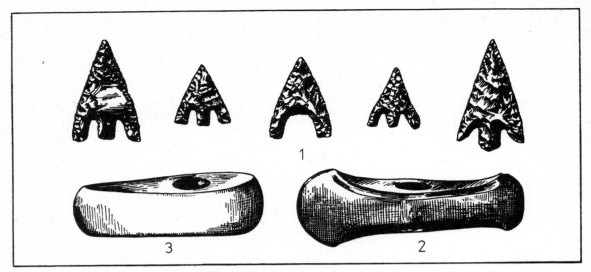

Fig. 3 Tanged-and-barbed flint arrowheads and stone battle-axes of the Early Bronze Age.

type, and these are found not only in these two areas but in the north generally and in Scotland. Food-vessel burials (both inhumations and cremations) are found beneath the very common bowl barrows and in flat graves without covering mounds. Although the Beaker people, and possibly also the Wessex people, were immigrants from the continent, the Food-vessel population seems to have been of native stock, possibly a result of the fusion of the existing Neolithic people with the Beaker arrivals, producing a new culture with its own clear characteristics. The material remains of the Food-vessel people include far less in the way of metal work than the Wessex culture. Some simple bronze daggers similar to Beaker types have been found, as well as one or two flat (as opposed to flanged) bronze axes, but the bulk of the equipment was still in stone and flint. Bronze was still something of a luxury in these northern regions. The most striking Food-vessel remains are the moon-shaped gold neck-ornaments (of Irish gold), and the similarly shaped necklaces of jet beads on which they appear to have been based by the Irish goldsmiths.

The Wessex and Food-vessel cultures are followed by the Middle Bronze Age (1400–1000 B.C.) and it was only during this period that bronze came into fairly widespread use. However, one of the most noticeable characteristics of the time was the virtually universal adoption of cremation as the burial rite. In the Beaker period inhumation had dominated the scene, while in the Wessex and Food-vessel cultures both rites had been in use. By Middle Bronze Age times, however, cremation was the dominant rite and this led to the development of a whole range of much larger pots than hitherto to contain the cremated remains. Cinerary urns were on average 10–15 in. high and up to 10 in. in diameter, although there are examples as much as 2 ft high and 18 in. in diameter. One of the commonest types, the overhanging-rim urn, had its origins in the Wessex culture, but developed fully only in the Middle Bronze Age. Another type, of similar dimensions, was the enlarged food-vessel, the origin of which is self-evident. Other types (encrusted urns, cordoned urns), formerly thought of as Late Bronze Age, are now known to have been contemporary with the others and what clearly existed was a whole range of pots of large size to meet the funerary needs of the Middle Bronze Age population. The cremated remains were either buried beneath newly built round mounds or were inserted as secondary burials into already existing mounds.

In the Middle Bronze Age metalworking industry a number of clear-cut types of tools and/or weapons had emerged. From the simple flat and flanged axes of the Early Bronze Age there had now developed the type known as the palstave, with a wide flared cutting edge, prominent cast flanges and a stop-ridge to prevent the butt of the blade being forced back into the wooden handle and splitting it (Fig. 4). A later addition is a loop through which a cord could be used to secure the blade more firmly to the handle. A similar technique was used on the bronze spearheads. The shaft was inserted into a socket and secured by loops on either side. Slim bronze rapiers are another characteristic Middle

Bronze Age type. These would appear to have developed out of the Early Bronze Age dagger and like them had riveted handles (Fig. 5). The normal concomitant of a sword is a shield, and some circular bronze shields may belong to this period, although they are usually attributed to the Late Bronze Age (Fig. 5). Circular wooden shields are certainly a likely part of the Middle Bronze Age armoury.

In recent years a new element has been added to the Middle Bronze Age at the expense of the Late Bronze Age. The Deverel-Rimbury culture was for long considered to be within the Late Bronze Age, but more detailed research has now established its true chronological position in the second half of the Middle Bronze Age, between 1200 and 1000 B.C. Like the other Middle Bronze Age people the Deverel-Rimbury folk practised cremation, but in flat urnfields rather than under barrows. The cremated remains were placed in distinctive forms of pottery, bucket-shaped, barrel-shaped and globular

Fig. 4   Bronze Age axes: 1, Flanged axe with stop ridge; 2, Palstave; 3, Socketed axe.

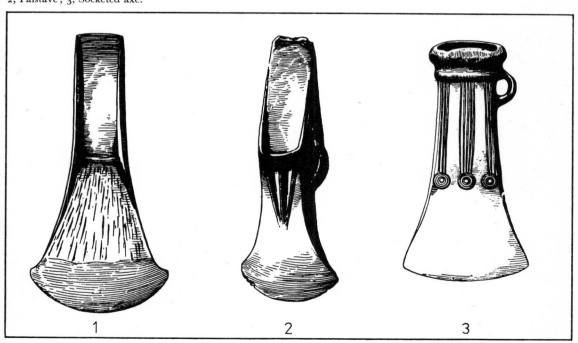

1   2   3

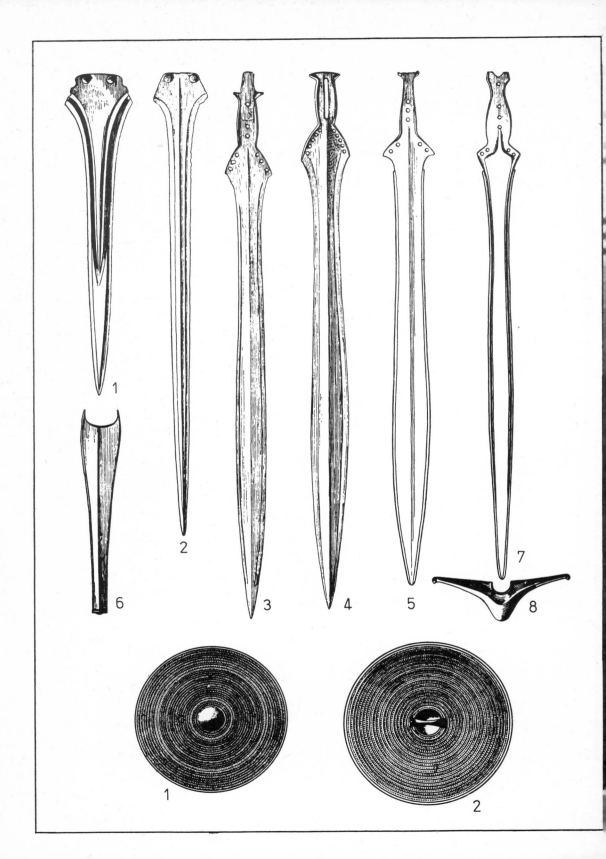

urns. The most significant aspect of the Deverel-Rimbury culture, however, are the farms and farming practice they brought with them from the continent, which can now be seen as a Middle rather than a Late Bronze Age development. The settlements will be dealt with in Chapter 2, but the farming practice seems to have involved ploughing and rectangular fields for the first time (rather than the hoe-culture and irregular plots which preceded it), and linear earthworks to which the name of ranch boundaries is frequently given. The Deverel-Rimbury people kept cattle, sheep and horses, and quite clearly practised mixed farming on a far more ambitious scale than had been possible hitherto. The pattern thus established occupied not only the second half of the Middle Bronze Age but probably much if not all of the Late Bronze Age (1000–500 B.C.). As will emerge later there are structural similarities which indicate continuity from Middle Bronze Age to Iron Age times.

The Late Bronze Age was marked by the variety and abundance of bronze equipment. This is, in fact, technologically the fully developed Bronze Age. Even in the Middle Bronze Age the types manufactured were limited to about half a dozen. In the Late Bronze Age, on the other hand, there is a virtual revolution, with a very wide range of specialist and general purpose tools and equipment. In military equipment there is an entirely new type of sword, known as leaf-shaped, much heavier than the bronze rapier, with its handle cast in one piece with the blade and suitable for both thrusting and slashing (Fig. 5). Such swords were carried in scabbards, probably of wood and leather, with bronze chapes or end pieces. The looped spearheads of the Middle Bronze Age are replaced by types held in position by pegs, although the loops sometimes survive as a purely decorative feature. A new type of axe appears, with the haft housed in a socket, so that there was little or no danger of splitting the handle in use (Fig. 4). Other Late Bronze Age equipment included socketed and tanged-and-riveted sickles, socketed-and-tanged knives, socketed hammers, chisels and gouges, and razors (Fig. 6). Perhaps the greatest innovation of the Late Bronze Age was the technique of sheet-metal work. Great bronze cauldrons, up to 2 ft in diameter, and tall bronze buckets, were manufactured from thin sheets of metal riveted together (Pl. 2). Other sheet-metal products included circular bronze shields and curving bronze trumpets.

Because of the removal of the Deverel-Rimbury culture to the Middle Bronze Age there is now something of a vacuum in the Late Bronze Age, with nothing to fill the gap between 1000 and 500 B.C., the generally accepted date for the beginning of the full Iron Age. The answer, or at least part of the answer, may be the extension back into the Late Bronze Age of part of the content of the following period, notably some of the numerous hillforts which have hitherto been thought of as exclusively Iron Age.

On the continent the Iron Age began c. 700 B.C. in the form of the Hallstatt culture centred on southern Germany. The first effects were felt here around 650 B.C., but only in a very small way, generally interpreted as sporadic raiding by war parties rather than invasion and settlement proper. The main Iron Age impact did not apparently take place until around 500 B.C., and this is taken as the beginning of the Iron Age period in the British Isles, which then lasted until the Roman conquest of A.D. 43 and the end of the prehistoric period as a whole, at least in southern Britain. Further north the prehistoric period lasted a few decades longer, while in Scotland and Ireland, largely unaffected by the conquest, the prehistoric tradition continued on for several centuries, only gradually giving way to more advanced modes of life.

The first stage of the Iron Age proper, usually termed Iron Age A, affected the classic triangular area of southern and eastern England, beginning c. 500 B.C. The people involved seem to have arrived from the

Fig. 5   Bronze rapiers and bronze leaf-shaped swords, bronze chapes (for scabbards), and bronze shields.

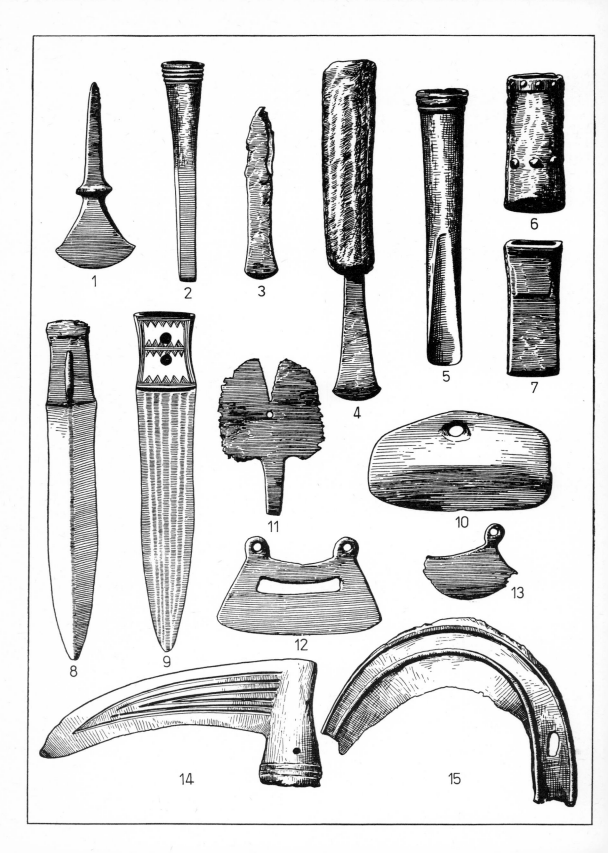

2 Late Bronze Age cauldron.

facing coasts of Europe, although it has been suggested that there was also a considerable survival here of the native, Late Bronze Age tradition. Whatever its composition the Iron Age A culture became established in the south-eastern triangle and beyond in the centuries between 500 and 250 B.C. The two major types of site are settlements and hillforts. The settlements indicate mixed farming at sites such as Little Woodbury with its large (50-ft diameter), circular farmhouse and ancillary structures. However, there were many other types of settlement as well, some indicating a continuance of Late Bronze Age traditions, and these are described in Chapter 2. The hillforts exist in their hundreds and at this stage are of the univallate (i.e. single rampart) type, and these are dealt with in

3 Iron Age pottery.

Fig. 6 Late Bronze Age equipment: tanged-and-socketed chisels (1–4); socketed gouge (5); socketed hammers (6 & 7); tanged-and-socketed knives (8 & 9); razors (11–13); tanged-and-socketed sickles (14 & 15).

Chapter 8. Iron Age A pottery is mostly in the form of shouldered jars closely resembling the bronze buckets of the Late Bronze Age (Pl. 3). Decoration is very simple and often entirely absent. One special class of pottery is coated with haematite (haematite ware) and seems to have been produced by specialist potters rather than domestically. Clay or chalk loom-weights, clay spindle-whorls and bone or antler weaving combs all indicate the widespread practice of spinning and weaving (Pl. 4). For dress fastening straight pins with ring or swans-neck heads and brooches of the safety-pin type were now very much in vogue.

During the development of the British Iron Age, in the centuries from 500 B.C. on, a new culture, known as La Tène, had replaced the older Hallstatt culture in Europe.

Eventually, between 300 and 250 B.C. the effects of these changes were felt in Britain and this stage is known as Iron Age B. Not all parts of the country were affected and in those areas Iron Age A continued, only gradually modified by the new ideas and fashions. Iron Age B influence is demonstrated most strikingly by the decorative art which came with the new migrants, a flowing curvilinear style which forms an important part of the repertoire of world art, of any period, ancient or modern. It is perhaps seen at its best in warriors' equipment, particularly in the decoration of scabbards, but also in shields, spears, helmets, etc. (Fig. 7). However, it appears perhaps even more strikingly in the decoration of such refined objects as circular bronze mirrors, polished mirror fashion on one side and elegantly decorated in La Tène style on the other, with an elegant

4   Iron Age weaving equipment: loom-weights, spindle-whorls, bobbins and weaving combs.

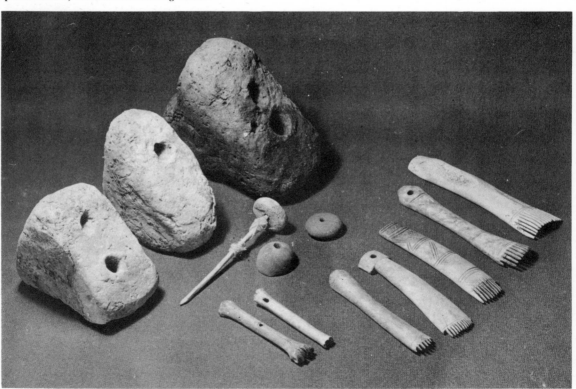

Fig. 7   Iron Age swords and scabbards decorated in La Tène style.

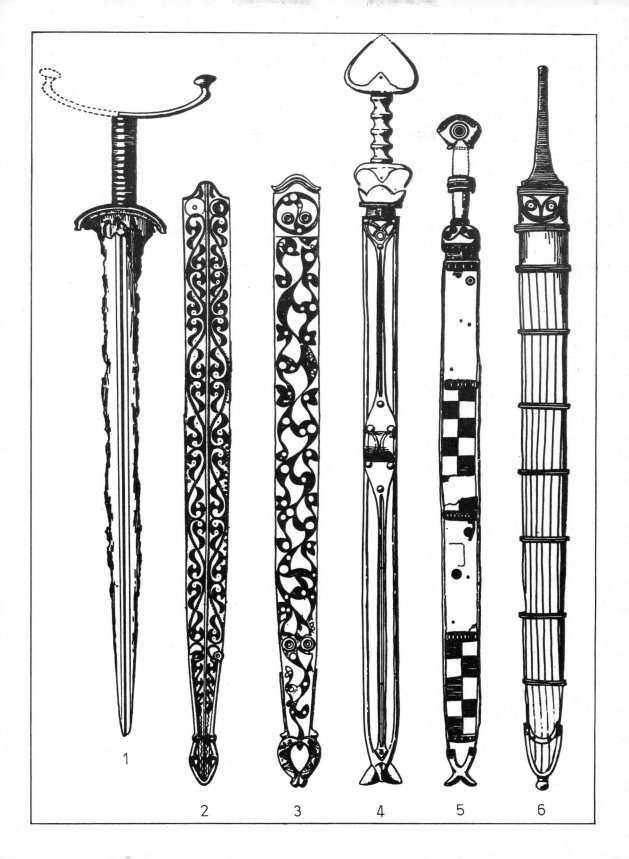

1　　　　2　　　　3　　　　4　　　　5　　　　6

handle for holding. During this period hillforts are deemed to have advanced to the multivallate (multiple-rampart) stage, but this is not necessarily a result of La Tène arrivals or ideas. It is more likely to be a native idea, a natural development from the single rampart stage, perhaps stimulated by the movements of people brought about by the La Tène migration into southern England. Other aspects of Iron Age B culture which can only be mentioned here are chariot burials (in eastern Yorkshire), iron currency bars, lathe-trimmed wooden vessels and the rotary quern for grain. Iron Age B pottery varied from area to area but was most frequently in the form of open bowls (rather than the high-shouldered jars of Iron Age A), with either La Tène style decoration or a simple beaded rim.

The last phase of the British Iron Age, known as the Iron Age C (Belgic) period, affected only southern and south-eastern Britain, from c. 100 B.C. onwards. Before the end of it, i.e. before the Roman conquest, southern Britain had become a series of petty kingdoms and it was the squabbles between these which provided the Roman opportunity for intervention in A.D. 43. By this time the Belgic people were importing wine, silverware and other luxuries from the continent, minting their own coinage, using the wheel for the production of pottery for the first time and, perhaps economically most important of all, were using a new, heavy plough which could cope with all sorts and conditions of soil so that much more land could be brought into cultivation. It was this relatively advanced farming which provided the economic basis for the much higher standard of living represented by the wide range of domestic equipment, imported and otherwise, and it was at this stage of development, at least in southern England, that the prehistoric period was brought to an end by the Roman conquest of A.D. 43.

As witnessed by its numerous hillforts, mainly in the Lowland zone south of the Clyde–Forth line, Scotland was very much involved in the broad pattern of events just described. In the Highland zone, however, the monuments take a different form, the Iron Age there being represented, in terms of monuments, by *duns*, small, stone-built forts, and by *brochs*, impressive stone-built towers, and these are dealt with in Chapter 9. This is an Iron Age, moreover, which was not brought to an abrupt end by the Roman conquest since even the temporary shift northwards of the frontier from the Tyne–Solway line (Hadrian's Wall) to the Clyde–Forth line (the Antonine Wall) still left the Highland zone and its monuments outside this northernmost frontier of the Roman Empire. In these remote regions there is no clear point at which the prehistoric period can be said to have ended, and prehistoric practices and traditions lingered on for centuries after they had ceased further south.

The Roman conquest brought to an end over 3,000 years of prehistoric building activity, among other things, following on the initial introduction of farming in the fourth millennium. During this time a wide range of structures had been devised and developed to meet the many needs of the population in the fields of accommodation, worship, burial, defence, etc., and these structures will be described and discussed in the following chapters.

2 Ancient Houses and Settlements

It has to be stated at the outset that remains of prehistoric houses and settlements in the British Isles are scarce, even in the Iron Age period which is best served in this respect. This is the more surprising in view of the extensive remains of other types of monument (Neolithic chambered tombs, Bronze Age round barrows and Iron Age hillforts) which exist in their thousands. Much of what is preserved of domestic accommodation is stone-built and located in the highland zone, in remote areas not much affected by agriculture. In the south and east, on the other hand, houses would have been timber-built and therefore much more vulnerable to decay; moreover, it is likely that many of them were located in the sheltered valleys where modern agriculture would have completely destroyed any visible remains. The picture of houses and settlements is therefore, at best, a patchy one, both geographically and chronologically, and this must be kept in mind in assessing what follows in this chapter.

The Neolithic Period

In spite of the paucity of the evidence one thing is clear: both in the Windmill Hill area, and in other regions as well, such remains as there are indicate a tradition of predominantly rectangular rather than round huts. A house at Haldon in Devon, for example, was apparently about 24 × 16 ft, its outline marked by stones, presumably the footings for the walls. Among the stones were post-holes for the original upright timbers. Three post-holes along the axis suggest a gabled roof, almost certainly covered with thatch. The (on average) 4-ft gaps between the uprights of the walls would probably have been filled with wattle and daub, woven panels of reeds or thin branches daubed with clay. There is clay on the site and the stone footing would make an ideal base for such a method of walling. A house of roughly similar size (c. 24 × 12 ft) is known from Clegyr Boia in Pembrokeshire, involving eight post-holes in two rows of four each. There are stone footings on one of the long sides and presumably the roof and walls were carried out in the same way as the Haldon house. Possibly contemporary with this rectangular house is a roughly circular hut and this association is interesting in view of the evidence from Lough Gur in Ireland (below). A Neolithic house at Mount Pleasant, Nottage, Glamorganshire, was found beneath a later Bronze Age burial mound (Fig. 8A). The plan was less clear-cut than Clegyr Boia but was rectangular or near-rectangular in layout, with timber uprights and stone footings. Two other rectangular timber-framed houses have been uncovered in the Isle of Man. One at Ronaldsway was

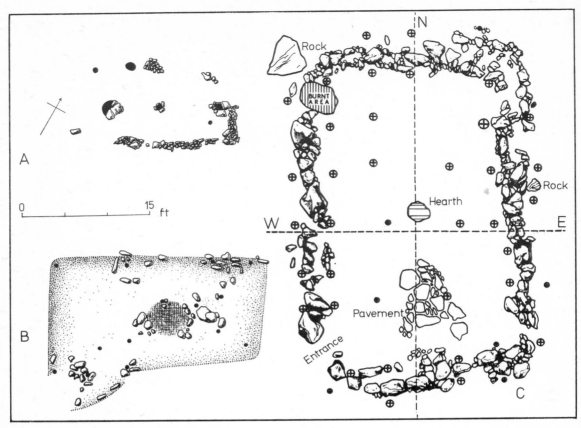

Fig. 8   Neolithic houses: A, Mount Pleasant,
Glamorganshire; B, Ronaldsway, Isle of Man;
C, Site A, Lough Gur, Ireland

sunk about 2 ft into the ground and its
dimensions, defined by post-holes, were
23 ft long by 13 ft wide at one end and
10 ft at the other (Fig. 8B). There was a
clearly defined entrance and a stone-lined
central hearth. Internal post-holes may
have been part of two rows parallel with
the long sides, an arrangement found also
at Lough Gur. The second house, at
Glencrutchery, was uncovered many years
ago although it was not recognised as such
at the time.

The largest body of evidence on Neolithic
timber-framed houses comes from Lough
Gur in Co. Limerick, Ireland, excavated by
the late Professor S. P. O'Riordain from

1936 onwards. The settlement contained
both round and rectangular huts, and in
this case there is no doubt that both types
belong to the Neolithic period and formed
part of the same settlement. The rectangular house uncovered on Site A was the most
informative in terms of structure (Fig. 8c).
It was large as compared with houses
described so far, 42 × 27 ft overall, with
its entrance in the south-west corner. The
walls were defined by pairs of post-holes
about 4 ft apart with stone foundations
between. Presumably whatever formed the
walls rested on the stone foundation and
was retained on either side by the upright
posts, forming walls 4 ft thick, although
these must have been composed of fairly
light materials. Two rows of internal post-

holes running lengthwise were presumably part of the roof supports. There was a hearth more or less at the centre of the internal space, which was c. 32 × 20 ft. Two circular houses on Site C were built on the same principles, with 3-ft-thick walls defining an internal space 18–22 ft in diameter. A third house was defined by a simple ring of 24 post-holes some 18 ft in diameter, with no indication of the double setting of the other houses.

The remaining evidence is scanty, apart from Scotland (below). There are circular stone huts at Carn Brea in Cornwall and Legis Tor in Devon which may be Neolithic, and part of a rectangular house at Easton Down, Wiltshire, which appears to pre-date a Beaker site. In a few cases what appear to have been actual houses have been found beneath burial mounds. The best example is at Kemp Howe in Yorkshire. The house was largely subterranean with a central row of post-holes indicating a pitched roof, and may represent an alternative Neolithic type to those considered so far. Recently (1973) R. W. Feachem has suggested that some of the simple circular stone huts of the moorland areas of the highland zone, traditionally regarded as Bronze Age/Iron Age, may, in fact, belong to the Neolithic period, albeit the later part of it. In the same year G. J. Wainwright published the plans of two groups of post-holes from the Neolithic levels of Eaton Heath, Norwich, Norfolk. One group of eight post-holes was roughly

5 General view of the Neolithic settlement at Skara Brae, Orkneys.

trapeze-shaped in plan and might, with some additional post-holes, have formed a house of similar shape, perhaps 20 × 10 ft, narrowing to 5 ft at the opposite end. The other group, of five post-holes, formed a rectangle c. 12 × 8 ft. At another Norfolk site, Broome Heath, Ditchingham, the same excavator uncovered another Neolithic settlement. The few post-holes found formed no coherent pattern but the settlement was partly enclosed by a closely set arrangement of two banks and two ditches.

The most striking evidence of Neolithic habitation comes from Scotland. Skara Brae in the Orkneys (Pl. 5) is one of the best preserved habitation sites in pre-historic Europe, particularly with regard to its furniture. In Period 1 there was already a stone-built settlement, although there is no clue as to what form it took. In Period 2 there is evidence for at least six houses, corresponding closely in type with those of the following period. They are smaller in area, with thinner walls, but they have the same basic features. These houses appear to have been dismantled to make way for the main settlement of Skara Brae. The Period 3 houses were larger and more substantial than those of Period 2, with double walls nearly 10 ft thick (Fig. 9). The inner, dry-stone wall, up to 4 ft thick, was built of the local flagstone. To prevent draughts, domestic refuse from the midden was piled against it, thus sealing the gaps. To keep this material in position an outer dry-stone wall was built, producing a composite wall, up to 10 ft in thickness. Most of the houses were rectangular with rounded corners, and

Fig. 9   Plan of Skara Brae, Orkneys.

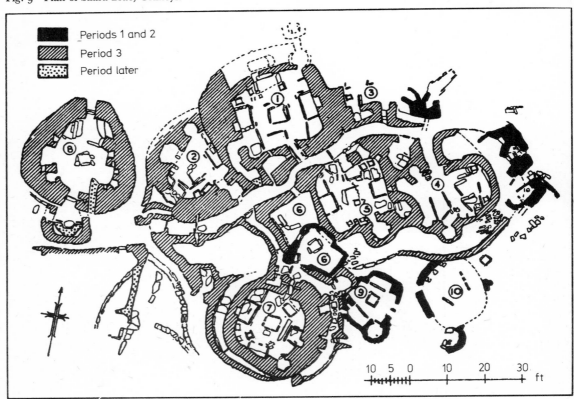

Periods 1 and 2
Period 3
Period later

10 5 0   10   20   30   ft

6 Hut No. 7, Skara Brae, Orkneys.

up to 21 ft square internally (House No. 1). The latter was noticeably larger than the others, presumably indicating some difference in wealth or rank. Access was via tunnel-like passages closed by doors locked in position with horizontal bars, the bar-holes for which are still visible.

One of the most striking features of Skara Brae is the uniformity, from house to house, of the stone furniture (Pl. 6). The central feature was a hearth, 4–5 ft square, edged with narrow kerb-stones, rising a few inches above floor level. Beyond the hearth, against the back wall, was what can only be described as a dresser. It consisted of two stone shelves, 5–7 ft long, resting on legs or piers projecting from the wall. This was presumably where the main domestic equipment was stored and, in fact, one pot was still standing on a dresser shelf when excavated. Against the right- and left-hand walls were the beds, stone slabs on edge enclosing spaces commensurate in size with modern single beds. These would have been filled with heather and grass, topped off with skins, to provide a warm and comfortable sleeping place. Above each bed was usually a cupboard-like recess for storage. Much smaller slab-lined boxes were let into the floor, the joints apparently sealed with clay. They are usually termed limpet boxes and may have been used for keeping limpets and other sea food. Other features include slab-lined drains, sometimes serving small cells in the thickness of the wall which may have acted as the family urinal.

Although the greater part of the house wall must have been sunk in midden debris the roof must have risen above it to allow for the emission of smoke. A low conical roof of turf or thatch, with a central smoke hole or chimney, seems the most likely, supported by whale jawbones (found on the site) or timbers, although no post-holes have been found. Houses 1–7 were linked by a system of narrow streets (unroofed) or corridors (roofed). It is quite clear that by Period 4 there were roofed corridors and this process of roofing over streets probably began in Period 3.

House No. 8 was detached from the main group. It contained a hearth but no dresser or beds and was therefore not a normal Skara Brae dwelling house. It was certainly used at one stage by a flint worker and may always have had an industrial rather than a domestic function.

The main feature of Period 4 was the piling up of midden material in the space remaining between the houses and over the now roofed corridors, transforming the village into a single mound. Thus Skara Brae finally became subterranean, but only as a result of a long-drawn-out process, starting from a village of free-standing houses.

Houses of virtually identical structure and furnishing have been excavated at Rinyo on the island of Rousay, likewise in Orkney. In addition to the Skara Brae features they possess also clay ovens, built on a flat slab placed against the hearth. They were about 15 in. square internally and at least 9 in. (probably originally 15 in.) high. They add an additional touch

Fig. 10 Plan of the Benie Hoose, Shetlands.

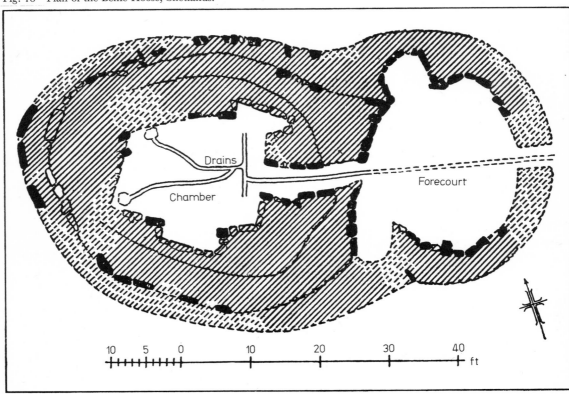

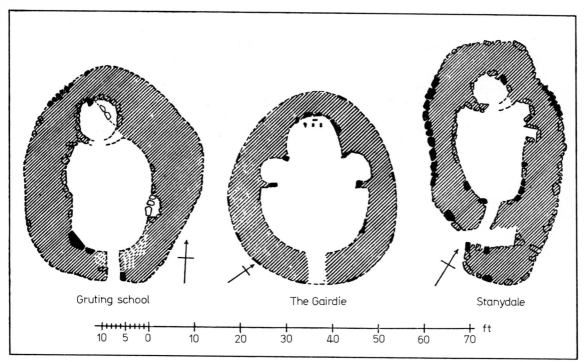

Fig. 11 Neolithic houses in the Shetlands.

Gruting school   The Gairdie   Stanydale

```
|++++|++++|——+——+——+——+——+——+——+——| ft
 10   5  0     10   20   30   40   50   60   70
```

to the already unusually full domestic picture presented by the range of furniture. There seems no reason to assume that domestic furniture was confined solely to Skara Brae and Rinyo. Indeed there is more reason to assume the opposite: that such furniture was part of a wider tradition of domestic equipment, normally executed in wood and therefore perishable, and it is as much for their implications in the field of domestic comfort as for their architecture that these sites in the Orkneys are so important.

In the Shetlands field work and excavation in the last twenty years have uncovered a whole new range of Neolithic houses which do not form tightly knit agglomerations linked by passages as at Skara Brae and Rinyo. These Shetland houses are closely linked in plan and structure with two (rare) structures, also in Shetland, usually interpreted as temples,

which are, in turn, closely linked to the megalithic tombs of the region. The Benie Hoose at Yoxie on the island of Whalsay stands within a hundred yards of one of the two temples mentioned above, which it resembles closely in plan, even to the extent of having an enclosed forecourt (Fig. 10). Because of this it has been suggested that it was the residence of the priests or attendants at the temple. The house is built with inner and outer dry-stone walls with a rubble filling between, producing an overall thickness of 12–15 ft. The house is some 80 ft long and over 40 ft wide with a D-shaped forecourt and a roughly rectangular main room, c. 20 × 15 ft, reached by a passage 15 × 3 ft. A system of drains served each corner of the main room and ran out through the passage, across the forecourt and through the outer entrance. There is no trace, either here or elsewhere in Shetland, of the elaborate furniture of the Orkney settlements.

The remaining Shetland houses lack the forecourt of the Benie Hoose but are otherwise of similar dimensions and structure (Fig. 11). They are usually oval in plan, up to 55 × 40 ft, with walls between 7 and 10 ft in thickness. An entrance passage at one end leads into a principal coal room, up to 20 × 15 ft in area, with subrectangular or semicircular recesses opening off to the sides. At the back, opposite the entrance, there is often a larger recess or apse, or even a roughly circular room, 8 or 9 ft in diameter. Associated with many of these houses are field-systems defined by dry-stone walls, suggesting that these were individual farms worked by a single family. Among the crops grown was barley, the carbonised remains of which have been found in excavation. Remains of animal bones indicate livestock that included horses, oxen, sheep, pigs and dogs. Since most of the houses are on or near the coast it is probable that the range of foods also included fish, shell-fish and marine mammals as well as sea-birds and their eggs; additional variety would have come from the gathering of wild fruits and berries.

The structure of these Shetland houses links them very closely to megalithic tombs and temples of the Neolithic period, and the pottery found in excavation tells the same story. The tombs belong to the later rather than the earlier part of the period and the presence of Early Bronze Age Beaker pottery in the houses, in addition to the Neolithic ware, indicates a late Neolithic/Early Bronze Age date for these Shetland houses, from perhaps 2300 to 1600 B.C.

The Bronze Age

The change from Neolithic to Bronze Age was a gradual one, with often a considerable time lag in the remoter parts of the British Isles, so that Late Neolithic there was contemporary with Early Bronze Age elsewhere. The houses and settlements in the Orkneys and Shetlands just described almost certainly continued well after 2000 B.C. and may well have been influenced by the Beaker cultures which heralded the opening of the Bronze Age. Other sites, principally Lough Gur in Ireland, showed continuity of occupation through Late Neolithic into Beaker times. At Lough Gur the evidence indicates that the Beaker occupants built oval rather than round or rectangular huts; the latter were quite clearly the work of the earlier Neolithic population. The Beaker structures consisted of a series of post-holes outlining two generally oval-shaped houses, about 23 × 15 ft, with one end flattened, presumably to house the entrance. Internal post-holes on the long axis were probably connected with the roof support, whatever form that took. Another Beaker house, at Downpatrick, Co. Down, has been claimed as circular, but in fact the post-holes by themselves define a shape and size (23 × 15 ft), very similar to the Lough Gur house, with a flattened end and a central line of posts. Associated with it was a smaller, circular house, some 13 ft in diameter. The surviving post-holes of a house at Beacon Hill, Flamborough, Yorkshire, define one end of an oval about 15 ft wide, which could well have been of the same type as those at Lough Gur and Downpatrick. Excavations at Belle Tout, Sussex, uncovered the corresponding portion of another oval house (unless it is complete as it stands).

The oval shape is not confined to timber structures or to the southern regions of the British Isles. At Northton in the island of Harris, Outer Hebrides, two stone-built Beaker houses (c. 28 × 14 ft) were sunk into the ground so that the walls served to retain the surrounding sand. A series of stake-holes 2–3 ft in from the wall were not strong enough to have supported anything heavier than a tent-like covering of skins (Fig. 12B). The Beaker structures at Easton Down flint mines, Wiltshire, were also sunk into the ground, although whether they were, in fact, houses is another matter. Certainly no hearths were

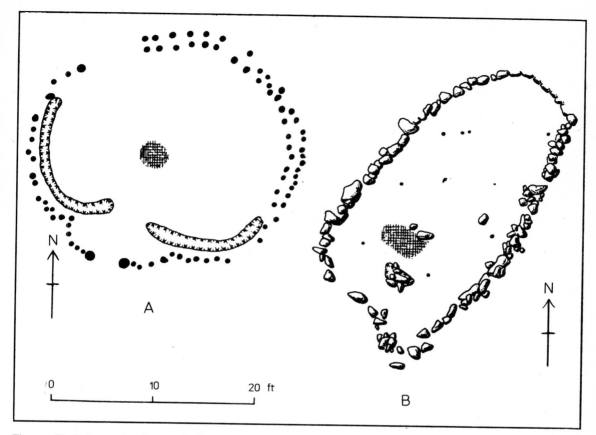

Fig. 12 Early Bronze Age houses: A, Gwithian, Cornwall; B, Northton, Outer Hebrides.

found in any of them. They consisted of oval hollows, up to 10 × 6 ft, sunk 1½ ft into the chalk, surrounded by oval or rectangular settings of posts.

The oval structures just described are somewhat unusual in terms of domestic architecture. They are in a sense more appropriate to a tent-like structure, and the houses at Northton may have given the clue. In addition to more substantial houses the Beaker people may have had a tradition, and a need, of something lighter and simpler, the essential part of which (the skin covering) could be transported as required, perhaps to meet purely seasonal needs.

The second Beaker hut at Downpatrick, mentioned earlier, was circular, as were some of the houses at Belle Tout in Sussex. The most elaborate circular Beaker house, however, is the one from Gwithian, Cornwall. The Phase 1 house was some 15 ft in diameter with a large centre post. This was replaced by a larger house (25 ft diameter) defined by a double setting of stake-holes and gullies, with a fairly elaborate porch-like arrangement at the entrance and a central hearth (Fig. 12A). There were no internal roof supports so that possibly the wall timbers were bent over to meet in the centre and then coated in some way to make the roof weatherproof. A stone-built, circular structure of probable Beaker date is recorded at Woodhead in Cumberland, but is not certainly a house; it may well have been a burial monument based on a house form.

The few remaining Beaker structures can be described as rectilinear. One of the houses at Belle Tout was trapeze-shaped (c. 22 × 13 × 5 ft), i.e. very similar in both shape and size to the possible Neolithic house at Eaton Heath, Norfolk. Some of the structures (presumably houses) in the settlement beneath a barrow at Swarkeston in Derbyshire were generally rectangular in shape, but the picture was confused by the large number of post-holes in the area. A recent excavation (1970) at Willington, Nottinghamshire, has uncovered two (possibly three) structures of Beaker date. The largest was some 50 × 30 ft, large by prehistoric standards, and very large for the Early Bronze Age.

The evidence for Early Bronze Age houses (Wessex and Food-vessel cultures) is meagre. At Coney Island, Lough Neagh, Armagh, Food-vessel sherds and tanged-and-barbed arrowheads were associated with the foundations of two rectangular houses (9 ft wide and up to 20 ft long), one of them built of turf supplemented by timber posts. At Carrigillihy, Co. Cork, the finds indicated an Early Bronze Age (possibly Beaker) date for an oval house (22 × 33 ft internally) with thick walls of rubble faced on either side with stone walling (Pl. 7). This stood within an oval enclosure (50 × 42 ft internally) surrounded by a dry-stone wall. The whole arrangement of a house standing within its own (farm?) yard looks very much later, but the evidence from Shearplace Hill, Dorset, supports the possibility of an Early Bronze Age date for a farming establishment.

The now generally accepted date (c. 1200–1000 B.C.) for the Deverel-Rimbury culture means that at least in the second half of the Middle Bronze Age there are a number of settlement sites to be considered, even if most of them continue also into the Late Bronze Age. The settlement most closely connected by its pottery with the type sites (Deverel and Rimbury in Dorset) is Shearplace Hill in the same county.

7 Model of the Early Bronze Age farmstead at Carrigillihy, Co. Cork.

Fig. 13 Reconstruction drawing of the Itford settlement, Sussex.

Although the main occupation was in the second half of the Middle Bronze Age, it is worth noting that there is some evidence of occupation in the earlier part of the period and possibly as early as the Wessex Early Bronze Age. Shearplace Hill (excavated 1958) consists of a series of linked earthwork enclosures forming the main feature of a complex of ancient fields and trackways. It is one of many such groups in Dorset which must be seen as Middle Bronze Age farmsteads. The Main Enclosure (c. 90 × 80 ft), defined by a bank and ditch, was flanked by the North Annexe (80 × 50 ft), the South Enclosure (80 × 40 ft) and the Outer South Enclosure (300 × 150 ft).

Of the two houses uncovered in the Main Enclosure, A was the larger. It had a 'marking-out groove' (34 ft in diameter) within which was a complex of post-holes defining a circular house (27 ft in diameter) with a fairly elaborate porch. House B was smaller (c. 16 ft diameter) but appeared to have a similar porch arrangement. It was suggested that House A was the principal dwelling and that B was a byre or servants' quarter.

More recently, however (1969), in an alternative interpretation, the 'marking-out groove' has been brought into the main structure of the house, and is seen as the setting for an outer wall of fairly light construction (possibly wattle and daub), with the main weight of the roof carried on the circle of timber uprights. The front of

39

the porch is now flush with the outer wall. The main importance of this interpretation lies in its significance for later and more elaborate Iron Age houses which Shearplace Hill now clearly appears to anticipate. Similar double-ringed round houses have been suggested for some of the other Middle/Late Bronze Age settlements to be considered next.

For the reasons given earlier, Itford Hill, Sussex, and a number of associated Bronze Age settlements must now be considered under the Middle Bronze Age heading, although the same type of settlement probably continued into the Late Bronze Age. Itford (Fig. 13) consisted of a linked group of earthwork enclosures and hut platforms, measuring overall 440 × 180 ft, with a small detached enclosure about 100 yds to the south-east. The principal enclosure (c. 120 × 80 ft) was surrounded by a timber fence and contained four circular huts, C, D, E and F. Hut D, the largest in the whole settlement, was 22 ft in diameter with a ring of timber uprights 10 in. in diameter and a porch 5 ft deep in front of the entrance. The other three huts were smaller (16–20 ft diameter) with no apparent entrances and may have been simply roofed shelters for livestock. Enclosures V, VI and VII contained among them another four huts while the remaining huts were to the north-west (A & B), the east (G) and the south-east (M & N). Although at first sight an assemblage of thirteen huts might look like a small village, the evidence suggests that only four of them were used as living accommodation. The rest would appear to have been used for farm purposes, so that the whole site can be seen as a farmstead, occupied by a single family, although of the extended (three-generation) variety. The excavators suggest a population of about twenty persons, which would agree with this. They also suggest that the occupants 'practised mixed farming by raising crops of barley and possibly other cereals, and by stock-raising with sheep and oxen'.

The reappraisal of house structure has been applied also to the Itford settlement. Briefly the rings of post-holes are now seen as inner rings of roof supports with a light outer wall beyond, the evidence for which has largely been destroyed. This would again make the porches which exist in some houses flush with the outer walls and it seems likely that the Itford houses, too, belong to the double-ring-and-porch type.

Like Itford, Thorny Down near Salisbury, Wiltshire, has had to be looked at again, both in terms of its date and its house type. The site consists of a single, roughly rectangular, earthwork enclosure (c. ½ an acre) containing the remains of at least nine timber-built huts, some larger than others, perhaps indicating, as at Itford, the varying needs of a farming establishment. Two of the larger huts (I and V) had porch arrangements, and once again it has been suggested that the ring of post-holes stood several feet inside the outer walls and carried the main weight of the roof, so that at Thorny Down, too, there would appear to have been houses of the double-ring-and-porch type in the Middle Bronze Age.

The most considerable group of Middle and Late (formerly Late) Bronze Age settlements is in Sussex where over a dozen sites are listed at the end of the Itford report. They include Plumpton Plain which, prior to the excavation of Itford, gave the clearest picture of such settlements. Although the others are quite clearly habitation sites, the remains are often such that the structural picture is not very clear. Plumpton Plain, however, was relatively well preserved. It consisted of four oval or subrectangular enclosures, surrounded by banks without ditches, the largest (c. 150 × 125 ft overall) linked together by a series of trackways defined by hollows and banks, the whole complex associated with a series of ancient fields, most, perhaps all, of which served the agricultural needs of the community involved. The post-holes found inside the enclosures do not indicate clear circular plans, and again the answer may be that they are the main internal supports of the roof and the porch, with a lighter wall beyond, all evidence of which has now gone, bringing Plumpton Plain in line with the other Middle/Late Bronze Age sites considered above.

A number of small, subrectangular earthworks recorded in Wessex and dated to the Late Bronze Age may be simpler, smaller versions of the farmsteads just described, or perhaps outlying units of a larger farmstead.

In south-west England the use of stone for building has led to the preservation of large numbers of occupation sites, particularly in the moorland regions. Recent work on the environment of prehistoric Dartmoor has shown that during the Late Neolithic and Early Bronze Age periods (c. 2400–1400 B.C.) there was widespread occupation of the area, probably in the form of clearings in the forest which still covered much of the landscape. The settlements consisted of groups of unenclosed circular stone huts with no evidence of field boundaries, but there is, nevertheless, clear botanical evidence of cultivation, and the absence of boundaries may not be significant in a forest clearance situation. The huts are small, below 20 ft in diameter, and consist of an inner wall with earth and stones packed against it, and either sloping down to ground level or retained by a second slighter outer wall, with overall thicknesses of 4–6 ft.

This is the simplest type of Dartmoor settlement. The remainder are grouped for the most part into three basic types which appear to be largely of Middle to Late Bronze Age date (1400–400 B.C.). Type A settlements consist of groups of huts enclosed by a stone wall forming a generally oval enclosure about 1–5 acres in area. Grimspound is one of the best-known examples. The surrounding wall (some 9 ft thick and originally up to 8 ft high) enclosed the remains of twenty-four circular stone huts scattered widely throughout the 4-acre enclosure. What are presumed to be stock pens stood against the inside of the pound wall. Single rings of upright slabs

are presumed to have been cattle shelters. About twelve huts showed evidence of human occupation, but few details of their structure are available. Dean Moor in the Avon valley (excavated 1954–6) is smaller than Grimspound (2½ acres). Inside the enclosing wall (c. 9 ft thick) were the remains of nine circular stone-built huts, scattered throughout the enclosed area which had been terraced to provide level floors. Internal diameters varied from 15 to 28 ft with walls 4–6 ft thick formed of inner and outer stone facings and a rubble filling. The roof was supported by a ring of posts 6–8 in. in diameter, set 3–6 ft in from the wall, together with a centre post. Some pounds consist of more than one enclosure, Rider's Rings, for example, with two (Pl. 8), and Legis Tor with four. These are only a few examples of several dozen such settlements. Presumably the relatively large space inside was to allow for the accommodation of livestock at night. Although there are one or two outliers, the bulk of such settlements are found in the southern and south-western parts of Dartmoor, around the valleys of the Avon, Erme, Yealm, Plym and Meavy.

The second type of settlement (B) is the unenclosed group of huts. These are less numerous than Type A and are found mostly on the western side of Dartmoor. They consist of groups of circular huts (up to seventy-four in one case) some of which are linked to each other by walls, thus forming small, irregular enclosures which could have been for cultivation or for livestock. Standon Down, high up the valley of the Tavy, has sixty-eight huts, spread over an area some 750 × 650 ft. Many of the huts are linked by walls which form a dozen or more irregular enclosures, up to 200 × 100 ft. Western Oke, in the same area, has seventy-four huts and follows the same pattern. Smaller settlements include Har Tor on the Meavy, and Langstone Moor on the Tavy. Type B sites are deemed to represent the settlements of people with a mixed agricultural economy, who not only reared cattle but also cultivated garden plots or small fields.

8 Enclosed settlement of Rider's Rings, Dartmoor, Devon.

In Type C settlements groups of huts are associated with rectilinear fields, indicating a predominantly agricultural economy. A small farm might consist of a single hut and two or three small fields defined by granite slabs and boulders. Rippon Tor, for example, has a single circular hut in a rectangular enclosure, c. 100 × 50 ft (a farmyard?). This is surrounded on three sides by small rectangular fields with a combined area of just over an acre. A larger farm, such as Blissmoor, has three huts and seven fields (c. 2 acres), and an even larger one, or perhaps a hamlet, such as Foale's Arrishes, has eight huts and some twenty fields (15–20 acres). One of the huts is placed within its own enclosure, a feature found also at Kestor (excavated 1951–2). The latter has some twenty huts and an area of rectangular fields half a mile long and a quarter of a mile wide. One of the two excavated huts proved to be an iron smelter's workshop, demonstrating the Late Bronze Age/Iron Age continuity in the area. The second hut had stone-faced walls some 5 ft thick and an internal diameter of 27 ft. As at Dean Moor the roof was supported by a ring of posts 4–5 ft in from the walls and a centre post. It looks very much as if this form of hut was standard, regardless of the type of settlement (enclosed, open or with rectangular fields), during Middle and Late Bronze Age and, indeed, Iron Age times. It is presumably the south-western version of the double-ring type described above in Wessex. The earlier huts (Early and Middle Bronze Age) were relatively small (15–20 ft internal diameter), while the later huts were up to 30 ft in diameter internally, and 40 ft externally. Type C sites occupy a distinct region of Dartmoor, the majority being on the eastern and north-eastern sides, in contrast to Types A and B which were largely confined to the south and west. Some forty such settlements have been listed and there are others in the remaining regions of the south-west, with probably many more yet to be discovered.

In other highland regions (North Wales, Yorkshire, the Lake District, Northumberland and Scotland) remains of a generally similar, but less spectacular, nature, indicate that in these regions, too, there was agricultural activity in the Middle to Late Bronze Age period, with the possibility, at least in some areas, of earlier activity in the Early Bronze Age and even Late Neolithic period, and the virtual certainty in many other areas of continuity into the Iron Age and Roman periods. Far less work has been done in these areas as compared with the south-west and the general picture is that much less clear. Three main types of settlement seem to be involved. First, small groups of huts associated with rather vague walled enclosures, which were presumably garden plots, in the Late Neolithic and Early/ Middle Bronze Age periods. Second, groups of huts associated with systems of irregular plots defined by lynchets and banks, in the Middle/Late Bronze Age. Third, more regular, rectangular fields, with associated huts, in Iron Age and later times. While the parallels are not exact there is sufficient similarity between these remains and those in the south-west to indicate a broadly similar experience in regions which were closely akin in geographical terms.

Beyond the Scottish mainland there are further Bronze Age remains in the Shetlands, most notably at the famous site of Jarlshof, occupied for some 3,000 years (1500 B.C.–A.D. 1500), during which there was Neolithic, Bronze Age, Iron Age, Viking and medieval occupation of the site. The first settlement of which there are substantial remains (Fig. 14) is Late Bronze Age and consisted of five stone-built houses, very much on lines of the Late Neolithic/Early Bronze Age houses mentioned earlier. The Jarlshof houses may not have all been occupied at the same time. The original excavator, Dr Curle (seasons 1931–5), suggested that at least some of them were occupied successively over a long period, House II replacing House I, and House III in turn replacing House II. All three conformed to the same plan. They were pear-shaped, 25–35 ft long and up to 35 ft wide with

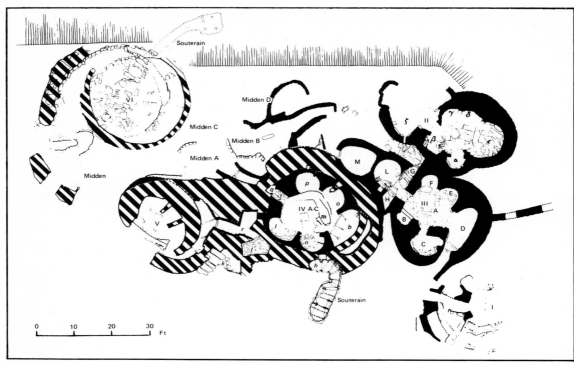

Fig. 14 Late Bronze Age (black) and Iron Age (black & white) settlements at Jarlshof, Shetlands.

dry-stone walls 4–6 ft thick. The entrance led into a central, roughly circular area (10–15 ft in diameter) almost certainly roofed over, beyond which was a large oval or semicircular room (c. 10–15 ft long and 6–9 ft wide). The remaining rooms or cells, four in each house, were placed in pairs symmetrically on either side of the central area. Later features included a walled courtyard in front of House II, a circular room (c. 7 ft diameter) opposite the entrance to House III (probably a potter's workshop), and another room (oval, c. 10 × 8 ft) adjacent to the latter, probably associated with House IV.

The inhabitants of this Late Bronze Age settlement lived largely by stock raising (sheep and cattle), although crops were cultivated as well. Fish (mainly cod), seals, sea-birds and shell-fish added variety to the diet. At a late stage in the history of the settlement a bronze-smith set up a workshop in one of the abandoned houses (III), and not very long after this new settlers arrived, bringing with them a new tradition of building and evidence of an Iron Age background.

Clickhimin, also in the Shetlands (excavated 1953–7), is known chiefly for its substantial, not to say spectacular, Iron Age remains. Beneath the later remains, however, was evidence of a Late Bronze Age farmstead, probably c. 700 B.C. Like Jarlshof, some twenty miles to the south, the main dwelling house was built in the long-standing Shetland tradition. It was oval in plan, 27 × 26 ft, with walls 5 ft thick. It had a southern entrance leading to a central hearth space (8 × 9 ft), and originally it possessed two lateral cells on each side of the hearth with a large compartment at the rear. At a later stage, outhouses were added to east and west and an enclosure wall was built around the crest of the islet on which the site stood, forming a farmyard 100 ft or so in diameter. Another Late Bronze Age farmstead of similar type is recorded at Wiltrow on the mainland coast between Jarlshof and Clickhimin.

The Iron Age

Any consideration of Iron Age houses and settlements must begin with the classic site of Little Woodbury near Salisbury, Wiltshire, excavated by Dr Gerhard Bersu in 1938 and 1939. The principal building was a large, circular timber house (50 ft in diameter). Other features included the remains of a timber palisade which took in an oval area (c. 400 × 300 ft) and defined what must be seen as the farmyard, within which the other building stood. The palisade appears to have consisted of upright stakes, possibly 5 or 6 ft high, set edge to edge in a trench about 1 ft deep.

The main house within the enclosure was clearly defined by four groups of post-holes (Fig. 15). Those in the outer ring were oval, probably for upright timbers (c. 18 × 10 in.) supporting the outer wall, with horizontal timbers between. The main support for the roof was probably provided by the second ring of posts, 12–15 in. in diameter and by the four central posts, up to 2 ft in diameter. Presumably both sets had continuous lintels on which rested the sloping rafters, linked by lighter horizontal timbers to which would be attached the outer roof covering, almost entirely of thatch. What happened at the apex is a matter for speculation. The four centre posts may have risen above the main roof to carry a separate canopy which would allow smoke to escape without admitting rain. In fact, a smoke-hole is not always necessary, particularly in a very large hut, the smoke simply dispersing through the roof space. In any case, the four-post setting may have had more to do with the provision of a loft (below) than with the emission of smoke for which it seems much too substantial.

The fourth and last group of post-holes,

eight in number, define an elaborate porch or entrance passage, some 15 ft long and 7–8 ft wide. This may be an indication that the outer wall of the house was relatively low, the passage providing adequate head-room for people and possibly vehicles. With regard to the latter it has been suggested recently that the great width of the entrance was to allow carts to be driven right into the building so that hay or similar materials could be unloaded directly into a loft in the roof space; a house 50 ft in diameter must have been 20–25 ft high so that it is perfectly feasible to envisage the utilisation of the upper portion in this way. Such a loft would go a long way to explain the presence of four massive posts at the centre of the hut.

House II, regarded by the excavator as later, but which could well have been simply an ancillary building, was of simpler construction. It was c. 33 ft in diameter with a ring of twenty-three post-holes, housing timbers c. 1 ft in diameter. A 10-ft gap on the eastern side was clearly the entrance, but much too wide for purely pedestrian traffic, so that something other than a purely domestic function has to be envisaged.

Within the palisade area some 190 carefully dug pits, up to 9 ft deep, were uncovered. These are generally interpreted as the storage system for the roasted grain, only a few of them being in use at any one time. Presumably they were lined with some sort of basket-work, otherwise the grain would have been very quickly affected by the dampness of the surrounding earth. The seed grain appears to have been stored in above-ground timber granaries standing on four legs; this is the usual interpretation of groups of four posts forming approximately 6 × 6 ft squares. Two-post settings (6–7 ft apart) are interpreted as corn-drying racks.

Everything points to the agricultural character of the Little Woodbury site and it must be seen as a complete farm, probably housing an extended (three-generation) family group. The large and substantial main

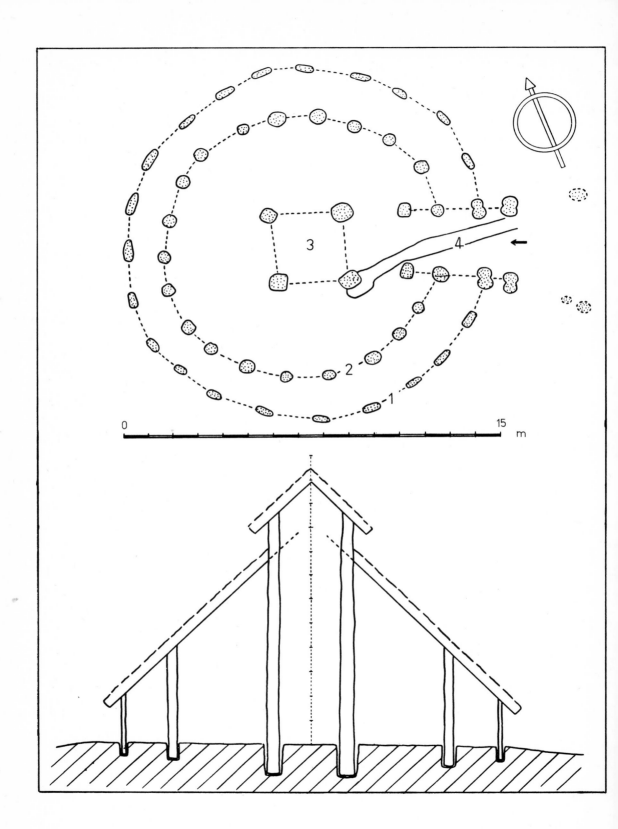

3

4

2

1

0   15
                                                 m

house (with nearly 2,000 square feet of floor space) indicates that it was a relatively prosperous establishment. How common such establishments were is difficult to say. Comparable sites have been discovered in recent years, but they are still not numerous and cannot be regarded as exclusively representative of Iron Age settlements. As will be seen later, many other types of Iron Age site are known.

The Little Woodbury palisaded enclosure is only one part of a much larger complex of earthworks. These include some small

enclosures, similar to the Late Bronze Age enclosures mentioned earlier, and may indicate continuity of occupation in Late Bronze Age/Iron Age times. However, the other notable feature of the complex is what is known as Great Woodbury, the ploughed-out remains of a much larger enclosure (c. 10 acres) about 500 yds to the west, linked to the smaller site by a ditch. Pairs of enclosures linked in this way (often described for obvious reasons as spectacles) are not uncommon in the chalk regions of Wessex and one such site at Pimperne, in Dorset, has produced remains comparable to those at Little Woodbury

9 Post-holes of the Iron Age house at Pimperne, Dorset.

Fig. 15 Plan and elevation of the Iron Age house at Little Woodbury, Wiltshire.

The site on Pimperne Down consisted of enclosure A (c. 1,000 × 650 ft) and enclosure B (c. 450 × 400 ft) about 150 ft apart, with a linking ditch, forming a 'spectacles' arrangement. Within the larger enclosure excavation has uncovered the post-holes of another large circular house (Pl. 9). Like Little Woodbury it had an outer ring of post-holes, an inner ring (c. 6 ft) inside these, and the post-holes of a substantial porch. What is most noticeably missing is the central four-post setting, and since this is missing from such other large Iron Age houses as exist, it would not appear to be an essential structural element of the type, and may have been designed to meet a particular need at Little Woodbury, perhaps the provision of the loft mentioned earlier.

Another large circular house (c. 50 ft overall diameter) was discovered at Longbridge Deverill, Wiltshire, as part of a complex broadly similar to Little Woodbury and Pimperne. The circular timber house (50 ft in diameter) consisted of three concentric rings of post-holes and a rectangular setting (the porch) at the entrance. The second (main) ring of posts (twenty-seven in number, 1 ft in diameter) were presumed to have been the main outer-wall supports, although this is not in keeping with the pattern of the other two sites. At the centre, there was an irregular ring of seven post-holes which may have supported some sort of simple loft.

Large circular houses do not appear to be confined to Wessex. At West Brandon, Co. Durham, an even larger example (58 ft diameter) stood within an enclosure of three-quarters of an acre, i.e. very much smaller than the Little Woodbury-type enclosures. The Phase I house had four concentric rings of posts. The house wall seems to have been on the second line (50 ft diameter), with the outer ring of smaller posts supporting the eaves. The third ring was some 9 ft inside the walls and presumably provided the main roof support. A fourth, rather irregular ring (12–13 ft diameter), may have supported a loft. There were additional

posts in the entrance area, but nothing as elaborate as the Little Woodbury-type porches. In Phase II the main wall was represented by a continuous groove or trench, in which the timber uprights could be set. An outer ring of light posts appears to have supported the eaves while internally there was a circular setting some 9 ft in from the wall, with additional posts at the centre. There was some elaboration of the doorway (c. 8 ft wide), although again nothing on the scale of the Little Woodbury porch. Enclosures of the West Brandon type are known elsewhere in the region so that the site is presumably representative of a series in the north-east.

The same house type is known also in Scotland, at West Plean, Stirlingshire. The remains consist of a ring groove, some 40 ft in diameter, with out-turned portions at the entrance similar to West Brandon. About 8 ft inside is a ring of eleven posts to support the roof. This is the smallest and simplest of the five 'large' houses considered so far, and is only slightly larger than the general run of Iron Age houses to be considered later. The distribution of the larger houses (in Wessex, north-east England and mid-Scotland) shows that the type is not simply a regional one but an integral part of the Iron Age building tradition in which there are both large and small houses. The various sizes would appear to indicate differing degrees of prosperity rather than a chronological development from small to large.

As indicated earlier, Little Woodbury, Pimperne, Longbridge Deverill, etc., represent only one type of Iron Age settlement. Other more modest types seem to have existed as well, consisting of smaller huts, of simpler construction, standing within comparatively small, often sub-rectangular, enclosures. These recall, both in size and shape, the Late Bronze Age enclosures mentioned earlier, and the native Late Bronze Age ancestry of these Iron age sites seems highly probable.

In this respect the excavation of the Iron Age settlement at Tollard Royal, Wiltshire, was most informative. It consisted of an angular, kite-shaped enclosure (c. ½ acre in area) with a simple round hut (c. 17 ft in diameter). Both enclosure and hut recall Middle/Late Bronze Age sites mentioned earlier such as Shearplace Hill, Thorny Down and Itford. Besides the single hut the enclosure also contained storage pits, working hollows and the post-holes for what are presumed to be granaries. These same features are recorded at two very famous nearby sites in Dorset, Rotherly and Woodcutts, excavated by General Pitt-Rivers at the end of the last century. The principal occupation at these two sites was during the Romano-British period but there is little doubt that their earliest phases, in the Late Iron Age, closely resembled Tollard Royal. Thus all three would appear to represent a long continuation in the Iron Age of a basically Late Bronze Age type of settlement. The settlement at Eldon's Seat, Dorset, also had a sequence of occupation from Late Bronze Age to Roman times. The Late Bronze Age settlement may have been enclosed by a timber palisade in the Itford manner, although there is no evidence on this point in the Iron Age settlement. One of the Iron Age huts (No. 6) quite clearly had a shallow porch, linking it structurally to Shearplace Hill and similar huts on the one hand and the Little Woodbury elaborate porches on the other.

Outside Wessex there are comparable small enclosures with fairly simple huts in a number of places in southern Britain. At Draughton, Northamptonshire, a small sub-rectangular enclosure, about 100 ft across, was surrounded by a bank and ditch. Inside were the remains of three huts, one c. 35 ft in diameter and the other two c. 20 ft. There was little indication as to the nature of the original structures. Presumably the larger hut was the main dwelling, with the two smaller as ancillary farm buildings. Colsterworth, Lincolnshire, was somewhat larger (240 × 210 ft internally), again originally surrounded by a bank and ditch. Inside were the remains of up to a dozen huts, not all of one period, mostly

between 20–35 ft in diameter, with one larger hut up to 44 ft across. Heathrow, Middlesex, was larger again, and roughly rectangular (c. 300 × 300 ft internally) surrounded originally by a substantial bank and ditch (Pl. 10). Inside were the remains of eleven huts, again not all of one period, up to 33 ft in diameter. Vinces Farm in Essex was also roughly rectangular, but much smaller, only c. 100 × 50 ft internally, and appeared to have contained only one circular house (c. 35 ft in diameter) with little detailed evidence as to its original structure. Staple Howe, in Yorkshire, was defined by a timber palisade, oval in plan (c. 200 × 90 ft). Inside were the remains of three huts, one, presumably the principal dwelling (c. 30 ft in diameter), and two smaller huts, one oval (30 × 20 ft), and one circular (c. 18ft diameter).

At West Harling, Norfolk, the two principal structures (II and III) were both circular but rather different in character. Site III was a circular hut (c. 36 ft in diameter), defined by post-holes but with no special structural features. It was surrounded by a very shallow circular ditch (c. 100 ft in diameter) which probably carried a thorn hedge. Site II was a more complex structure which has been the subject of a number of interpretations. It consists of a bank and ditch, with two entrances, north and west, closely surrounding a circular setting of posts (c. 50 ft in diameter). The excavators point to the difficulty of roofing such a structure with the range of post-holes uncovered, and suggest that the central area was an unroofed yard or court, surrounded by a range of buildings backed against the surrounding bank, although the bank can never have been very substantial. More recently a variation of this arrangement has been suggested in connection with the structures in some Scottish forts.

The Little Woodbury-type settlements and those smaller settlements in the late Bronze Age tradition appear to have existed alongside each other, representing two

10 Reconstruction drawing of the Iron Age settlement at Heathrow, Middlesex, by Alan Sorrell.

aspects of Iron Age life. Other aspects are represented by enclosures, known mostly from aerial photography, which differ from both of these, and by settlements within Iron Age forts (Chapter 8). In Hampshire a series of enclosures, all apparently of Iron Age date, indicate a much wider variety of settlement patterns than that encountered so far. A few settlements of the Little Woodbury type do exist but are heavily outnumbered by other types. One of these consists of an inner enclosure (c. 2–3 acres) contained by an outer enclosure (5–6 acres), with crossbanks dividing the space between (c. 100–125 ft wide) into segments. Another type is based on a so-called 'banjo' enclosure; a small inner enclosure ($\frac{1}{2}$–$1\frac{1}{2}$ acres) is approached by parallel ditches (forming

the banjo shape), which then swing outwards to form, in many cases, a second enclosure completely embracing the first. Other types recorded include enclosures of Little Woodbury size, but without its features (pits, working hollows, etc.), smaller enclosures, presumably in the same Late Bronze Age tradition as those described earlier, and what appear to be unenclosed or open settlements, groups of storage pits and working hollows with no visible surrounding earthworks. All this indicates the wide range of variations in Iron Age economy, the physical size and shape of the settlements presumably reflecting the nature and needs of the farming carried on. Under the broad heading of mixed farming differing balances of crop cultivation on the one hand and animal production on the other would have required different types of establishment and this is presumably the explanation of the variety of Iron Age settlement types in Wessex.

Yet one more type of settlement exists, both in Wessex and elsewhere, within Iron Age forts. Only about 5 per cent of such sites show visible evidence of hut circles (although the original number was probably much greater), and in Wessex this amounts to half a dozen or so forts. In most cases the groups are no larger than those encountered so far, but in at least two cases several hundred huts are involved, at Hod Hill and Hambledon Hill in Dorset, and there are similar numbers in other large forts as well (Fig. 64, for example). These cannot be described in the terms used so far and must be seen, in social terms, as (defended) villages or small towns and, in economic terms, as market centres where the surplus production of the farms could be exchanged for goods and services not otherwise available to farming communities. Thus in the late Iron Age, at the very end of the prehistoric period, it is possible to discern the first simple beginnings of urban life as opposed to the purely rural patterns which had existed hitherto.

In south-west England the pattern of settlements described for the Middle and Late Bronze Age appear to have continued largely unchanged into the Iron Age. At Kestor the one unequivocally Iron Age structure, the iron-smelter's hut with abundant remains of iron slag, was of the same type as all the other huts, with a double-skinned stone wall 5 ft thick and an internal range of timber post-holes to support the roof. At Bodrifty, near Penzance, a settlement which produced largely Iron Age pottery consisted of a group of a dozen or so huts within an oval pound some 400 ft long. The huts were very much in the Bronze Age tradition and some of them were linked to each other by lengths of wall which in some cases appear to have formed small enclosures. Settlements of this type hark back to the local Bronze Age on the one hand, and on the other closely

resemble the small enclosed settlements of Late Bronze Age tradition in Wessex and other parts of southern Britain, as described earlier.

As in Wessex, hut groups within hill forts represent another facet of Iron Age settlement. In the south-west, however, many of the forts are very small, 1–3 acres in area, known locally as 'rounds', so that any settlement within them is more likely to be a defended homestead rather than a defended village. Trevisker, mentioned earlier, is a case in point. In its first Iron Age phase it was a very small fort (c. ½ acre in area), with a single house (c. 42 ft diameter) within. At a later stage this was replaced by a larger fort (c. 3 acres in area) with three or more houses inside. Rounds, and non-circular forts of similar size, are very common in the south-west and many, perhaps all of them, are, like Trevisker, defended farmsteads. At the larger size (c. 3 acres) they may well be the south-western equivalents of Little Woodbury, while the smaller settlements may be closer to the surviving Late Bronze Age tradition.

Perhaps the most celebrated of all archaeological sites in south-west England are Glastonbury, Meare and Chysauster. Glastonbury and Meare in Somerset have long been famous as 'lake-villages', although this term has been questioned recently and the alternative term 'lakeside villages' proposed. Certainly there is now no question of these sites being artificial islands surrounded by open water, or even by marshes, as they have frequently been visualised. The precise environmental conditions of the period are still not clear, and may not have been exactly the same at the two villages. In general, conditions at Glastonbury appear to have been wetter than those at Meare and the Glastonbury settlement may well have been on the edge of the former Meare pool, so that a foundation or platform was required, although nothing on the scale which would have been required if the settlement had been the artificial island so often invoked. In its main period of occupation the site

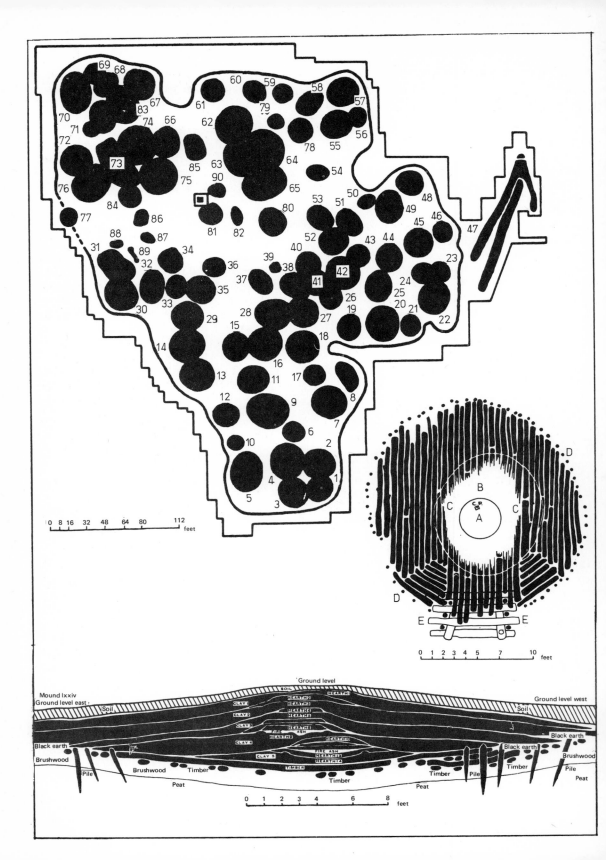

0 8 16 32 48 64 80 112
feet

D

B
C C R C
A

D

E E

0 1 2 3 4 5 7 10
feet

Mound lxxiv
Ground level east
Soil

Ground level
SOIL
HEARTH5 HEARTH
CLAY 1
HEARTH3
CLAY 2
HEARTH1
CLAY 3
HEARTH1
FIRE ASH
CLAY 4
HEARTH9 HEARTH10
FIRE ASH
CLAY 5
HEARTH13
TIMBER HEARTH14
TIMBER

Ground level west
Soil

Black earth
Brushwood

Black earth

Black earth
Brushwood

Brushwood Timber Timber
Pile Pile
Peat Peat
Peat

0 1 2 3 4 6 8
feet

consisted of an irregular 2-acre area, enclosed by a timber palisade, and containing eighty-nine fairly closely packed circular huts (Fig. 16). The foundation on which this settlement was built included timbers which have recently been recognised as forming part of an earlier Iron Age settlement consisting of rectangular, timber-framed huts, many c. 10 ft square, with plank floors, resting on oak piles driven into the peat. This settlement, possibly of the fourth century B.C., was replaced during the first century B.C. by the better-known Glastonbury settlement, the circular huts of which were 20–30 ft in diameter, with a centre post and clay floors. The latter needed frequent renewal,

as many as ten times in some cases, because they gradually sagged, due to the softness of the ground beneath.

Recent work at the Meare settlement has established a similar sequence. However, conditions seem to have been generally drier there and the settlement may not have been actually on the lake side, but some distance away. The most substantial structural remains, at both Meare and Glastonbury, have always been the mounds formed by superimposed layers of clay and these have always been interpreted as hut floors. However, the recent reinvestigation has indicated that by no means all such mounds were originally huts, and the estimated number of dwellings in the two parts of the Meare village (c. sixty huts each) may be rather less than has generally been assumed. The

11   Oblique aerial view of the Iron Age village at Chysauster, Cornwall.

53

Fig. 16   Plan of Glastonbury settlement; plan and section of hut 74.

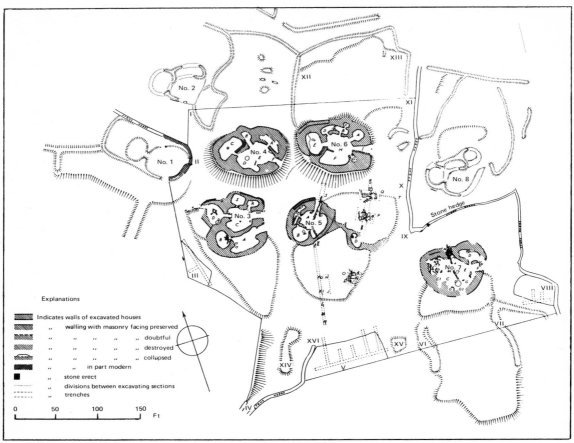

Fig. 17 Plan of the Iron Age village of Chysauster, Cornwall.

same reservation may, of course, apply also to the eighty-nine huts of the Glastonbury village. Although there are no other sites comparable to these two, they are unlikely to have been unique and they must be seen as another facet of the Iron Age settlement pattern. Even if the numbers of huts need to be reduced they must still be seen as villages rather than single homesteads, and as such are comparable with the larger groupings noted already within hillforts in Wessex and other regions.

Chysauster, in Cornwall, is equally famous in archaeological literature, because of its well-preserved and very large, elaborate houses (Pl. 11). Although the main occupation of these was in the Roman period, and many such houses were apparently only built then, there is some evidence of earlier occupation and the type is almost certainly in the prehistoric tradition and must therefore be included here. Although very much larger, it is very much in the style of the oval, Late Neolithic/Bronze Age houses in Scotland considered earlier, in which the rooms were contrived in the thickness of the structure. There the central area was roofed as well. In Cornwall the much greater size makes this extremely difficult and the central area is an open courtyard, hence the name courtyard houses. None the less, in spite of this difference and the difference in size, it seems perfectly feasible to see such houses as a more developed form of a long-established native type of house in the highland zone.

There are between thirty and forty settlements in Cornwall which have court-yard houses, sometimes mixed in with round huts, but Chysauster provides the best range of excavated examples. Its eight houses were strung out in two rows of four each, about 50 ft apart (Fig. 17). The houses were generally oval in plan, up to 90 × 70 ft. The entrance, on the eastern side, gave access to the central, open courtyard, from which opened a varying number of rooms, although these nearly always included three basic rooms. At the back of the court, opposite the entrance, was always a large round or oval room, usually paved and up to 30 ft in one dimension. This was presumably the main living-room of the house. The space on the left-hand side of the courtyard appears to have been roofed but open-fronted, possibly as some sort of shelter for livestock. On the right-hand side there was usually a long, narrow room, possibly used for storage. Beyond these basic areas (court-yard, living-room, shelter and store) there were often additional rooms which varied from house to house. Drains were a common feature of the houses, as were associated terraced areas, interpreted as (vegetable) garden plots.

As in the south-west, there is a mixed body of evidence on settlements in North Wales, without very much satisfactory dating evidence. There is quite clearly continuity from Late Bronze Age to Iron Age, par-ticularly in the smaller, simpler sites, such as the small groups of unenclosed huts which exist in fairly large numbers in Caernarvon-shire and adjacent areas. Equally there is clear evidence of continuity from the Iron Age to the Roman period, so that isolating specifically Iron Age types of settlement will always be difficult. One type which is dated by excavation evidence to the second and third centuries A.D. is the 'enclosed homesteads' which has also been described

as a courtyard house. This immediately suggests a link with the courtyard houses just considered in Cornwall, a link which has been suggested by some and denied by others. One of the arguments against the link has been the Roman date of the North Wales sites but, as indicated earlier, the Cornish sites are now seen as primarily Roman so there are no chronological reasons why the two types should not be connected. They are generally similar in size and shape and, although not identical in layout, they follow the same broad principle of an open courtyard area with a rooms opening from it. Although occupied mainly in the Roman period the North Wales sites may well have originated in the latter part of the Iron Age and, like Chysauster and similar sites, be seen as a developed form of a traditional native type with a long history in the highland zone. Some of the differences between the south-western and Welsh sites may be due to the fact that the latter are not grouped in villages but are apparently isolated farmsteads.

Sites consisting of concentric circles, the innermost one of which is a hut circle, are another type in North Wales which may well be Iron Age. The circles consist of dry-stone walls and can be two or three in number with overall diameters up to 200 ft. Those with two rings, a single hut within a roughly circular enclosure, may be similar to some sites noted in the south-west such as the iron-workers' establishment at Kestor in which a stone hut stood within the so-called Round. Sites with three rings are presumably a more elaborate version of the same type of establishment. An excavated example at Penygroes, Caernar-vonshire, had diameters of 40, 85 and 200 ft for the inner, middle and outer rings. Middle and outer rings were linked in the entrance area by parallel walls forming a passageway. The structure of the hut (with a double-skinned wall c. 5 ft thick) was similar to those in the south-west. Both two- and three-ring sites were presumably connected with the enclosure or pounding of livestock. In the two-ring type they would occupy the area immediately around the hut. In the three-ring type they would be contained between the middle and outer rings, leaving the area immediately around the hut free for other purposes.

As in other regions Iron Age settlement is represented also by hut groups within hillforts. Because it is a largely stone-using region these are particularly well represented in Caernarvonshire. The number of huts at some sites indicate a fairly considerable social group, comparable with those in the larger sites in Wessex. At Garn Boduan, for example, there are the remains of some 160 round huts, between 15 and 25 ft in diameter, and there are similar numbers, at other sites, such as Tre'r Ceiri and Carn Fadrun. There are similar numbers, too, at some sites in south-west Wales, at Carn Ingli and Moel Trigarn in Pembrokeshire.

Some indication of the Iron Age settlement pattern in north-east England and southern Scotland has already been given, with reference to the sites at West Brandon, Co. Durham, and West Plean, Stirlingshire. Such sites suggest that at least to some degree these northern regions shared the experience of Wessex with regard to the construction of advanced types of Iron Age houses. As pointed out earlier, the West Brandon house stood within a relatively small enclosure, in what was taken to be the Late Bronze Age tradition, and such enclosures are not infrequent in the area, many of them of the palisade type, containing single huts, some of them presumably of West Brandon size, but many more probably of more modest dimensions (20–35 ft) representing the commoner type of house. Palisaded enclosures also contained larger settlements, groups of a dozen or more huts, perhaps the northern counterparts of some of the sites discussed earlier with similar numbers of huts in the southern half of Britain. The same may be true of the so-called 'scooped enclosures' found in the north-east. These consist of a series of enclosures and platforms cut in the slope of a hill and surrounded by a stone wall. These have been compared to southern sites such as Itford which, in turn, is deemed to be ancestral to the types of Iron Age sites just mentioned, so that again the broad experience of north-east England and southern Scotland may have been very similar to that of southern Britain with regard to Iron Age settlement as a whole.

This receives further confirmation from the settlements inside the numerous hillforts of the area. Many of them are quite small, similar to those in south-west England, and may represent fortified homesteads rather than any more ambitious type of fortification. Some of them, indeed, seem to have had earlier phases, before the defences as such were built, when they were surrounded simply by palisades as described earlier. There are also larger groupings inside more extensive forts, as noted for North Wales and southern England. Yevering Bell, Northumberland, for example, has some 130 hut sites visible within its rampart, while Eildon Hill North, Roxburghshire, still has about 300, with a possible original total of c. 500, quite clearly a very substantial settlement and something much more than a group of farming families. Social groups of this size must have embraced many people who were not themselves food producers but nevertheless occupied essential economic positions: middlemen, traders, specialists in metal work and other crafts, exchanging their skills for the produce of those engaged directly in farming. Thus the broad settlement pattern in north-east England and lowland Scotland, while not identical to that in southern England, nevertheless has many areas of resemblance; such variations as do exist may be due as much to environmental differences as anything else.

The earlier phases (Neolithic and Bronze Age) of some of the Iron Age sites in the far north of Scotland have been mentioned already, most notably at Jarlshof and Clickhimin, in the Shetlands. At Jarlshof the first Iron Age settlement was built above the buried remains of the Late Bronze Age site (Fig. 14). It consisted of three structures with an associated series of souterrains or underground chambers. The main structures were circular or oval in plan and were partly subdivided by radial walls projecting inwards from the main surrounding walls. Judging by the remains found, one of the huts was a workshop rather than a dwelling, while another was quite clearly open on one side and was, therefore, presumably a shelter for live-stock. Only one of the three was used for normal living purposes, so that the site would appear to have been a single family establishment rather than a three-hut hamlet. In spite of the change from bronze to iron (in any case only a gradual process), the basic economy probably remained much the same: the rearing of cattle and sheep and some crop growing, both supplemented by hunting and food gathering. Eventually, this settlement too was abandoned and was covered with drifting sand by the time the next Iron Age settlement came to be built.

Before dealing with this a number of sites comparable to that just described need to be dealt with. At Clickhimin, which likewise had a preceding Bronze Age farmstead, structural remains of the first Iron Age settlement were largely destroyed by later developments (Fig. 68). However, enough remains to indicate that the main dwelling house had walls 4–6 ft thick enclosing a circular space some 25 ft in diameter, probably partly subdivided by radial walls in the Jarlshof manner. At a later stage the old Bronze Age house was utilised as an outhouse. The same type of dwelling is encountered also in the Orkneys where two sites provide much clearer structural evidence. At Howmae the structures were sunk into the sand dunes so that the walls were relatively thin, but the internal layout recalled Jarlshof. Oval or roughly circular rooms up to 25 ft in diameter had radial walls, up to 5 ft long, projecting inwards from the main walls. At the Calf of Eday, on the other hand,

the structure was free-standing with walls up to 8 ft thick and a more or less circular interior space, again c. 25 ft in diameter. Radial walls up to 5 ft long divided the space near the wall into nine separate compartments, each c. 7 × 5 ft. The broad uniformity in size and layout of these examples suggests that farmsteads of this type were a fairly widespread feature of Iron Age settlement in the Orkneys and Shetlands, and probably in the adjacent regions of the Scottish mainland as well. The nature of the sites, and the general absence of fortification, suggest that this was a period of peaceful farming settle-ment, probably during the last few cen-turies B.C. This era of peace eventually came to an end (probably during the first century A.D.), to judge by the appearance in the Hebrides, Orkneys, Shetlands and northern and western Scotland, of some hundreds of stone-built circular towers, known as brochs, which form the subject of Chapter 9. The brochs were, in their turn, followed by the last two house types to be considered in this chapter, aisled roundhouses and wheelhouses. These developments can best be followed in the long sequence at Jarlshof.

At Jarlshof the new Iron Age structures were built a little to the west of the now sand-covered Late Bronze Age and Iron Age settlements (Fig. 18). The first struc-ture (Phase I) was, in fact, a broch; with an attached oval courtyard on its west side; the southern half of both broch and courtyard have been lost through erosion by the sea. Since the broch will be dealt with in Chapter 9 the first phase to be considered here is Phase II, which probably followed quite shortly after Phase I, during which a large roundhouse was built in the northern part of the broch courtyard. The house was, in fact, slightly oval (37 × 34 ft internally), with walls 4 ft thick, although it was flanked for about two-thirds of its circumference by the remains of the broch and the courtyard wall. The surviving height of the house wall (7 ft 7 in.), and the existence of a ledge or scarcement at

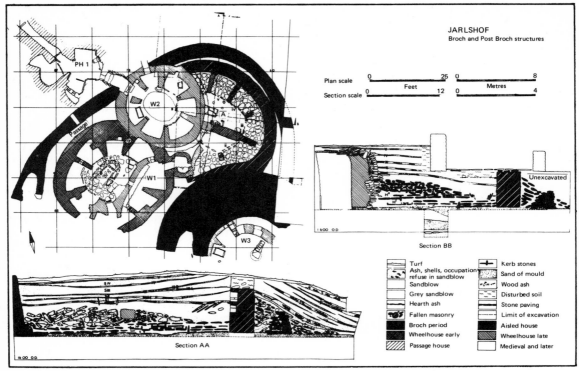

Fig. 18 Plan of the broch courtyard, the aisled house (A), and the wheelhouses (W1–3) at Jarlshof, Shetlands.

5 ft 4 in. to support the upper floor, indicate that the roundhouse was a two-storey structure. The upper floor seems to have consisted of a gallery extending some 6 ft out from the wall, leaving a circular open space at the centre. It was supported by the ledge and, as first built, by timber uprights around the central area which probably extended upwards to support the the roof which was probably cone-shaped with a central opening. At a later stage the timber uprights were replaced by eight massive free-standing stone piers which would have supported a much more substantial roof. A number of structural features call for comment in this house. The circular setting of timber posts inside the roundhouse is very much on the lines of timber structures inside brochs, and this is hardly surprising since the house abuts and

immediately succeeds a broch, so that the building tradition involved was obviously still very much alive. This was followed by the arrangement of stone piers which recalls radial walls of the Iron Age houses described earlier and looks ahead to the true wheelhouses which followed in Phase III at Jarlshof.

The effect of the stone piers which stood free of the house wall was to leave a sort of aisle around the circumference and such houses have been designated aisled roundhouses. The type is not confined to the Shetland region. There are closely comparable aisled roundhouses in the Outer Hebrides, in North and South Uist. At Clettraval, N. Uist, there were eight piers, as at Jarlshof, standing within a circular house, internally 28 ft in diameter, externally 46 ft (Fig. 19). The difference of 18 ft is accounted for by the great thickness of the house wall, which is, in fact, double, with a turf and rubble filling between inner and outer walls each c. 2½ ft thick. Another aisled roundhouse at Kilpheder, S. Uist, was of similar dimensions (29 ft diameter internally) with a double wall at least 10 ft thick, and eleven stone piers, two of them flanking the entrance.

Returning to the sequence at Jarlshof again, the aisled roundhouse of Phase II was followed, probably during the second and third centuries A.D., when the broch tower was now in ruins, by the wheelhouses of Phase III (Fig. 18). That a close family relationship exists between the aisled roundhouses and wheelhouses is apparent from the fact that the term wheelhouse is sometimes applied to both groups indiscriminately. In a recent work on the Iron Age, the Kilpheder aisled roundhouse is described as a wheelhouse. Both types are, in fact, wheel-like in plan, as indeed are many of the earlier Iron Age houses in northern Scotland, and all must be seen as

closely interrelated types. As used here the term wheelhouse is descriptive of houses of the type exemplified in Phase III at Jarlshof, where four examples have been uncovered in excavation. The typical wheelhouse is circular in plan (30–40 ft in overall diameter) with dry-stone walls 3–4 ft thick, i.e. somewhat smaller and less massive than the average aisled roundhouse. Internally it has radial walls (rather than free-standing piers), which in most cases taper in plan towards the centre. The compartments thus formed are roofed with flat stone slabs (preserved in one house at Jarlshof at a height of 9 ft), covered with further dry-stone work (part of the corbelling for the central part of the roof), topped off with turf. There is no indication of a second storey and to that extent wheelhouses are simpler structures than aisled roundhouses. In a sense they represent a return to the earlier Iron Age type which contained most of the elements of a wheelhouse without its more formal regular layout. The aisled roundhouses can be seen as a more sophisticated interlude in the

Fig. 19   Plan of the aisled round house at Clettraval, Outer Hebrides.

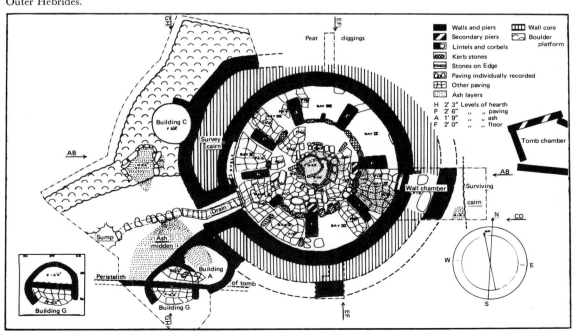

59

basic native tradition, perhaps under the influence of broch architecture which preceded them.

Of the four wheelhouses at Jarlshof only two are well preserved. The third was built inside the broch of which half is missing and the remains of the fourth were fragmentary. It seems likely that there were other wheelhouses in the now destroyed southern half of the courtyard. At Clickhimin the simple wheelhouse was likewise built inside the remains of the broch tower, and the same seems to have happened at a number of other sites in the Shetlands. In the Orkneys and the adjacent mainland (Caithness and Sutherland), on the other hand, broch and post-broch settlements seem to have taken the form of rather irregular clusters of huts of no particular shape or tradition around the broch tower, best seen at Gurness and Lingro in the Orkneys. In the Hebrides, on the other hand, the pattern is more akin to that in the Shetlands. Villages of the type just mentioned seem to be absent and where there is evidence of subsequent occupation it takes the form either of squatting in the remains of the broch or of aisled round-houses and wheelhouses of the Shetland type.

In the following development of houses and settlements in these northerly regions, outside the province of Roman Britain, the story has been carried far beyond the end of the prehistoric period in the south (A.D. 43). Wheelhouses were, indeed, still very much in use after the Romans had withdrawn from Britain and probably continued to be used until the sixth or seventh century A.D. But even in the south the story had to be taken beyond the actual date of the Roman conquest because it was quite clear that in many areas the native tradition remained strong and the full story of prehistoric houses and settlements could not be told without venturing into, and indeed going beyond, the period of Roman occupation.

Recent work in two hillforts has produced evidence which adds significantly to the picture of prehistoric housing presented here. At Moel y Gaer, Rhosesmor, Flintshire, round huts were uncovered, of the double-ring-and-porch variety discussed earlier. The huts were 25–30 ft in diameter with a stake-built outer wall and an internal ring (c. 18–22 ft in diameter) of about a dozen posts which provided the main support of the roof. At the entrance a setting of four posts formed a porch about 10 ft wide and about 6 ft deep. Associated with these huts were rectangular structures represented by settings of four post-holes about 10–12 ft square. These have been encountered in one or two other sites and will be further considered below. At the second hillfort, Crickley Hill, Gloucestershire, the houses uncovered were rectangular, and of unusual size, up to 80 ft long and 20 ft wide. Their main structural features were two rows of posts about 10 ft apart running the length of the hut; the posts in the rows were at 8–10 ft intervals and provided the main support of the roof. Crickley Hill demonstrates clearly that the Late Bronze Age/Iron Age tradition was not exclusively one of round houses.

Four- (and occasionally six-) post square structures have been encountered also at other hillforts, including Danebury, Hampshire, Croft Ambrey, Herefordshire, and Fridd Faldwyn, Montgomeryshire. Their precise function is uncertain. They seem too small to be houses, at least by the standard of most of the houses considered in this chapter, and at Moel y Gaer they stand alongside a group of round huts, as described above, as if they were something other than dwellings. At Little Woodbury, rectangular settings of four posts were presumed to be the remains of above-ground granaries and this is one possible explanation of these larger settings. Another possibility is that these posts are the main supports for above-ground dwellings, which could have been stepped out by several feet on all four sides, thus achieving dimensions normally accepted as commensurate with those of a dwelling (c. 14–18 ft square).

3 The Windmill Hill People

Apart from its portable remains the Neolithic of southern England, the Windmill Hill culture, is represented by a considerable group of monuments, including some of the most puzzling types of the whole prehistoric period. Among these are the so-called *causewayed enclosures*, the outstanding example of which is Windmill Hill, Wiltshire, which gives its name to the whole culture. The other monuments represented are earthen (or unchambered) *long barrows*, for burial purposes, *cursus earthworks*, another very puzzling type, and *flint mines*, not strictly monuments in the same sense as the other three types but none the less an important part of the non-portable remains of the Windmill Hill culture. The location of these sites, supplemented by the distribution of smaller finds (pottery, etc.), indicates the area occupied by the Windmill Hill people; that part of England south and east of a line from the Severn to the Wash, with an extension northwards into Lincolnshire and Yorkshire (Fig. 20).

Causewayed enclosures (Fig. 21)

The sites included under this heading consist of either a single roughly circular or oval enclosure, or two, three or four more or less concentric enclosures, formed of banks with outer ditches. The ditches, however, are not continuous, being interrupted by the most characteristic feature of this type of monument, numerous undug sections forming causeways across the ditch, hence the name, causewayed enclosures. The older name, causewayed camps, has now been generally discarded since it suggested a function, that of habitation, which we now know not to be true. Current views on what such sites were intended for will be dealt with later.

Seventeen causewayed enclosures are known at present, including Crickley Hill in Gloucestershire, discovered only in 1971. Of these, seven are in Wessex (Wiltshire, five; Dorset, two), and four in Sussex. Apart from two in Devon, the remainder form a scatter to the north, one each in Gloucestershire, Berkshire, Bedfordshire and Middlesex. Such a distribution leaves some very obvious gaps, most noticeably between Wessex and Sussex, and in any case covers only part of the Wessex culture area as defined above, so that the seventeen known enclosures are unlikely to represent the original total of such sites. Crop marks of sites with interrupted ditches have been noted in eastern counties as far north as Lincolnshire, and if these are indeed causewayed enclosures then they fill out the distribution pattern to very nearly the full extent of the Windmill Hill culture as a whole. On the basis of crop marks alone the total could be doubled, and there are additional reasons for supposing that original numbers could have been higher

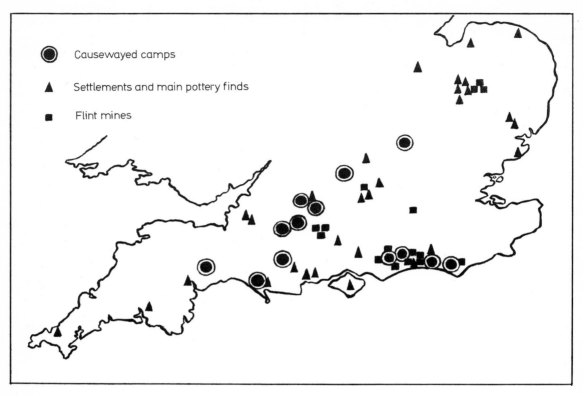

Fig. 20 Map of southern Britain showing the area occupied by the Windmill Hill people.

Legend:
- ⊙ Causewayed camps
- ▲ Settlements and main pottery finds
- ■ Flint mines

again. As will emerge below, there is evidence that the ditches were deliberately filled in again by the Windmill Hill people so that not very much would remain standing above ground. This, and the effects of long-term agricultural activity, would make them very difficult to identify on the ground and the chances are that a good number of causewayed enclosures remain to be discovered. On this basis it seems reasonable to suggest an original total of something over fifty causewayed enclosures built by the Windmill Hill people.

Of the seventeen known causewayed enclosures eleven are sufficiently well preserved to permit some discussion of size and layout. The smallest sites, Combe Hill, Sussex, and Rybury, Wiltshire, are between 3 and 4 acres in area, while the largest site, Windmill Hill itself (Fig. 21B), is around 21 acres in area. In fact, on the basis of size the eleven sites fall into two groups. About two-thirds of them are below 8 acres in area; with these can probably be included Whitehawk in Sussex (11–12 acres). The three remaining sites, however, are very much larger and are all located in Wessex: Maiden Castle, Dorset (17–18 acres), Hambledon Hill, Dorset (19–20 acres), and Windmill Hill, Wiltshire (20–21 acres). As will be seen later the size of these three may be of great significance in discussing the possible functions of causewayed enclosures.

As indicated earlier each site consists of from one to four rings of earthwork. In fact, nine out of the eleven sites have either one ring (five sites) or two rings (four sites). Of the two remaining sites one has three rings (Windmill Hill), and one four rings (Whitehawk, Sussex). A site at The Trundle,

Sussex (not included in the eleven because its plan is incomplete), has two rings inside the later Iron Age fort defences: the outer ring overlaps itself on the west so that there are three lines of earthwork on this side.

Moreover, another section of causewayed earthwork emerges from beneath the Iron Age defences on the north making a fourth line. Although the plan is incomplete, therefore, The Trundle would appear to belong in the same group as Whitehawk

Fig. 21 Plans of causewayed enclosures in Wessex.

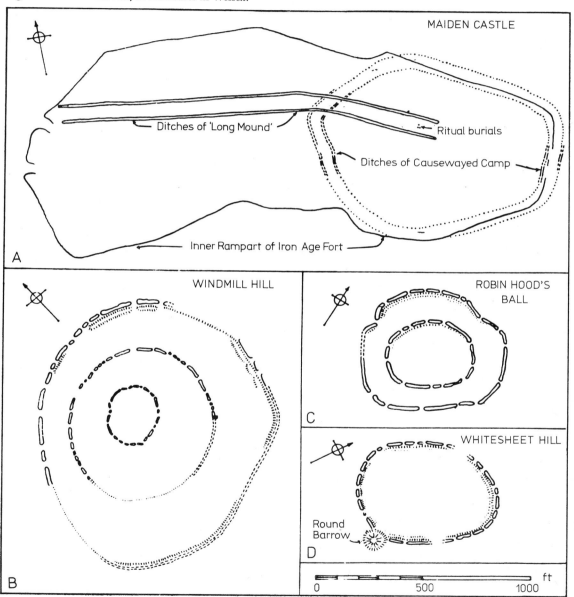

MAIDEN CASTLE

Ditches of 'Long Mound'

Ritual burials

Ditches of Causewayed Camp

Inner Rampart of Iron Age Fort

A

WINDMILL HILL

B

ROBIN HOOD'S BALL

C

WHITESHEET HILL

Round Barrow

D

0   500   1000   ft

and Windmill Hill. None the less, the commoner type of causewayed enclosure has only one or two rings of earthwork.

The evidence available for even a brief descriptive account varies considerably from site to site. Not much can be said about Maiden Bower, Bedfordshire, Abingdon, Berkshire, or High Peak, Devon, apart from the fact that they are (or were when complete) causewayed enclosures; nor about Crickley Hill, Gloucestershire, until more information is forthcoming. Of the two other sites not included in the group of eleven, The Trundle, Sussex, and Hembury, Devon, the former has been mentioned already. Its inner enclosure was 400 ft in overall diameter, with the second ring 25–75 ft beyond; on the west the overlapping sections of the latter were about 100 ft apart. If the causewayed ditches to the north were part of an outer enclosure buried by the hillfort rampart then the overall diameter of the whole causewayed site would have been in the region of 950 ft, very much the same sort of size as the three large Wessex sites. Hembury, too, is partly obscured by a later Iron Age fort. As far as can be observed it consists of an arc of causewayed earthwork cutting off the end of a promontory, i.e. not the usual circular plan, the natural slopes presumably forming the two remaining sides of the enclosure, unless there are causewayed earthworks beneath the Iron Age ramparts, or as yet unidentified outside.

The five sites with a single ring of earthwork are all more or less oval in plan with their greater diameters mostly between 500 and 750 ft: Rybury, Wiltshire, 520 × 470 ft; Knap Hill, Wiltshire, 650 × 430 ft; Whitesheet Hill, Wiltshire, 640 × 450 ft (Fig. 21D); Barkhale, Sussex, 750 × 550 ft. The exception is Hambledon Hill, Dorset, which, although consisting of a single ring, is nevertheless one of the small group of large sites mentioned earlier (19–20 acres): 1,050 × 900 ft. The enclosure is located on a hill at the junction of three ridges. About 40 yds outside on the south and east there are earthworks (closely spaced double

ditches) across the ridges. There was probably a third earthwork on the ridge to the west in a position now covered by the outer defences of Hambledon Iron Age fort.

The four sites with double rings of causewayed earthwork are in Dorset, Wiltshire, Middlesex and Sussex. At Maiden Castle, Dorset, the two lines of causewayed ditch, about 50 ft apart, are visible only on the west. Elsewhere they are presumed to be buried beneath the rampart of the later Iron Age fort, giving the causewayed site an area of 17–18 acres (Fig. 21A). At Robin Hood's Ball, Wiltshire, the two rings are about 100 ft apart. The inner oval ring is 350 × 275 ft, and the outer, more irregular ring is 650 × 550 ft (Fig. 21C). At Staines, Middlesex, the two rings were 70 ft apart with the maximum diameter of the outer ring in the region of 600 ft. Combe Hill, Sussex, is broadly similar in size and layout to Robin Hood's Ball. Its oval inner ring is 375 × 275 ft with the outer ring about 100 ft beyond. The outer ring, however, has very considerable gaps, up to 300 ft long and may never have been complete on the south and east. In both rings a steep natural slope takes the place of the earthworks on the north side.

Of those sites with more than two concentric rings The Trundle, Sussex, has been mentioned already as a probable example. The two certain examples are Windmill Hill, Wiltshire, with three rings, and Whitehawk, Sussex, with four. At Windmill Hill (Fig. 21B), the inner oval enclosure is 275 × 250 ft. The second enclosure (700 × 650 ft) is between 150 ft beyond on the north-west and 300 ft beyond on the south-east. The outer enclosure, at similar distances again, is 1,300 × 1,000 ft overall. The three rings at Windmill Hill are more or less evenly spaced and fairly regular ovals. The layout at Whitehawk, Sussex, is much less regular. The two oval inner rings are very closely spaced, only 25–30 ft apart, with the overall dimensions of the second ring 400 × 325 ft.

The third ring (650 × 550 ft) varies between 50 and 125 ft beyond. At this stage White-hawk bears a close resemblance, both in size and plan, to another Sussex site, The Trundle, in spite of the latter's overlapping feature. The fourth ring (900 × 650 ft) is 50–100 ft beyond the third and is replaced on the eastern side by a steep natural scarp. This outer ring may correspond with the postulated outer ring at The Trundle.

So far nothing has been said about the original structure of causewayed enclosures as revealed by excavation. Indeed, nothing much can be said about the banks since they are largely denuded or entirely absent. This, as pointed out earlier, is due not to erosion but to a deliberate refilling of the ditches in Neolithic times, and such a process must come into any discussion of the function of causewayed enclosures. In a number of cases it is clear that the turf was stripped off the area where the bank was to be built. It is also clear that puddled chalk (i.e. chalk mixed with water) was a component of some banks, with rubble mixed in to form a firmly concreted mass, now represented where it survives at all by a stub, a foot or two high, of the original bank. There is some slight evidence of timberwork associated with the banks, but precisely what form it took is very difficult to say. The frequent gaps or causeways across the ditches are not matched by equal numbers of gaps in the accompanying banks. It is possible that the banks were originally continuous, except for entrances, with the ditches regarded simply as a series of quarries to provide building material. Because of the absence or reduced state of the banks it is difficult to make any pronouncements on this, but some at least of the existing gaps in them may be due to wear caused by human and animal traffic crossing the earthwork where there was a causeway across the ditch. Again, the question of entrances must come into any discussion of function.

The main body of evidence on causewayed enclosures, in terms of both structure and finds, comes from the ditches which by their nature are much better preserved than the banks. The undug causeway between the various sections of ditch vary considerably in width, from a foot to as much as 25 ft, so that it looks as if size was not particularly significant and that the particular gap was a matter of chance rather than design. Excavation showed the ditches to be mostly flat bottomed and 3–7 ft deep. Allowing for erosion the sides must have been very steep when first dug. The flat bottoms are between 5 and 10 ft wide, unlike later Iron Age defensive ditches which are normally V-shaped. Although the ditches in any one ring were more or less of the same depth, in multiple-ring sites there was a tendency for ditches to be progressively deeper from inner to outer rings. At Windmill Hill, for instance, the inner ring ditch averaged 3 ft in depth, the middle 4½ ft and the outer 7 ft. The Trundle is an exception to this, the pattern there being reversed. Whatever the direction, however, such deliberate arrangements must have had some significance for the builders although what this was will always be difficult to deduce. In plan view most ditches are rather untidy looking, the sides rarely being parallel so that it looks as if their finished appearance was not of any great importance. They may indeed be simply linear quarries placed as close as possible to the banks for which they were to provide the material. The greater depth of the outer ditches may be simply an indication that, for reasons we cannot now perceive, the outer banks needed, or were desired to be, bigger than those inside. Although the ditches are usually now the most prominent feature of causewayed enclosures it may well be that originally it was the banks that were the significant element in such sites, the ditches being no more than quarries for the building material.

Whatever the ditches were, however, there is no question that the deposits in them 'remain', according to Isobel Smith, 'the most prolific source of information about Neolithic subsistence economy, material culture and intercommunal relationships'.

The evidence clearly indicates a mixed farming economy based on the raising of cattle, sheep, goats and pigs and the growing of wheat and barley. Bones of wild animals were comparatively few, although there was some evidence of the gathering of wild plants for additional food. Apart from animal bones the ditches yielded abundant remains of pottery, grain-rubbing stones and querns, and, in a late Neolithic phase of the site, when the ditches were almost completely refilled, a large number and variety of stone axes, originating in many different parts of the country. The contents of the ditches, both early and late, must have a considerable bearing on the next topic to be considered, the fundamental one of function.

It was long assumed that these enclosures were settlement sites, some sort of defended or protected village, hence the now dis-carded term causewayed *camp*. The abundant domestic refuse in the ditches led to their interpretation as the actual habitations of the Neolithic population. By 1954 this idea was effectively disposed of by Professor Stuart Piggott and a new sug-gestion was put forward. One of the arguments against their being defensive works were the numerous entrances which would make such a structure quite ineffec-tive. Another was the fact that often the best position was ignored in favour of one that was weaker in terms of defence. Professor Piggott's suggestion was that causewayed enclosures were used for an annual round up of livestock at the end of the summer, at which time many of the younger beasts were slaughtered (and eaten at feasts, hence the great quantities of bone in the ditches), because of the difficulties of providing them with winter feed. However, closer analysis of the bones revealed that most of the animals slaughtered, at Windmill Hill at least, were mature beasts, which had quite clearly been supported through a considerable number of winters already. Again the numerous gaps argue against enclosures for livestock, as does the fact that the banks were

deliberately levelled and the ditches filled in. By 1965 a new suggestion had been made as to the function of causewayed enclosures.

As already stated, it is now quite clear that banks were deliberately pushed back into the ditches and this immediately suggests a ritual rather than a practical function; in normal circumstances a structure for which there was no further use would simply be left to decay in its own time. The ritual interpretation is further reinforced by the realisation that the ditches had been recut on more than one occasion; in other words, this process of building and subsequent reduction had been repeated several times. The period over which this process took place is indicated by the contents and stratigraphy of the ditches which show that these sites were in use for several centuries. Quite clearly they were not dug and refilled every year, so that use at some longer interval is indicated and this again would argue against a purely practical function which would almost certainly have been based on a yearly cycle. The contents of the ditches also indicate use of the sites by people coming from a considerable distance, even when the sites had been finally filled in, as if the sanctity of these causewayed enclosures was still widely acknowledged.

All this evidence is now generally under-stood to mean that causewayed enclosures were the rallying point for periodical gatherings of interrelated but widely scattered communities, coming together only at intervals to perform certain necessary rituals and to celebrate them and the meeting with friends and family by large-scale feasting, hence the large quan-tities of animal bones in the ditches. The burials of whole animals cannot be thus explained and these must represent sacri-ficial offerings, again in keeping with the suggested function of these sites. Finds of stone and flint implements, some for geo-logical reasons obviously not local, indicate that trading was carried on and this is not unlikely at such large gatherings of normally widely dispersed customers.

Until any evidence to the contrary is produced it looks as if causewayed enclosures must be seen as ceremonial centres of the Windmill Hill people, not apparently the only ones (see below, cursus earthworks), but ones which may have an important bearing on the origins of the henge monuments of Chapter 5. There is no obvious source outside the British Isles for these, and unless they sprang into being fully formed, then their antecedents must lie within these islands. It seems highly improbable that within the Neolithic period as a whole two entirely separate traditions of large ceremonial enclosures would have developed, often in the same areas. It seems much more logical to accept that there is a link between the two, with the causewayed sites occupying the earlier position. Carbon-14 determinations indicate their period of use as being from just before 3000 B.C. to about 2500 B.C., as a group, and the period of use of henge monuments as beginning 2500 B.C. so that the suggestion that the latter had their origins in causewayed enclosure has good chronological support. On this basis the somewhat untidy and irregular causewayed sites may, by 2500 B.C., have been formalised into the single and more regular ring of the henge monument. This may be an over-simplification of a more complex process but nevertheless on present evidence it would appear to represent the broad pattern of events in the third millennium B.C.

Long barrows

Corresponding closely in distribution with the causewayed enclosures are the earthen long barrows of the Windmill Hill people. These burial monuments are termed earthen or unchambered long barrows to distinguish them from the stone-built chambered long barrows of other regions which will be considered in Chapter 4. Beyond the area of the causewayed enclosures there is an additional spread of earthen long barrows in Lincolnshire and Yorkshire. About 200 earthen long barrows are known in all, most of them (c. 170) in Dorset, Wiltshire, Hampshire and Sussex, with the bulk of the remainder (c. 30) in Yorkshire and Lincolnshire. Of these only about twenty have been excavated in recent times and most of our knowledge of internal structure is based on this 10 per cent sample. Without anticipating the survey of structure below it can safely be said that the internal arrangements of the long barrows under discussion are rather more complex than is implied by the terms *earthen* or *unchambered*, which tend to suggest an unrelieved covering mass of earth.

The designation long, to distinguish these mounds from round barrows, covers a considerable range of dimensions, from around 70 ft to, in an extreme case, over 1,800 ft. However, the bulk of earthen long barrows (about 150 of them) are between 100 and 300 ft in length. There are, in fact, only four over 500 ft in length, most of the remaining sites being at the other end of the scale, between 70 and 100 ft. Closely related to length is the question of shape. Earthen long barrows are frequently described as being trapeze-shaped in plan, with the broader end higher than the narrower end, and this is true for many of the 200 known sites, but by no means all. Many of the shorter long barrows, for example (those below 100 ft in length), are, in fact, oval in plan, and only marginally different from round barrows of similar dimensions. The largest variant group, however, embraces those sites which are parallel or rectangular rather than trapezoidal, with no distinguishable higher end. Many, but not all, of these are at the upper end of the size range (i.e. over 200 ft in length), but there are also shorter examples (below 200 ft), just as there are trapeze-shaped barrows over this length. The two groups are not mutually exclusive in terms of size. The very long examples (over 500 ft) of parallel-sided long barrows are known as bank barrows, of which four examples are known (Pl. 12). The out-

12 Oblique aerial view of the bank barrow at Long
Bredy, Dorset.

standing example is the one uncovered
during the excavation of Maiden Castle,
Dorset (Fig. 21A). Although little of the
actual mound remained it appeared to
have had a turf core with the remainder
consisting of chalk rubble. Shape and
dimensions were indicated by the surviving
parallel ditches which were about 15 ft
wide, just over 50 ft apart, and no less
than 1,800 ft long, with a change of
direction about two-thirds of the way
along. Because of its great length the
structure has sometimes been seen as a
possible *cursus*, but work subsequent to the
original excavation showed that it was
indeed a long barrow, of the bank barrow

variety. In terms of shape, therefore, long
earthen burial mounds can be described as
either oval, trapeze-shaped, rectangular or
bank barrows. It is noticeable that the
mound, instead of being round-topped, not
infrequently has a distinct ridge on its long
axis, and that is a point which will be
returned to when the origins of long
barrows are being discussed.

The material from which these often
very large mounds were built was derived
from ditches of roughly commensurate size
which form another distinctive feature of
the type. In most cases there are two
ditches, flanking the two long sides of the
mound. Usually a berm or area of flat
ground was left between the mound and the
ditches on either side, and in many cases

this berm can still be distinguished in surface examination. Where no berm is now visible presumably it was of relatively small size and has been reduced by erosion. Flanking ditches were sometimes carried around the end of the barrow to form a U-shaped ditch, and, in other, fewer cases, the mound was completely encircled by an oval ditch, interrupted by causeways of undug ground (Fig. 22).

There is a noticeable pattern in the orientation of earthen long barrows, i.e. in the direction in which they face. In nearly every regional group the largest number face more or less due east. The exceptions are one or two groups in which the majority face south-east, and south-east, moreover, occupies second position in those groups where an eastern orientation was dominant. The majority of the remainder are on various other points in the eastern half of the compass, i.e. from north to south via the eastern side. There are a few sites facing partially west (north-west, south-west) but no sites facing due west and as a whole sites on the western half of the compass form a very small proportion of the total. Quite clearly considerable significance must be attached to this pattern and this again will need to be brought into the later discussion.

As already indicated only about twenty earthen long barrows have been excavated to a satisfactory standard and our knowledge of the original structure is based on these. Excavation of the ditches has revealed two main points of interest. As originally dug, they appear to have been steep or even vertical-sided, the present wide, V-shaped appearance being the result of erosion. This means that the berms, where they are visible, between mound and ditch were originally even wider than they now appear, and even in sites where no berm showed on the surface, such as Fussell's Lodge, Wiltshire, the intervening space was actually as much as 20 ft wide. The second point emerged from only one long mound, Wor Barrow, Dorset, meticulously dug in the nineteenth

century by General Pitt-Rivers, although there is supporting evidence from two other non-barrow sites. At Wor Barrow the quarry ditch, which completely encircled the mound, appeared to have largely but not entirely destroyed an earlier much smaller ditch of similar plan. A similar enclosure, but without a superimposed long barrow, has been uncovered on Normanton Down, Wiltshire, and there is another at Dorchester, Oxfordshire, associated with a complex of henge structures. To these have been given the name mortuary enclosures and they are presumed to have preceded the actual construction of the barrow with its accompanying quarry ditches. This generally oval plan may explain why some barrows have an encircling ditch (rather than the more usual twin flanking ditches), this following and reflecting the plan of the mortuary enclosure which may well have preceded it. Presumably such enclosures were a temporary expedient where bodies could be stored until such time as it was decided to construct the actual burial mound.

The long barrows built from the ditch material can be divided into two groups, those in which there is evidence of a structure to retain or revet the edge of the mound, and those in which there is no such evidence, the main part of the mound being simply of the dump variety. Most excavated barrows (about two-thirds of the total) belong, in fact, to the second group, although they are by no means lacking in evidence of other structural features. The commonest of these are mortuary houses, relatively small structures as compared with the mound as a whole, in which were placed the actual burials. Mortuary houses are under barrows of both groups, as are the less common but none the less interesting timber façades.

There are six long barrows in the first group, which have evidence of a revetment for the mound material. One of the best examples of the type is Fussell's Lodge, Wiltshire, excavated in 1958. In the old ground surface beneath the mound was a

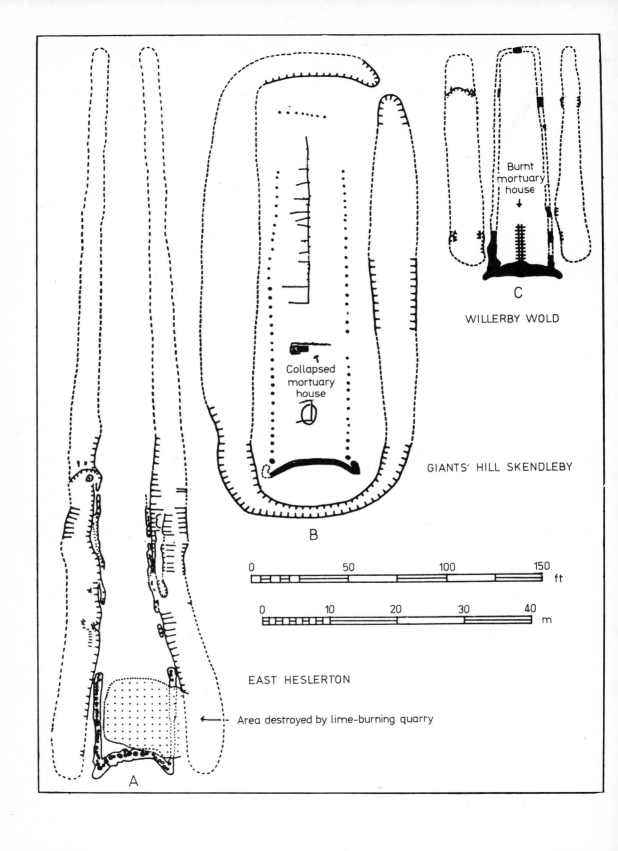

C

WILLERBY WOLD

Burnt
mortuary
house

Collapsed
mortuary
house

B

GIANTS' HILL SKENDLEBY

0   50   100   150
ft

0   10   20   30   40
m

EAST HESLERTON

Area destroyed by lime-burning quarry

A

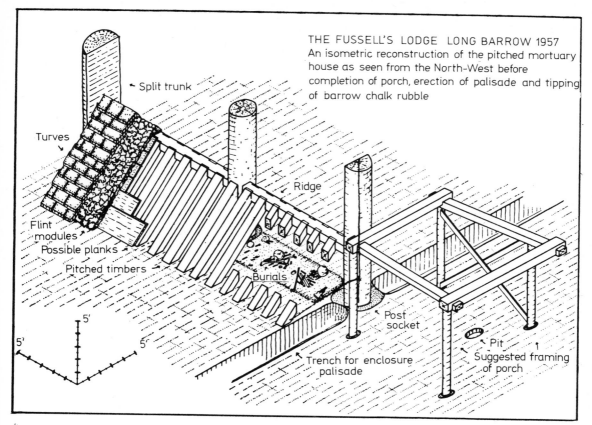

THE FUSSELL'S LODGE LONG BARROW 1957
An isometric reconstruction of the pitched mortuary
house as seen from the North-West before
completion of porch, erection of palisade and tipping
of barrow chalk rubble

Split trunk

Turves

Ridge

Flint
modules
Possible planks
Pitched timbers

Burials

Post
socket

Trench for enclosure
palisade

Pit
Suggested framing
of porch

Fig. 23   Isometric reconstruction of the mortuary house
of the Fussell's Lodge long barrow, Wiltshire.

continuous bedding trench, 4–5 ft deep and
15–18 in. wide, defining a trapeze-shaped
area 135 ft long, 20 ft wide at the narrow
end and 40 ft at the broader end which
was slightly convex in plan. There was an
entrance at this end fronted by a porch-
like arrangement of four posts. This
bedding trench almost certainly housed a
substantial timber wall, perhaps up to 6 ft
high, which edged or retained the mound
material (Figs. 23 & 24). At Wor Barrow,
Dorset, the bedding trench was rectangular
in plan (90 × 35 ft), again with a porch-
like feature at one end. Doubts have been
expressed whether the timbers in such a
trench could retain a mound which then
still stood some 12 ft above the old ground

surface. But if it were originally even
higher (as has, probably correctly, been
suggested), however, the retaining wall
would not need to be as high. From the
crest of a 35 ft-wide mound the surface
would slope down on either side to a
revetment which would need to be only 7–8
ft high. In any case, there is no reason why
some of the material should not have been
piled against the outside of the revetment
as a buttress, in the manner of the extra
revetment material in chamber megalithic
tombs. Wayland's Smithy, Berkshire, discovered beneath the remains of a later,
stone-chambered megalithic tomb, was oval
in plan (60 × 30 ft) and had a stone instead
of a timber revetment wall. A trapezoidal
setting of post-holes at one end was probably

Fig. 22   Plans of earthen long barrows in the north.

Fig. 24   Reconstruction drawing of the Fussell's Lodge long barrow, Wiltshire.

for a timber porch in the manner of the Fussell's Lodge barrow.

The three remaining long barrows with evidence of timber revetment are in the north. All three show, in addition, clear evidence of elaborate timber façades. Willerby Wold, Yorkshire, is trapeze-shaped (125 × 35 × 22 ft), not dissimilar in size and proportions to Fussell's Lodge (Fig. 22C). At the wider, eastern end of Willerby Wold, however, there is the foundation trench for a crescent-shaped façade, some 40 ft wide, i.e. wider than the trapeze-shaped structure behind, and presumably also higher, forming some sort of monumental front to the finished structure, justifying the term façade. At Giant's Hills, Lincolnshire, the façade forms an even more marked crescent, some 50 ft wide, and returns or doubles back at each end (Fig. 22B). It appears to have been composed of massive, split tree trunks, with the bark side facing outwards, set in a wide foundation trench. The revetment behind was set in post-holes rather than a continuous trench and was 200 × 40 ft for just over half its length. Thereafter it tapered to about 30 ft at the narrower end. The façade at East Heslerton, Yorkshire, was even more deeply incurved (Fig. 22A). Its bedding trench was 40 ft wide and had contained upright tree trunks, up to 2 ft in diameter, with only narrow spaces between them. The outer ends of the bedding trench returned to form the bedding trenches for the revetment to the mound. This was 40 ft wide and parallel sided for about 60 ft. Thereafter it narrowed considerably and the bedding trench became discontinuous. As indicated by the flanking ditches the East Heslerton barrow was nearly 400 ft long, but the revetment trench survived for only about 150 ft back from the façade.

There is some evidence that the wider, slightly (outward) curving end of Fussell's Lodge was treated as a façade (wider foundation trench, larger timbers), but apart from that the remaining façades are associated with mounds which do not appear to have been revetted on the three remaining sides. The barrow was simply a mound sloping down to ground level at sides and back. Only at the front was there a vertical, retaining element in the form of a façade. Not much is known of the façade at Heddington, Wiltshire, apart from the fact that there was a transverse trench running across the mound at the wider end. At Hanging Grimston the façade was about 50 ft wide. The outer sections were straight. The centre section (about one-third) turned inwards in a shallow V-shape and impinged on one of the post-holes of the mortuary house. The most complex site of the three is Nutbane, Hampshire, where the façade is only one of a number of phases. Apart from the actual burial and their mortuary structures (below) there appear to have been at least two timber buildings across the wider, eastern end of the mound. The first was relatively simple (16 × 14 ft), supported on four corner posts. This was replaced by a larger, more complex structure consisting of a rectangular building 22 × 18 ft wide with the eastern side extended to north and south to link at right angles with two free-standing timber walls, each about 25 ft long. The result is a façade, part of which is the side wall of the rectangular building, with two supporting side walls, and the whole may have been designed to revet the eastern end of the mound which was otherwise unrevetted. That the eastern end was intended to be a façade is suggested by the forward projection of the corners, leaving the centre part, the east wall of the rectangular building, recessed by several feet.

The remaining barrows about which there is reasonably reliable information appear to have neither revetments to the mounds (timber or otherwise) nor façades.

One thing they do appear to have, however, is evidence for mortuary houses, relatively small structures forming the immediate covering of the burials, and this they share with all the barrows considered so far and probably with all earthen long barrows. Certainly many nineteenth-century accounts mention features which, in the light of present-day knowledge, we can reasonably assume to have been the remains of mortuary houses. It is also worth noting that the suggestion has been made more than once that earthen long barrows are unchambered only in the sense that no chamber has survived because it was built in perishable timber rather than stone. In other words, earthen long barrows are the timber counterparts of the stone-chambered long barrows, those, for example, in the immediately adjacent Cotswold region.

The mortuary houses containing the burials were normally placed under the wider end of the barrow, immediately behind the façade where one existed, or in a corresponding position where this feature was lacking. Much of the evidence indicates a tent-like structure sloping to ground level on either side of a central ridge, often of considerable size, up to 25 ft in length. Post-holes in many cases show that there were two considerable posts (often split, half tree trunks), one at each end, between which presumably ran a ridge-pole, and the rest of the structure seems to have been built around these elements. At Wayland's Smithy, Berkshire, mentioned earlier, there were the remains of a mortuary house some 20 × 8 ft inside the oval stone revetment of the mound, just behind the (presumed) porch. In the words of the excavator, Professor R. J. C. Atkinson, 'the evidence leaves no doubt that the burials were deposited within a wooden chamber resembling a low ridge-tent, with a massive post at either end, between which a ridge-pole was supported by mortised joints. The combined sides and roof were presumably formed of close-set timbers resting at their . . . upper ends on the ridge-pole and at their lower . . . ends on the ground. . . .' This timber structure may have had a further covering of stones, and the whole thing would in any case have been covered by the barrow proper when the whole burial process was completed. From the packing around them it was quite clear that the two main posts were D-shaped, half tree trunks, with their flat sides facing each other.

The same feature is found at Fussell's Lodge. There, the D-shaped posts are 2 ft in diameter and about 22 ft apart (Fig. 23). Because of this there is a fully circular post, 2 ft in diameter, about half way along. Between these three ran a ridge-post, against which on either side rested a series of sloping timbers forming the framework of a structure, triangular in cross-section, about 5 ft high and 8–10 ft wide at ground level. The sloping timbers may have been covered with planking, covered in turn by a layer of flint nodules, the whole building finished off with a layer of turves. This considerable structure lay immediately behind the gap in the wide end of the timber palisade, with the porch in front of it.

Less complete evidence from other sites would, nevertheless, appear to indicate that tent-like mortuary houses were a fairly regular type under earthen long barrows. The evidence often takes the form of a pair of post-holes, on the long axis of the mound at the wider end, presumably for the two main uprights supporting the ridge. In between, covering the burials, are mounds of flints, stones, chalk nodules, turves, etc., which are presumed to be the collapsed remains of the structure, originally supported by sloping timbers resting on the ridge-pole. At Nutbane such a pitched mortuary house stood within a rectangular timber enclosure which lay immediately behind the roofed timber structures described earlier.

However, not all mortuary houses were of the pitched variety, nor were they all at the wider end of the barrow. In some cases they occupied a more central position. In at least one such case the mortuary house was defined by four corner posts so that it is unlikely to have been of the pitched type. In other cases no posts were involved, the whole structure being apparently built of turf. At Thickthorn Down, Dorset, the excavated remains indicate two parallel walls, about 3 ft high and 6 ft apart built of turf, and these are presumably the main walls of a turf-built mortuary house. The outer faces of the walls were not vertical, but sloped down to ground level on either side, recalling the cross-section of the timber-built pitched houses. No doubt more careful excavation and recording in the past would have revealed further variations on the mortuary house theme.

Beneath the mortuary houses, and often crushed by their collapse, lay the reason for the often elaborate structures described so far, the burials. As compared with the space occupied by the barrow and its accompanying ditches the burials occupy a very modest area. They consist for the most part of skeletal remains, grave goods (pottery, tools, weapons) being comparatively rare in earthen long barrows. The skeletal remains are either complete, articulated skeletons, indicating that the complete body, flesh and all, was buried, or they are groups of disarticulated bones, indicating that the flesh had been allowed to rot away before burial, the surviving bones then being buried as a group.

The burials can be divided also into burned and unburned remains. However, the burned burials do not appear to have been cremations in the same sense as the cremated burials of the Middle Bronze Age. It has in the past been assumed that some of them had been cremated where they were found, in the barrow, and for these the term *cremation in situ* has been used. Although this is now known to be incorrect, in the sense that cremation proper was not involved, it does supply the clue to what actually happened. The bodies were *in situ* (i.e. on the spot where they were found) when they were burned, but the burning was not designed to cremate the bodies. It appears, in fact, to have been directed to the burning of the mortuary house, possibly as a last act before the erection of the covering mound. In the process, the bodies were inevitably burned, but only partially, and in some cases bones were only blackened; the process certainly fell far short of the complete cremation which Neolithic people were quite capable of achieving.

Articulated skeletons were normally deposited in a crouched or contracted position, i.e. with the knees drawn up towards the chin, with the body lying on its side. Occasionally such burials were accompanied, in the same mortuary house, by burials of disarticulated bones although the type usually occupied separate parts of the structure. In disarticulated burials the deposits are sometimes those of single individuals and sometimes of groups of people. At Fussell's Lodge, for example, all the bones were in four separate heaps, accounting for well over fifty people, the bones of each person being confined to a particular heap and not scattered throughout the four. The number of people represented (between fifty-three and fifty-seven) at Fussell's Lodge was arrived at by a close scrutiny of every piece of bone from the burial area. It was very much greater than the on-the-spot estimate made at the time of excavation and raises the question of whether many other such estimates have greatly underrated the number of persons buried at other sites. Numbers such as those at Fussell's Lodge suggest a veritable cemetery rather than simply a family or collective grave. As far as can be ascertained very few of the inviduals buried under earthen long barrows were over fifty years of age at death.

The origins of the practice of burial under long earthen mounds of either trapezoidal or rectangular form (Fig. 24) can be discussed only in the most general terms. The distinctive trapezoidal plan will be encountered again in the British Isles when megalithic tombs are being dealt with in Chapter 4, and presumably both earthen and chambered types stem from the same source.

Outside the British Isles, in northern Europe generally, both pitched mortuary houses and trapezoidal and rectangular long mounds are recorded, so that possibly the origins of this aspect of the Windmill Hill culture are to be found to the east, in north Germany and Poland. In those areas, and to the south, in central Europe, trapezoidal and rectangular plans appear also in domestic architecture, with long-houses, often of considerable size, up to 150 ft long. In many cultures there is a close link between the houses of the living and the houses of the dead, and it seems probable that in these long trapezoidal and rectangular houses of central and northern Europe we have the models for the burial places of the dead, solid structures of earth, retained by stone or timber revetments, with the plan, and possibly the external elevation of a house of the living. The story may well be much more complex than as stated here, but these, nevertheless, appear to be the essential ingredients. What does seem unlikely is that there is no link at all between trapezoidal houses and trapezoidal burial mounds of similar dimensions. The reasons behind the trapezoidal house plan are strictly outside the scope of this survey, but may be connected with the practice of housing both human beings and livestock under one roof. This is a common practice in many agricultural communities and the great size of some of the houses involved makes it the more likely. The trapezoidal plan may have developed out of the ordinary rectangular long-house by the widening of one end to provide more space for livestock. This would avoid any structural break which would arise if the house were widened simply at one point. The trapeze-shaped house could be built virtually in the same way as a parallel-sided house, but without its limitations with regard to the accommodation of livestock. The rectangular house was by no means ousted and both types would appear to have given their plan to the houses of the dead, the long burial mounds.

Cursus earthworks

It was mentioned earlier that because of its great length (1,800 ft) the Maiden Castle long barrow had been suspected of being a 'cursus' (Fig. 21A). Although this suspicion is no longer justified, it does indicate the linear nature of this rather puzzling class of earthworks. In fact, although the Maiden Castle barrow is very long in terms of earthen barrows, it is quite small in the context of cursus earthworks. In spite of their length, however, cursuses are still enclosures, albeit very long and narrow ones. They consist of banks with external ditches forming enclosures up to 430 ft wide and up to six and a half miles long! The long sides form two regular parallel lines and the ends are squared. The Latin term *cursus* was first given to one near Stonehenge, by the famous antiquary William Stukeley in the eighteenth century, on the assumption that it was some sort of racecourse. Just what the original purpose of these earthworks was we simply do not know, but perhaps Professor R. J. C. Atkinson's suggestion that they were intended for some sort of 'ritual linear activity' is as close as any. The question of function will be further commented on below.

There are, in fact, two cursuses near Stonehenge, known as the Greater Cursus and the Lesser Cursus (Fig. 48). The Greater Cursus runs east and west about 800 yds north of Stonehenge. Excavation has indicated that it is almost certainly contemporary with the first phase of the latter represented by the bank and ditch and the Aubrey holes. It is about one and three-quarter miles long and about 330 ft wide at the eastern end. From there it widens gradually to about 430 ft near the western end and then narrows again to its original width at the opposite end. Apart from its close proximity to Stonehenge there appears to be a clear link between cursus earthworks and earthen long barrows. The eastern end of the Greater Cursus is, in fact, formed by a long barrow

set transversely across the line of the parallel banks and ditches, and there is an even closer association in the Dorset Cursus (below). The Lesser Cursus, to the north-west, is much smaller, 1,200 × 150 ft. It is noticeable that both cursuses are surrounded by numerous Bronze Age round barrows, including many forming cemeteries, some of linear type.

Unquestionably the most spectacular of all such monuments is the Dorset Cursus, which is no less than six and a half miles long, running from Thickthorn Down to Pentridge, more or less parallel to (and about half a mile south-east of) the Blandford to Salisbury road (Fig. 25). It consists of parallel banks and external ditches with an overall width of just over 300 ft and this is virtually constant throughout its length. Its great length appears to have been achieved by one and possibly two extensions. About one and a half miles from the well-preserved south-western end on Thickthorn Down there are two long barrows, one of them set transversely across the line of the earthwork which may have been an end of the cursus at one stage, in the same way as the transverse barrow at the Greater Curses at Stonehenge. About the same distance beyond, on Wyke Down, there is quite clearly an original squared-off end, indicating that at one stage the cursus was just over two and a half miles long, from Wyke Down to Pentridge. Incorporated in the north-western side is an earthen long barrow which would appear to be earlier, since it is not precisely on the same alignment as the cursus. The three long barrows mentioned so far do not, however, account for all such barrows associated with the Dorset Cursus. At the south-western end, and more or less in line with the squared end of the cursus, are two long barrows one of which has been referred to earlier, the Thickthorn barrow. Equally, at the north-eastern end are two more long barrows, not aligned in quite the same way but just as close. Since the long barrows are probably earlier than the cursus it looks as if the latter was laid

Fig. 25   Plan of the Dorset cursus.

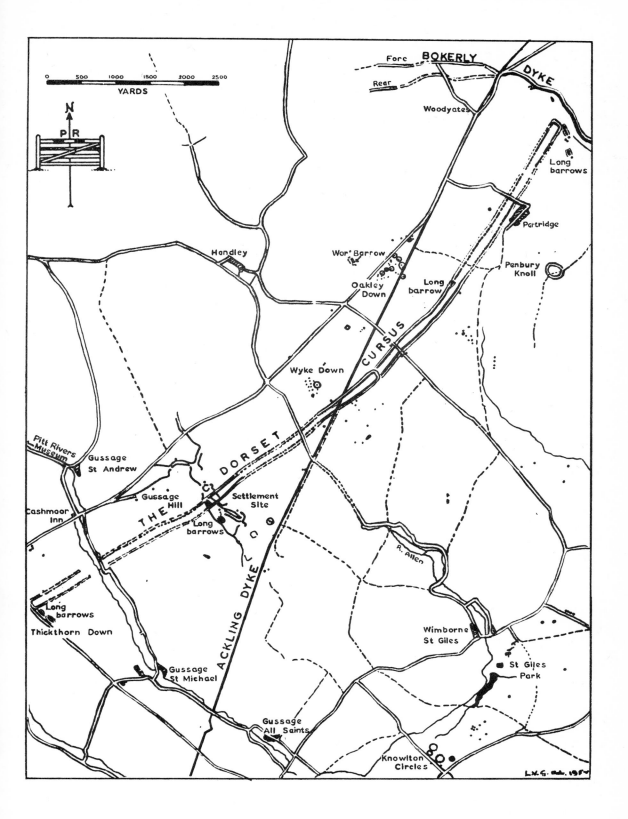

out according to the disposition of the various barrows and this may account for its slightly curving track.

Other cursus earthworks are known in the Windmill Hill area but almost entirely from aerial photographs in which their presence is revealed by crop and soil marks. Little or nothing is visible on the ground. One at Dorchester, Oxfordshire, cut through a long mortuary enclosure which it was suggested earlier represented the first structural phase of some long barrows, further emphasising the link between them and cursus earthwork.

In the absence of evidence any consideration of the original function of cursuses is bound to be highly speculative. However, the length of the structures and the twin, parallel and relatively closely spaced banks do suggest some sort of lengthwise movement. This was seen by Stukeley as racing, perhaps of a ritual nature. An alternative view is that such enclosures were some sort of processional way, marked off by earthworks because of their sanctity, which is demonstrated by the way in which later, Bronze Age barrow groups cluster around them. Why a processional way in this particular form was needed is an entirely different question. They may have some connection with the avenues (both in earthwork and upright stones) leading up to some henges and stone circles, in which it would seem reasonable to assume that some sort of processional activity took place. Because of the sanctity of such monuments these processions may have been limited to a small select group of people, priests and chiefs, perhaps. The cursus may have been designed to allow a re-enactment of such processions by the population as a whole, hence, perhaps, their greater width. Beyond this speculation becomes mere guesswork. Linear earthworks are notoriously difficult to interpret. Even total excavation, an enormous undertaking in the case, for example, of the Dorset cursus, would not necessarily provide the answer. In the meantime, beyond noting their existence

and characteristics, one can do little but await some future clue as to their original purpose.

Flint mines

Flint mines are not structures in the same way, for example, as barrows or stone circles, but they are, nevertheless, archaeological monuments and as such will be included here. In spite of the difference in name they are the southern counterpart of the axe-factories of the north and west referred to in the introductory chapter. The difference is that in the south the raw material had to be mined before the factory activity could take place. Flint occurs naturally in chalk and if he was not already aware of its existence from the exposed chalk cliff-faces of the Sussex coast, man would very quickly have learned this basic geological fact from digging the ditches of earthen long barrows and causewayed enclosures. Where it does occur the flint is in a series of relatively thin horizontal layers separated by perhaps four or five feet of sterile chalk. Quite clearly the upper layers can be reached by a simple open-cast technique and there is plenty of evidence that a great deal of flint was mined in this way. However, the best flint for tool-making is in the lower layers, perhaps twenty or thirty feet down, and this led to the development of a true mining technique. Once the flint seam at the bottom of a deep pit has been exhausted it is simpler and more economical to extend laterally by means of galleries, following the seam, than to sink a new pit, and it is these deep pits with their maze of side galleries which are great monuments of the Neolithic mining industry (Fig. 26). That it was an industry, run by specialist miners-cum-traders, there can be little doubt. Although the existence of quite a few flint mines (as opposed to open-cast sites) is known, not unnaturally most of them are completely blocked and inaccessible. At the site of Grime's Graves, Norfolk, however, two of the excavated

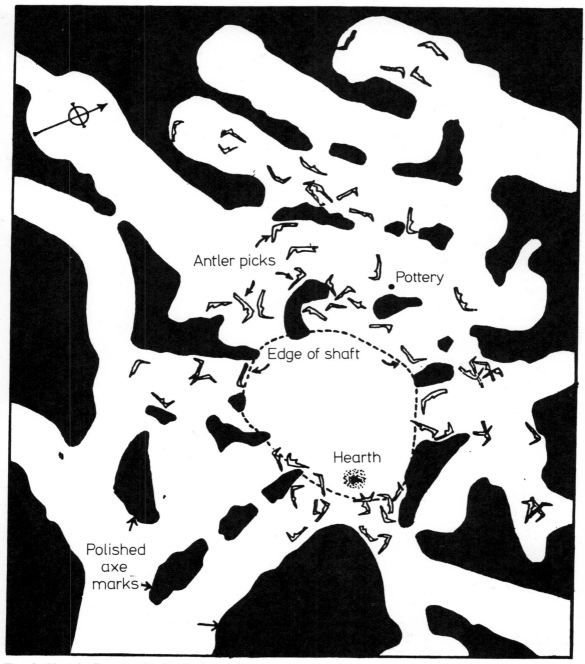

Fig. 26   Plan of a flint mine (Pit No. 2), Grime's Graves,
Norfolk.

shafts have been kept open for visitors by
the Department of the Environment and
show very vividly just what was involved
in such an undertaking. A shaft some 12–
13 ft wide (now much wider at the top due
to erosion) was sunk about 27–28 ft into the
chalk, passing through two seams of flint
and ending at the third. At this level a
series of galleries radiating outwards was
opened up to follow this particular seam
(Pl. 13). The galleries extended for 30–
40 ft, in many cases only a couple of feet
high, and are often dangerously close to
each other, with only a thin wall of undug
chalk between. Although this is the only
site where the whole pattern can be seen
there must have been many such in the
Windmill Hill culture region to meet the
needs of the population during the long
span of the Neolithic period.

13   Neolithic flint mine at Grime's Graves, Norfolk:
entrance to galleries in Pit 1.

4 Megalithic Tombs

The rugged northern and western coasts of Britain and the greater part of Ireland provide the setting for a very unusual group of burial monuments, known variously as megalithic tombs, chambered tombs or collective tombs. They are built for the most part of very large stones, often many tons in weight, hence one of their descriptive terms, megalithic, from the Greek *megas,* large, and *lithos,* stone. The alternative designations indicate two other important characteristics, namely that they contain burial chambers and that the burials therein are collective or group burials rather than individual burials. The two thousand or so megalithic tombs which still exist in the British Isles are only part of a larger European picture, embracing some forty to fifty thousand tombs in the west Mediterranean islands, Spain, Portugal, France, Holland, North Germany, Denmark and southern Sweden (Fig. 1). Such large numbers are accounted for, in part at least, by the long period, some 1,500 years, during which they were built and used, from c. 3000 B.C. to c. 1500 B.C., that is during the Neolithic and Early Bronze Age periods. Individual tombs were in use over a period of generations, if not centuries, and the latter part of the 'megalithic period' is probably accounted for more by the use of existing tombs than the construction of new ones.

The origins of what may be termed European megalithic architecture will be discussed in a later section, but one or two general points bearing on the European background can be made here. Traditionally, all megalithic tombs have been divided into two broad sub-categories which we call Passage Graves and Gallery Graves, based on the form of their internal stone structure. In a Passage Grave there are two main elements, a passage and a burial chamber, clearly distinguishable from each other, the passage usually being both lower and narrower than the chamber. In a Gallery Grave, on the other hand, there is only one element, a parallel-sided passage or gallery which fills the function of both passage and chamber. The mounds or cairns which cover these tombs also fall into two main groups, based on their shape, circular, usually covering Passage Graves, and long, usually covering Gallery Graves. However, this apparently clear picture of circular Passage Graves (Fig. 30B, for example) and long Gallery Graves (Fig. 29, for example) is now regarded by most archaeologists as an over-simplification of a very complex pattern. Both types do, in fact, exist, but they by no means account for all of the many thousands of tombs in Europe. As will be seen later, even within the British Isles there is a very wide range of variations with many sites difficult to classify in terms of a simple two-fold system.

The term collective tomb is descriptive of the way in which these structures were used, an aspect which is at least as important as their architecture. It is quite clear from the skeletal remains found in them that such tombs were collective burial places, used over a considerable period of time for a number (sometimes a very large number) of burials. This, of course, is one of the reasons why a stone internal structure (i.e. a chamber or gallery) was necessary, so that access was always possible, even if a temporary blocking had to be removed each time a burial was made. In some European tombs the remains of a hundred or more individuals have been found, although in the British Isles the numbers are usually considerably less. Although there are many examples of cremation, none the less, the commoner rite in collective tombs was inhumation, i.e. the deposition of the bodies in an unburnt condition. In fact, inhumation seems to have taken two forms; either the bodies were deposited as they were, flesh and all, or else they were first exposed in some temporary structure until the flesh had rotted away and were then deposited in the tomb as skeletons. In some cases the skeletons are incomplete, suggesting that, possibly for ritual reasons, some portion of the skeleton was held back from burial, or was removed at a later date. The practice of collective burial suggests that megalithic tombs served the needs of a particular community, or perhaps only the leading families thereof, or were more simply family graves.

Thus far the covering mounds have been described simply as either round or long. In fact the latter term covers a considerable range of shapes as will be seen when the various regional groups are considered. But whatever the shape it is normally defined by a kerb of upright stone slabs or dry-stone walling, often very carefully built. In spite of the care taken, however, such kerbs were not intended to be seen. Additional cairn material (extra-revetment material) was piled against them completely masking

their existence. Quite clearly there were compelling reasons for defining the shape of the mound by means of a kerb and these will be discussed later. The same kerb also in many cases defined a forecourt, semicircular or triangular in shape, standing in front of the entrance to the tomb. The stones surrounding the forecourt were usually much higher than the rest of the kerb and quite clearly an architectural effect was aimed at. Presumably the forecourt was provided as a setting for some of the ceremonial connected with the burial rites. Again, however, the forecourt was filled with blocking material between burials so that the often elaborate stonework was hidden from view. Where there was no forecourt there was often a flat façade, an arrangement of large upright slabs on either side of the entrance, again intended to impress but again concealed when the tomb was not in use.

There are still some two thousand identifiable tombs in the British Isles, although the original number was probably well in excess of three thousand. The surviving tombs are spread throughout northern and western regions in a series of groups distinguished for the most part on a geographical basis, and these provide a convenient framework within which all megalithic tombs in the British Isles can be considered.

Megalithic tombs in England and Wales

The joint English and Welsh share of the overall total is only about three hundred and fifty tombs (c. 17 per cent), situated, with the exception of one very small group, in the western parts of southern Britain. In fact, the three hundred and fifty tombs can be divided into one major group, the Cotswold-Severn group, accounting for about half the total, and a series of smaller groups accounting for the other half, which will be considered first.

The exception to the generally western distribution pattern is the Medway group of five sites in Kent, i.e. in south-east

England, far removed from any other megalithic group. As well as being geographically remote these few sites differ from all other megalithic tombs in the British Isles in that their covering mounds, defined by stone kerbs, are rectangular rather than round or trapeze-shaped, and in this respect they resemble tombs in southern Scandinavia and north Germany, and it is probably in that direction that their origin is to be sought.

At the other extremity of southern Britain is a group of about fifty sites in the Scilly Islands, together with another four of the same type on the mainland of Cornwall. These all have circular covering mounds defined by massive stone kerbs, and average between 20 and 40 ft in diameter, although the largest is up to 75 ft in diameter. This circular covering mound

would appear to indicate the Passage Grave tradition, but internally there are structures which look more like Gallery Graves. The fact that they do not fall neatly into either the Passage Grave or Gallery Grave category illustrates the point made earlier about the shortcomings of the system, rather than any peculiarity of the Scillonian group of tombs. Also in the south-west is the Penwith group of about a dozen sites in Cornwall, Devon and Dorset. These appear to have simple rectangular chambers set for the most part in long mounds.

In south-west Wales there are about thirty-five certain sites and a similar number of doubtful examples. Two sites, Longhouse and Burton, may well have been Passage Graves. They have large polygonal chambers and, in the case of Burton, what could be interpreted as the remains of a short passage. In neither site

Fig. 27 Plans and elevations of two Passage Graves in Anglesey: A, Barclodiad y Gawres; B, Bryn Celli Ddu.

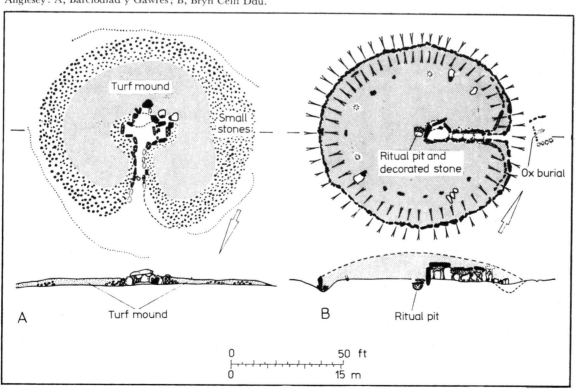

A   Turf mound

B   Ritual pit

0   50 ft

0   15 m

14   Entrance to the circular Passage Grave of Bryn Celli Ddu, Anglesey.

is the covering mound preserved. Many of the remaining tombs are difficult to classify because of their ruined state. They consist for the most part of a capstone supported by a few uprights, with no trace of a covering mound.

In North Wales there are about seventy sites, many of them again difficult to classify. The greatest numbers occur in Anglesey (twenty-nine sites), and include two well-preserved and extensively excavated Passage Graves. Barclodiad y Gawres, a circular mound some 90 ft in diameter, contains a cruciform Passage Grave, and only example of such an arrangement in England and Wales (Fig. 27A). Bryn Celli Ddu, about 80 ft in diameter, has a simpler internal arrange-

ment of a passage and polygonal chamber (Fig. 27B & Pl. 14). Of the remaining tombs in North Wales many have only the remains of the internal stone structures. Such mounds as do remain appear to be long rather than round. Dyffryn Aududwy, Merionethshire, proved, on excavation, to have two internal structures, an earlier tomb of the Portal Dolmen type in a roughly circular mound, incorporated in a later long mound with a rectangular chamber at one end. In two other long mounds, Capel Garmon and Tyddyn Bleiddyn, Denbighshire, access to the chambers seems to have been from the side rather than the end, the usual practice in long mounds.

In Derbyshire half a dozen tombs again indicate a mixture of traditions. Mining-low, Five Wells and Green Low all have

Fig. 28   Plans of Cotswold-Severn megalithic tombs: A, with terminal chamber; B, with transepted chamber; C, with lateral chambers.

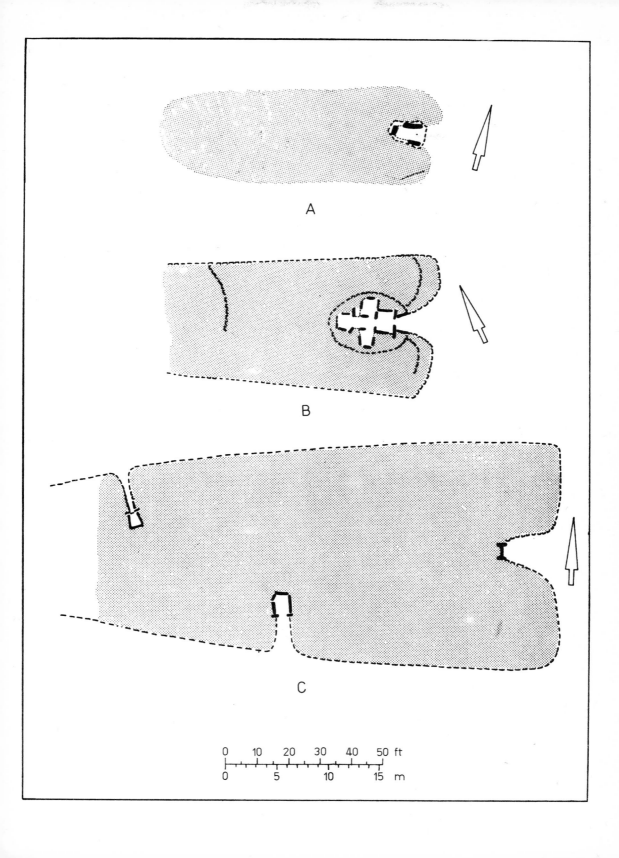

A

B

C

| 0 | 10 | 20 | 30 | 40 | 50 ft |
| 0 | 5 | | 10 | | 15 m |

internal passage-and-chamber structures under round cairns and to that extent represent the orthodox Passage Grave type. But Mininglow, for example, had no less than five separate internal structures, only two of which (probably) had separately distinguishable passages and chambers. There were two passage-and-chamber structures, back to back, at Five Wells and only one, the more usual arrangement, at Green Low. The single megalithic tomb in Cheshire, The Bridestones, consisted of a parallel-sided gallery set in a long covering mound, i.e. Gallery rather than Passage Grave tradition.

The Cotswold-Severn tombs (Fig. 28).

The Cotswold-Severn group (c. 180 sites) is one of the major concentrations of megalithic tombs in the British Isles. Its covering mounds belong to the long barrow tradition while its internal arrangements show a degree of variety which makes it difficult to use the term Gallery Grave without a great deal of qualification. Although there are many irregular mounds the typical Cotswold-Severn cairn can be described as trapeze-shaped in plan, i.e. wider at one end than the other, the majority being between 100 and 175 ft long. Widths vary from 50–60 ft at the broader end to 30–40 ft at the narrower end. At the broader end the mound curves inwards towards the entrance, forming the funnel-like approach or forecourt. The plan of the covering mound is defined by a well-built dry-stone wall (less frequently a wall of upright slabs), perhaps 3–4 ft high, bonded into the cairn material behind. In spite of the quality of the walling, however, this feature was not intended to be seen, additional material (generally called extra-revetment material) being piled against it, completely masking it. There are, therefore, presumably compelling ritual reasons for this trapeze-shaped plan, and for its concealment, and this aspect will be discussed in a later section.

The internal structures of these Cots-wold-Severn tombs can be divided into three groups: terminal chambers, transepted chambers and lateral chambers. Terminal chambers consist of rectangular chambers standing immediately behind the forecourt (Fig. 28A). In some cases they are almost square in plan, but in others they are much longer than they are wide, approximating to the true 'gallery' form. A massive example of the first type is provided by Tinkinswood, Glamorganshire, where the chamber is 16 × 12 ft, although the majority are very much less than this; and an example of the second type by Heston Brake, Monmouthshire, where the gallery-like chamber is 23 × 5 ft.

Transepted chambers consist of a central passage with up to three pairs of side chambers or transepts opening on either side (Fig. 28B). One of the finest examples is Stoney Littleton, Somerset, where the interior structure (c. 50 ft long) consists of a square ante-chamber (c. 5 × 5 ft), a central passage (3–4 ft wide), three pairs of side chambers (up to 7 × 4 ft) and an end chamber (c. 6 × 4 ft). The whole structure is roofed by means of corbelling. Other tombs (Notgrove, Hetty Pegler's Tump and Parc le Breos Cwm) have two pairs of transepts, and others (Nympsfield, Penmaen Burrows and Wayland's Smithy) only one pair. The latter is unusual in having a flat façade instead of a forecourt. The West Kennet long barrow (Pl. 15) also had a flat façade, concealing an earlier crescentic forecourt, instead of the more usual funnel-shaped type of the Cotswold-Severn region.

In the third group (lateral chambers), the internal structures of the mound are entered from one or both of the long sides, or more rarely from the back (Fig. 28c). The most interesting aspect of these lateral chambers, however, is the fact that many of them appear to be of Passage Grave type. The reasons for this combination of two traditions will be discussed later, but at least some of these lateral Passage Graves have been shown by excavation to represent an early structural phase when they were covered by their own free-

15 Interior view of the West Kennet long barrow.

standing circular mounds, and only at a later stage were they incorporated, mound and all, in the long barrow structure.

Megalithic tombs in Scotland

Megalithic tombs in Scotland (between 600 and 700 in number) occur in two major concentrations, in the south-west, from the Solway Firth to the island of Mull, and in the north-east, from the Moray Firth to Caithness and the Orkneys. Apart from a scatter of sites in eastern Scotland the remainder of the distribution is made up of two smaller groups, one in the Hebrides and one in the Shetlands.

The south-western tombs include the (main) Clyde group, and a smaller Bargrennan group (about a dozen sites),

the latter of the Passage Grave type. They consist mostly of round cairns (45–60 ft in diameter) with rectangular or wedge-shaped chambers, approached by long passages, and there is sometimes more than one chamber under each cairn.

The Clyde group consists of about a hundred tombs, together with about sixty ruinous sites which may have been originally of the same type. They show a number of points of similarity with the Cotswold-Severn tombs, most notably in their trapeze-shaped plan. At the broader end there was, most frequently, a forecourt, in this case semicircular rather than funnel-shaped (Fig. 29). The internal structures are sometimes single rectangular chambers but more frequently they are longer and subdivided into a series of compartments, from two to five in number, by septal

87

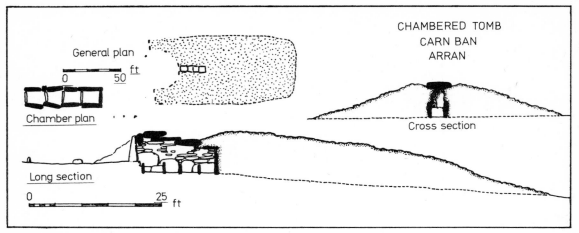

CHAMBERED TOMB
CARN BAN
ARRAN

General plan

0   50 ft

Chamber plan

Cross section

Long section

0   25 ft

Fig. 29   Plan and sections of the Clyde-type megalithic tomb at Carn Ban, Arran.

slabs. These are slabs of stone placed across the gallery at right angles but rising only a couple of feet in height, so that although the compartments are clearly marked off from each other, there is little or no difficulty in moving from one end of the gallery to the other. Although there are no transepted chambers in the Clyde cairns, the internal arrangements do include lateral chambers, apparently for the same reasons as in the Cotswold-Severn group.

The only other megalithic tombs on the western side of Scotland are those in the Hebrides (c. fifty in number), which appear to be mostly of the passage-and-chamber type. The covering mounds include round, long and a few, unusual, square cairns with projecting corners. In many cases the short passages are approached through triangular forecourts. The slab-built chambers are noticeably massive in construction and up to 19 × 12 ft in size.

Megalithic tombs in north-eastern Scotland can be divided into four groups: the Clava, Orkney-Cromarty, Maes Howe and Shetland groups. The Clava tombs (c. fifty in number) are grouped around the Moray Firth. They include two types of structure, Passage Graves and ring-cairns.

The Passage Graves are of classic form with stone kerbs, straight passages and circular corbelled chambers (10–13 ft in diameter), beneath circular cairns (Fig. 30B). They are in most cases surrounded by a ring of free-standing stones, as are the ring-cairns. The most noticeable feature of the latter, however, is the absence of a passage and the size of the chamber area (16–34 ft in diameter), which makes it virtually certain that ring-cairns were never roofed. Presumably whatever took place in this central area (burial, ritual or both) was sealed at the end by filling it to the top of the inner kerb-stones.

Megalithic tombs in the Shetlands (some sixty in number) are known as heel-shaped, on account of the plan of the cairn, or, in some cases, the platform on which the (circular) cairn stands. The internal structures are mostly of the Passage Grave type with cruciform, roughly circular or rectangular chambers. Most cairns have an incurving façade or shallow forecourt on one side and it was probably the combination of this feature with a circular mound which produced the unusual heel-shaped plan.

Fig. 30   Plans of megalithic tombs in N.E. Scotland: A, Camster Round; B, Balnuaran of Clava; C, Camster Long.

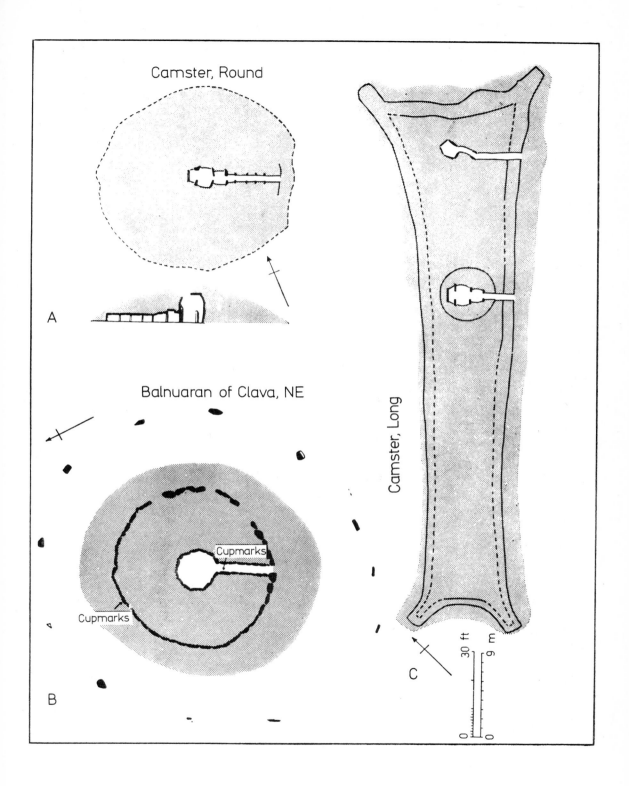

Camster, Round

A

Balnuaran of Clava, NE

Cupmarks

Cupmarks

B

Camster, Long

C

30 ft

9 m

0

16　Oblique aerial view of the Maes Howe megalithic tomb, Orkneys.

The Maes Howe group

Maes Howe, one of the great achievements of prehistoric architecture, is the principal tomb of the Maes Howe group of ten Passage Graves situated in the Orkney Islands (Fig. 31A). Its covering mound (c. 124 × 105 ft) is surrounded by a wide berm, beyond which is a ditch between 30 and 60 ft wide (Pl. 16). The entrance passage is 3 ft wide and 4½ ft high and consists of coursed masonry for the first 8 ft. Beyond this, however, for nearly 20 ft, the two walls and the roof are formed of three huge stone slabs, between 18 and 20 ft long,

nearly 4½ ft wide and 7 in. thick, an outstanding example of megalithic technique (Pl. 17). About 50 ft in from the edge of the mound is the chief glory of Maes Howe, its chamber, some 15 ft square with each corner occupied by a substantial buttress. The chamber walls rise vertically for about 4½ ft and then incline inwards for another 4 ft. Above this again the courses are stepped out to form a square corbelled vault which still survives to a height of 12½ ft; in its original state the chamber must have been 16–18 ft high. Each of the corner buttresses consists of a large stone slab up to 10 ft high, with the other face of coursed masonry, providing additional support to take the thrust of the corbelled

17　Maes Howe megalithic tomb, view along entrance
passage towards exterior.

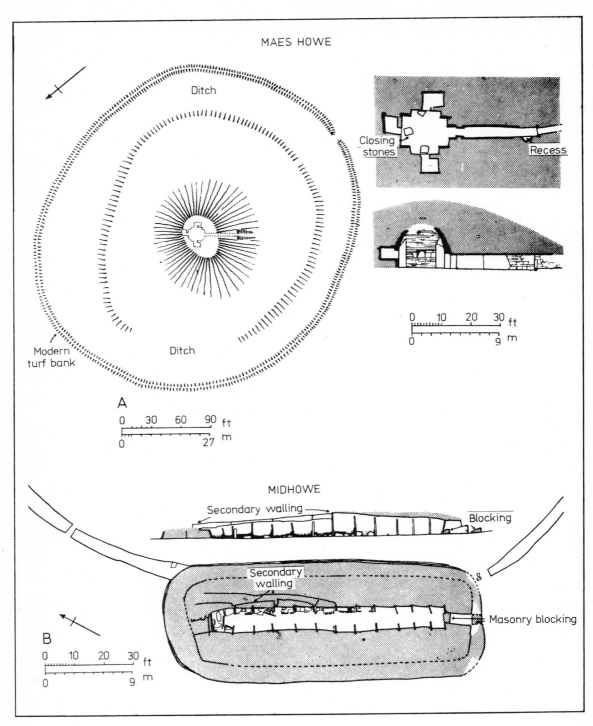

MAES HOWE

Ditch

Closing
stones

Recess

Modern
turf bank

Ditch

A

0   30   60   90 ft
0   27 m

0   10   20   30 ft
0   9 m

MIDHOWE

Secondary walling

Blocking

Secondary
walling

g

Masonry blocking

B

0   10   20   30 ft
0   9 m

Fig. 31   Plans and sections of megalithic tombs in the
Orkneys: A Maes Howe; B, Midhowe.

ceiling. The most striking feature of the chamber is the sheer quality of the masonry. The wall faces are flush, with fine joints between regular, rectangular blocks. Many of the courses consist of a single stone slab, c. 10 ft long, from buttress to buttress. Opening from the west, north and east sides of the chamber are three cells up to 7 ft long, 5 ft wide and 3½ ft high. They are, however, placed about 3 ft above the floor level of the main chamber, and access to them is via window-like openings (c. 2½ ft square), rather than doorways. Three large stones on the chamber floor were presumably intended as blocking stones to seal the cells. Other sites of the Maes Howe group (Quanterness, Quoyness, Vinquoy, Wideford Hill and Cuween), are less spectacular but nevertheless still of great architectural interest.

The Orkney-Cromarty group

The Orkney-Cromarty group of about 200 tombs is in many ways one of the most interesting of all megalithic groups in the British Isles both because of its variety and its architecture. Its covering mounds range from round and oval cairns to two different kinds of long cairn. Internally the (normally) corbelled roof is partially supported by slabs of stone projecting from the chamber walls, dividing the space into a series (in many cases three pairs) of stall-like recesses, hence the term of *stalled cairns*. At Camster in Caithness two fine tombs, Camster Round and Camster Long, illustrate two of the major types in north-eastern Scotland (Fig. 30A, C). From the eastern side of the round cairn (c. 60 ft in diameter) a passage 18 × 2½ ft leads (via an antechamber 4½ ft wide) to a main, corbelled chamber 10 ft high, subdivided into a main section 6½ ft wide and a rear section 4 ft wide. The three sections are marked off from each other by projecting slabs of stone. Camster Round gives its name to the *Camster type*, a circular Passage Grave with the stalled construction peculiar to north-eastern Scotland.

In the second major Orkney-Cromarty type, the Yarrow type, the internal structures are virtually the same as in Camster Round but, in marked contrast, the covering mound is long (Fig. 30C). At the

18   Interior of the Midhowe stalled cairn, Orkneys.

broader end it has a wide, crescentic fore-court, flanked by horn-like projections (hence the term horned cairns). At the narrower end there is a matching crescentic arrangement, again flanked by two horn-like projections. Camster Long follows the Yarrows plan (c. 195 ft long), but its chambers are entered from the side of the mound in the manner of the Cotswold-Severn lateral chambers. Significantly, the larger chamber, of the tripartite, stalled variety, appears originally to have been a separate tomb with its own, circular cairn.

There are, however, other types of long cairn in the Orkney-Cromarty group. At Midhowe on the island of Rousay in the Orkneys there is a stalled chamber, of twelve sections, some 76 ft long with a passage on the same axis nearly 13 ft long, beneath a mound about 107 × 42 ft, rectangular in plan with rounded corners and no trace of projecting horns (Fig. 31B & Pl. 18). In a generally similar tomb at Blackhammer in the same island access is from one of the long sides, passage and chamber (seven sections) forming a T-shape in plan, and there is a T-shaped arrangement at Unstan on the mainland of the Orkneys, in this case, however, under a cairn which is almost circular in plan. Such T-shaped structures recall some of the tombs of the Maes Howe group, mostly under round cairns, but most particularly Holm of Papa Westray, of very much the same sort of shape and size as Midhowe, but entered from the long side, as at Blackhammer. Quite clearly where the two groups came into contact with each other, in the Orkneys, there was a certain mingling, at least of architectural traditions and practices.

Megalithic tombs in Ireland

Megalithic tombs in Ireland are more numerous than elsewhere in the British Isles, with a total greater than the com-bined total (c. 1,000) for the other three countries. The main groups involved are the Passage Graves of the Boyne culture,

the (long) Court cairns of northern and north-eastern Ireland, the so-called wedge-shaped tombs (northern and southern varieties), the Tramore group and the Portal Dolmens.

The Boyne tombs

Like Maes Howe in Orkney, many of the Boyne Passage Graves (c. 200 in number) are outstanding examples of prehistoric architecture. More than half of them are grouped in five cemeteries: Boyne, Four-knocks, Loughcrew, Carrowkeel and Carrowmore. The Boyne cemetery is situated in the bend of the River Boyne about twenty miles from Dublin and consists of a dozen or so circular mounds, at least five of which are certainly Passage Graves. New Grange (Fig. 32) is 280 ft in diameter, over 40 ft high, and occupies about an acre of ground (c. 5,000 square yds). Surrounding it are twelve large stones, presumably the remains of an originally complete ring of free-standing stones about 350 ft in diameter. Internally the passage, about 60 × 3 ft, built of upright slabs and capstones, gives access to a main chamber and three side chambers, in plan like a cross, hence the term *cruciform* Passage Grave. The main chamber is about 10 ft square and no less than 19 ft 6 in. high, achieved by corbelling. All three side chambers, roofed with capstones, contained large stone basins, which will be encountered again in other Boyne tombs.

Dowth, just over a mile away, is of the same dimensions (c. 280 ft in diameter, 47 ft high), with the edge of the mound defined by a kerb of large stones. It houses two Passage Grave structures, both roofed with capstones. Dowth north is cruciform, with a 27-ft passage leading to an octagonal central chamber about 9 ft across and 11 ft high. In the centre is a large oval basin carved in a roughly rectangular slab of stone c. 6 × 3½ ft. Three side chambers complete the cruciform plan. Beyond the south chamber there is also an unusual extension in the form of a narrow chamber

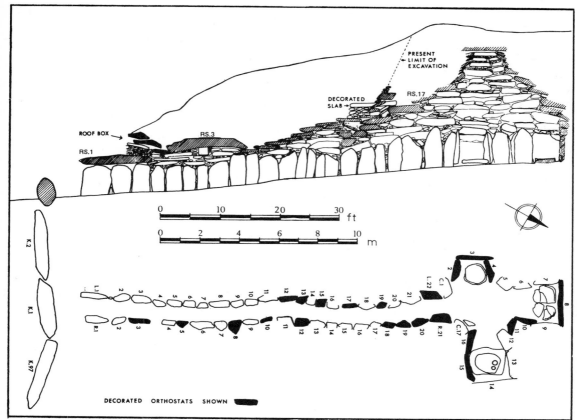

Fig. 32   Plan and section of the cruciform internal
structure at the Passage Grave of New Grange, Ireland.

or passage with two side chambers. Dowth
south is much simpler, with a short passage
(11½ ft long) leading to a circular chamber
15 ft in diameter with a single, trapeze-
shaped side chamber (9 × 7 ft) on the
south side.

The third major tomb in the Boyne
cemetery is Knowth, of the same dimensions as the other two (Pl. 19). As a result
of excavations in 1967 and 1968 not one
but two internal structures were found, on
opposite sides of the mound. The eastern
tomb is cruciform with a passage about
2½ ft wide and originally about 115 ft long.
A stone basin c. 4 ft in diameter was discovered in the right-hand chamber. In the
western tomb the passage (c. 100 ft long)

is about 2 ft wide and 3½ ft high. At the
inner end it widens to about 4 ft to form a
simple rectangular chamber c. 5 ft × 4 ft.
Both passage and chamber are roofed with
capstones. In the passage a stone basin c.
2½ ft in diameter was found (Pl. 20). One
of the most remarkable features at Knowth
was the discovery of fifteen small Passage
Graves (c. 40 ft in diameter), surrounding
the main mound, forming a complete
cemetery, within the main Boyne cemetery.

Much less is known about the last two
Passage Graves, sites J and K. Site J has a
hexagonal corbelled chamber about 10 ft
across and 8 ft high, with five small side
chambers; no trace of a passage has been
found as yet. At site K there is surface
evidence of both passage and chamber,
although the plan of the latter is unknown.

19 General view of the Knowth Passage Grave, Co.
Meath, during excavation.

The main tomb (I) at the Fourknocks
cemetery, about ten miles north of Dublin,
is a cruciform Passage Grave about 60 ft
in diameter. A short passage, about 18 ×
4 ft, leads into an oval chamber (c. 21 ×
18 ft) with three small side chambers. The
lower courses of a corbelled roof were
found, although whether such a large
chamber could be roofed by corbelling
alone is a matter for speculation. Fourknocks II had a passage but no chamber
and may have been simply the crematorium
for the main mound. Fourknocks III proved
to be of Bronze Age date.

The three largest cairns (D, L and T) at
the Loughcrew cemetery (c. thirty tombs)
are 180, 135 and 115 ft in diameter
respectively. D appears to be unchambered,
but the other two have passages and corbelled chambers and T is of classic cruciform type (Fig. 33A). Tomb L has no less
than eight side chambers, in two of which
there were stone basins. Many of the
remaining mounds in the cemetery were of
smaller dimensions than the three mentioned.

At Carrowkeel in north-west Ireland,
Co. Sligo, there are thirteen round cairns,
eight or nine of which have passages and
chambers, many of them of cruciform
type. Cairn K is about 70 ft in diameter
and about 18 ft high (Fig. 33B). Internally
a short passage leads to a corbelled central
chamber 11 ft high, with three side
chambers in the classic cruciform plan.

At Carrowmore there are now remains of
about sixty tombs, although there were
originally at least a hundred. The cairns are
relatively small, c. 40 ft in diameter, and
the internal arrangements correspondingly
simple, with no traces of corbelling, for
example (Fig. 33C). Passages are either
very short or non-existent and in many
cases the internal structure consists of a
closed, slab-built chamber with no formal
means of access.

These five cemeteries account for more
than half the tombs in the Boyne group.
The remaining tombs occur in ones and
twos mainly in the eastern half of the

country although there are some in the west as well.

The remaining megalithic tombs will be dealt with more briefly. Some 300 long mounds, in the northern part of Ireland, are known as Court cairns (Fig. 34). Most of them are broadly similar to the Clyde cairns of south-west Scotland. The best examples have the same trapeze-shaped plan, a semicircular forecourt and an internal, gallery-type structure of separate compartments divided by low septal slabs. In some cases, however, the open forecourt has been extended to form an enclosed court. In other cases, two separate tombs face each other across a closed court. In still other cases, two tombs are joined back to back so that there is a semicircular court at each end of the mound.

The third large group of Irish megalithic tombs, up to 400 in number, are known as Wedge-shaped Graves, and are divided into northern and southern types. The Southern Wedges are angular in plan with a gallery which is wider and higher at the front than at the back, hence the name (Fig. 35B). The Northern Wedges have a portico or antechamber in front of the gallery, the back of which tends to be rounded in plan (Fig. 35A). In many

20 Decorated stone basin in the Knowth Passage Grave, Co. Meath.

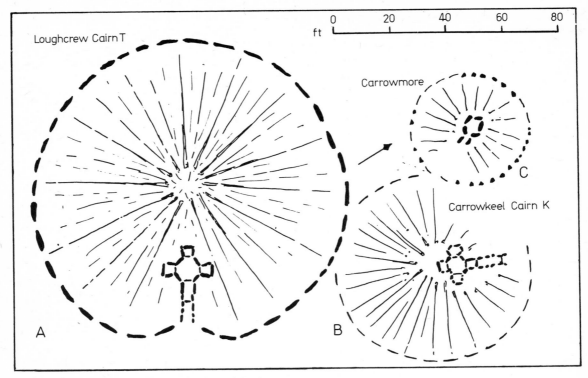

Fig. 33   Passage Graves of the Boyne culture (plans):
A, Loughcrew; B, Carrowkeel; C, Carrowmore.

examples, of both types, the walls defining the gallery are double, two rows of upright slabs with a filling of small stones between. Southern Wedges (up to 250 in number) occur mainly in the south-west, while the less numerous Northern Wedges are found in Ulster and adjacent areas (Fig. 36).

The term Dolmen (from a Breton word for a stone table) is applied to a type of simple, but none the less impressive, megalithic structure consisting simply of a chamber of upright slabs and a capstone, often of considerable size and weight (Pl. 21). Most if not all trace of the covering mound has long since gone, hence the table or altar-like appearance of the now free-standing stone structure. A special form of this type of structure is the so-called Portal Dolmen which is fairly common in the eastern parts of Ireland and occurs also in Wales (Fig. 35c). In such structures two of

the upright stones, usually taller than the rest, are so placed as to form a pair defining a sort of porch or portal to the chamber proper, hence the term Portal Dolmen. Such evidence as there is suggests that the original covering mounds were both long and round.

The last group of Irish megalithic tombs is quite small and consists of some half-dozen graves in the Tramore region of southern Ireland. These are virtually identical to those in the Scilly Islands and the two are sometimes combined as an Anglo-Irish assemblage under the title of the Scilly-Tramore group.

For the source of what was quite clearly a powerful influence on western Europe in the years from 3000 B.C. on, one must look to the eastern Mediterranean. The reasons behind a movement into the west may have been trade in general and copper in particular, for which the demand, once metallurgy had been discovered, must have been considerable. A number of settlements, presumed to have been built by traders, are known in Spain, Portugal and France, and their stone architecture, and particularly their defensive walls, point very clearly to the civilisations of the eastern Mediterranean. However, megalithic tombs as such do not exist in the east Mediterranean area, so that quite clearly the whole answer does not lie there. Among the most striking funerary monuments that do exist are the famous *tholos* tombs, known at Mycenae and elsewhere, which have been suggested as the inspiration for west Mediterranean Passage Graves; but the dates of the Mycenaen *tholoi*, at least, are fairly well established, between 1500 and 1350 B.C., much too late to be the inspiration of megalithic tombs of similar plan in the west. On the other hand

Fig. 34 Plans of Court cairns in Ireland.

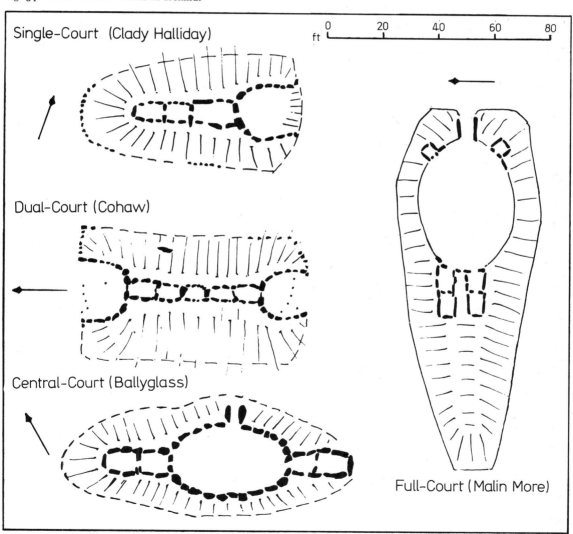

Single-Court (Clady Halliday)

ft 0   20   40   60   80

Dual-Court (Cohaw)

Central-Court (Ballyglass)

Full-Court (Malin More)

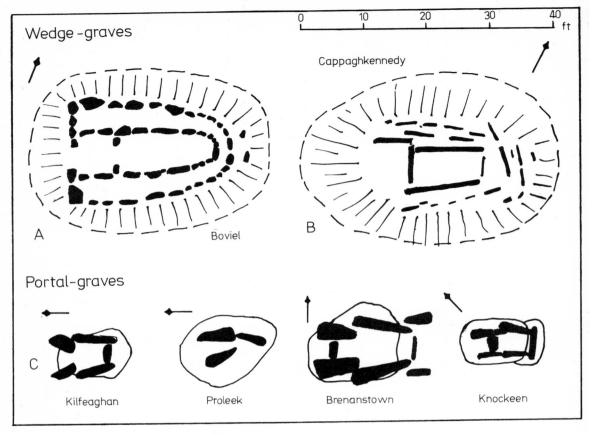

Fig. 35 Plans of Wedge-shaped tombs and Portal Dolmens in Ireland.

such *tholos* tombs must have had a very long period of development behind them, so that it is feasible to suggest that Passage Graves and *tholoi* are similar, not because one is the parent of the other, but because they are cousins, with a common ancestor, at a date sufficiently early to allow both types to develop on separate lines to the form in which we see them today.

If megalithic tombs as such do not exist in the east Mediterranean area, then at least some of the ideas, beliefs and practices which appear to lie behind them can be shown to have existed there. The practice of collective burial was widespread in the Aegean, but quite different from the practice in the surrounding territories of Anatolia, Mesopotamia and Egypt. Moreover, some of these collective burials were in natural caves, and it has often been suggested that a megalithic tomb was an attempt to create an artificial cave, a man-made cavern beneath a mound of earth. Cave burials are also recorded in the west Mediterranean, among the people who immediately preceded the period when megalithic tombs were in use. In both areas also there is the use of rock-cut tombs which in a sense stand even closer to the idea of the natural cave. Finally, apart from the ideas of collective burial and cave burial, there is the idea of burial in a chamber, in whatever form it took.

These three basic concepts, cave burial, collective burial and chamber burial, widespread in the east Mediterranean area, provide a more than adequate background out of which could have developed the whole idea and practice of collective burial in megalithic chamber tombs. What is new in the west is the method of building, the megalithic technique, and this must be regarded as the contribution of the western Mediterranean to the practice of collective, chamber burial.

From this key area began a dispersal over those areas of western and northern Europe described earlier, both overland across France and Spain and by sea via the Western sea route, ultimately as far as the Orkneys and Shetlands, bringing to the British Isles the practice of burial in megalithic tombs which, over a period of many centuries, resulted in the pattern as we see it today. The time aspect is important in understanding megalithic tombs, here as elsewhere. As pointed out at the beginning of the chapter even in the British Isles megalithic tombs were in use for around 1,500 years so that some groups or types could have been long out of use

before others appeared. It would be misleading to see the development of megalithic tombs as a single event, with all types and all regional groups in existence together. Acknowledgment of the time factor allows matters of changing style and fashion to be brought into the discussion and these may explain many of the variations described in the chapter, rather than differences of origin.

With regard to origins, Dr J. X. W. P. Corcoran's work on the Cotswold-Severn tombs has shown how a type can come into being in Britain without any single, obvious prototype in Europe. Rather than treating the tomb as a whole he deals separately with their covering mounds, with some (circular) mounds concealed within them and with their internal arrangements. The nearest possible source for the trapeze-shaped cairns are the long barrows of the Windmill Hill culture. Carbon-14 dates (3230 B.C.) show that the Windmill Hill barrows were certainly early enough to have provided this inspiration for the Cotswold-Severn cairns. The simple terminal chambers may have been derived

Fig. 36   Reconstruction drawing of a Wedge-shaped tomb in Ireland.

21   Trethevy Quoit dolmen, Cornwall.

from the same source, being stone versions of (presumed) timber chambers. The most complex of the internal structures, transepted chambers, have clear links with Brittany and this component may be presumed to have been derived from there. As pointed out earlier, the lateral chambers are of Passage Grave type, and it now appears that, as originally built, they were housed not in long mounds but in their own circular mounds. Only at a later stage, and presumably as a result of changing fashion, were they incorporated in long mounds, completely masking their original appearance. The new covering was so placed as to still leave access to them, hence the effect of lateral chambers. This suggests that in the Cotswold-Severn region there were at least two major events in the development of megalithic tombs. The first would appear to have been the arrival of people building small, circular Passage Graves. The next event marked an important change, the use of long, trapeze-shaped mounds housing different types of chamber. Existing round Passage Graves were concealed by the new constructions, so that, prior to excavation, the area looked to be firmly in the Passage Grave tradition. This second event was probably more complex than the first, as indicated by the origin and variety of its components. Lateral chambers and evidence of concealed circular mounds have been found also in Scotland, and a broadly similar sequence can be envisaged there as well.

It has been suggested that the orthodox type of megalithic tomb is a Passage Grave under a round cairn, and that all other types of megalithic tomb are unorthodox variations resulting from local adaptions of, and borrowings from, the basic tradition. One other fact should be kept in mind. Carbon-14 dates indicated that the great Passage Graves such as New Grange and Maes Howe are late rather than early in the story, c. 2000 B.C. or thereabouts. The earliest arrivals of megalithic tomb builders seem to be represented by small, relatively simple Passage Graves under round cairns in the Cotswold-Severn region, in Scotland, and possibly generally in the British Isles. These have their counterparts in Europe and such tombs seem to represent the orthodox megalithic tradition at an early stage, possibly c. 3000 B.C. In the Cotswold-Severn region, as indicated above, these early tombs were replaced by an entirely different tradition of more complex origins. The most elaborate internal structures (the transepted chambers) have clear links with Brittany. The new long, trapeze-shaped covering mound was seen as a result of close contact with the Windmill Hill culture and its own trapeze-shaped, but earthen, long barrows, and it is the possible origins of the latter which add another European dimension to the picture. Briefly, in the Neolithic period in central and north central Europe there was a clear-cut tradition of large, trapeze-shaped houses; the generally accepted links between the houses of the living and the house of the dead (i.e. tombs) make it likely that the Windmill Hill long barrows were based ultimately on the European trapeze-shaped house and that this represents a contribution to megalithic tomb architecture from an entirely outside source. In the same way the circular Passage Grave would appear to be based on the round hut, the common type in the Mediterranean area. Thus it is feasible to suggest that, via the Windmill Hill culture, the trapeze-shaped cairn was brought into the megalithic tradition, appearing first of all in the Cotswold-Severn tombs where it supplanted the circular Passage Graves. Dates for such events are always difficult,

but somewhere between 2750 and 2500 B.C. is a possibility for the beginning of trapeze-shaped megalithic tombs. The two types of internal structure may represent different sub-phases. The terminal chambers may be simply stone versions of Windmill Hill timber chambers, and as such are likely to be earlier. The more complex transepted chambers represent influence from another direction, Brittany, and may form the last phase of the Cotswold-Severn culture.

Apart from scattered sites in North Wales, the next major concentration of trapeze-shaped cairns is in south-west Scotland, in the form of the Clyde cairns mentioned earlier. There are other parallels as well, indicating a strong link between the two. If the derivation of the trapeze-shape from the Windmill Hill culture is correct, then the Cotswold-Severn tombs are presumably earlier than trapeze-shaped tombs in the Clyde area, and in other areas as well, such as Ireland and in north-east Scotland. This accounts for a very considerable part of the megalithic tombs in the British Isles, none of which would have clear-cut continental prototypes, for the reasons just outlined. This very considerable development of megalithic tombs is due to internal developments within the British Isles, and as far as the north is concerned can be bracketed in broad terms between c. 2500 and 2000 B.C.

The developments just outlined have not taken account of the major groups of Passage Graves. Presumably at some stage the small, relatively simple Passage Graves mentioned earlier gave place to much more grandiose tombs, both in the British Isles and abroad. These appear to be relatively late in the sequence, c. 2000 B.C., and there is some suggestion of a connection with the Beaker people, in much the same way as the later developments of Stonehenge. The building of the larger Passage Graves would appear to indicate continuing contacts up and down the Western seaway, and the endurance of the orthodox megalithic tradition between 3000 and 2000 B.C., and probably later as well.

The Passage Graves account for another

substantial part of the megalithic tombs in the British Isles. Inevitably, the two lines of development outlined above impinged on each other at certain times and in certain areas to produce further variants on the megalithic theme which again are peculiar to the British Isles and can have no prototypes in Europe. For example, it was probably the attempt to add a fore-court to a round cairn which produced the peculiar heel-shaped cairns of the Shet-lands. Equally, it was the elaboration of the stalled chambers of Passage Graves which led to the development of certain long mounds which were rectangular with rounded corners rather than trapeze-shaped in the classic tradition. This happened in the Orkney-Cromarty area, one of the regions where much intermingling of tradi-tions seems to have taken place, which may explain why it contains some of the most interesting megalithic tombs in the British Isles.

As pointed out earlier the full story of megalithic tombs in the British Isles has still to be worked out. There are still many gaps in the account and many unexplained developments. These are problems for future excavation. What has been outlined here is that part of the picture which is now fairly well established and is not likely to be fundamentally changed by future discoveries.

5 Ceremonial Sites

There can be few people either here or abroad who have not heard of the most celebrated of all henge monuments, Stonehenge, from which the name of the group as a whole is derived. The word 'henge' is simply an old form of the verb 'to hang', used to describe the lintels or horizontal members at Stonehenge which were supported by, or hung on, the uprights. The implication of the term, as currently used, is that all circular sanctuaries had uprights and lintels in the Stonehenge manner, but modern research has established that this is not so. In fact, the only undisputed evidence of true henge or hanging features is at Stonehenge itself, which must be regarded as a very special and unusual form of henge monument. Elsewhere the evidence, where it is available, is of a variety of less spectacular features to none of which the description 'henge' is strictly applicable. However, the term has now achieved wide currency and it is difficult to suggest a suitable and equally convenient alternative. It will, therefore, be used here as the general designation of a group of circular sanctuaries of the Late Neolithic/Early Bronze Age period (c. 2500–1500 B.C.) without any implication as to structure, except where this is clearly established, namely at Stonehenge itself.

As thus defined there are between eighty and one hundred henge monuments still identifiable in the British Isles. Their surface remains display a series of common features which warrant their inclusion in a single group. The first such feature is the plan which, with only one or two exceptions, is circular or near circular, the irregularities occurring on the whole in the larger sanctuaries where the practical difficulties of laying out the site would be the greater. The most notable exceptions to the circular arrangement are Marden, Wiltshire (Fig. 42D), and Waulud's Bank, Bedfordshire (if the latter is indeed a henge), which are irregularly oval in plan with one side formed by a river. In overall size henges range from around 30 ft up to 1,700 ft (Durrington Walls, Wiltshire, Fig. 42A) in diameter, although it has been suggested that the smaller sites, notably at Dorchester, Oxfordshire, are not true henges but more probably burial monuments based on the henge model. Leaving the half-dozen smaller sites to one side the average diameter of the remainder is something over 200 ft.

The major visible features defining these circular areas are, for the majority of sites, a bank and a ditch. In most cases the bank is outside the ditch, unlike a defensive work where the opposite is true, and, in the absence of visible internal structures, this is the major diagnostic feature of henge monuments. The effect produced is that of an amphitheatre, the ditch defining and separating a circular plateau, presumably the sacred area reserved for priests, with excavated material thrown outwards to form a bank from which spectators, presumably the population as a whole, could witness whatever ceremonies were taking place inside. Some such bank and ditch arrangements were of considerable size and the resulting structure must have been quite imposing. At Avebury, Wiltshire (Fig. 42B), for example, the ditch as excavated is up to 70 ft wide and 30 ft deep (Pl. 22), with an outside bank of commensurate size, defining a sacred area some 1,150 ft in diameter (28½ acres). In some cases the ditch is outside the bank, as at Stonehenge, where both features are in any case of very modest dimensions, and in other cases there are two ditches, inner and outer, with the bank between.

Another surface feature, the entrance, is the basis on which henge monuments are currently classified. Most henges have either one entrance or two diametrically opposed entrances and these are designated Class I and Class II henges respectively. Class I henges are somewhat more numerous than Class II, forming about 60 per cent of the total. In fact, Class II embraces also those few sites with more than two entrances, the most notable examples being Avebury, Wiltshire, and Mount Pleasant, Dorset, each of which has four entrances (Fig. 42 B, C). Sub-classes IA and IIA indicate those henges in which there are two ditches with the bank between, as mentioned in the last paragraph.

The remaining henge features, mostly in the sacred area, are much more varied in type and are best dealt with separately as they occur. They can, however, be sum-

22　The ditch at Avebury henge monument, Wiltshire, during excavation.

marised briefly as part of the general picture of henge monuments. Apart from stone structures they are known only from excavation, which means that the information is still incomplete, although recent work has added greatly to our knowledge. Stone circles occur in only thirteen henge monuments so that, in spite of the pre-eminence of Stonehenge, they would not appear to be an integral part of the henge tradition. Timber circles are known (from excavation) in eight or nine henges and the chances are that more will be found as a result of future excavations; it is unlikely, on the other hand, that any more stone circles will be found, since some traces of these normally survive on the surface. Other features include circles of pits, central features (stones, cairns, burials, etc.), entrance features (stone or timber posts) and outlying stone or timber posts, beyond the sacred area and its enclosing earthworks. It must be clear from this that, apart from the circular plan, the ditch, the external bank and the entrance arrangements, which are common to most henge monuments, there is a great deal of variety in the additional structures which makes any general statement about them impossible. One thing which must be clear is that Stonehenge, far from being typical is, in fact, unique, not only in the context of henge monuments but in the prehistoric world as a whole.

The hundred or so confirmed and possible henge monuments are widely distributed throughout the British Isles, for the most part in a series of fairly compact groups, with very large blank areas between. The Cornish group consists of three certain and two doubtful henges. The most interesting site is probably the Stipple Stones, a Class I henge some 225 ft in diameter with an irregular circle of twenty-eight stones within and a single stone at the centre. The ditch was originally 9 ft wide and 3 ft deep and was inside the enclosing bank. Castilly, also Class I, is of the same general dimensions but has no trace of internal structures. Castlewich is somewhat

larger (c. 300 ft in diameter) and like them is Class I. Again there is no surviving evidence of any internal structures.

In south-west Wales, Meini-Gwyr, Carmarthenshire, is perhaps the most interesting in that it contains visible stone structures. Apart from stones lining the entrance it has a circle of seventeen stones within the enclosure (120 ft diameter). The other Carmarthenshire site, Ffynnon-Brodyr, is very much larger and distinctly oval in plan (440 × 350 ft). Castle Bucket and Dan y Coed, Pembrokeshire, are 250 ft and 160 ft in diameter respectively, with their single entrances facing generally west, as do those of the two sites considered already.

Apart from two uncertain sites the small group in north-west Wales consists of the henges at Llandegai, just outside Bangor, known as Llandegai North and Llandegai South (226 ft and 223 ft diameter). Llandegai North, however, was of Class I, with its ditch outside the bank, while Llandegai South was of Class II with the more usual henge arrangement of the ditch inside the bank. At both sites excavation revealed the existence of pits outside the entrance, some of them containing cremated burials. Both henges were discovered only as a result of aerial survey and were excavated in advance of a building development which now covers the site.

The Derbyshire group also includes two certain and two doubtful sites. Arbor Low, a Class II site, is one of the outstanding henge monuments in the British Isles (Fig. 37 & Pl. 23). It has an overall diameter of about 300 ft. Within the bank, c. 7 ft high, is a ditch 30 ft wide defining a central circular area some 160 ft in diameter. Around the edge of this is a ring of about fifty large stones, recumbent not upright, with a cove or U-shaped setting of stones at the centre. Excavation in the early part of the century failed to uncover any sockets in the ground for the recumbent stones. Either they were kept upright in some other way, or were intended to be recumbent, or else the monument was

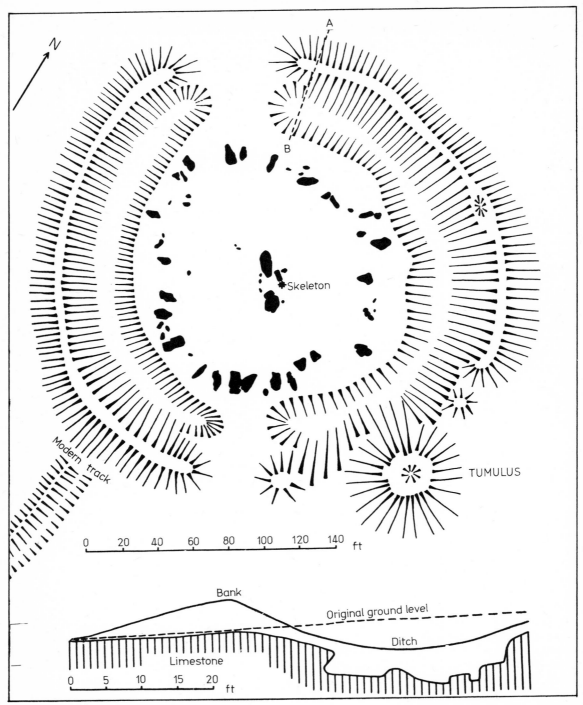

Fig. 37 Plan of the henge monument at Arbor Low, Derbyshire.

23 Oblique aerial view of the Arbor Low henge monument, Derbyshire.

simply not completed. A round, presumably Bronze Age burial mound (c. 70 ft in diameter) was built against the outside of the bank just east of the south entrance, and there is another, Gib Hill, about 350 yds to the south-west which still stands some 15 ft high. Both contained cremations placed in stone cists within the mound.

The Bull Ring, in Dove Holes, is of the same class (II) and size (c. 300 ft diameter) as Arbor Low, and there are other resemblances as well. Although no stone structure now survives there are written records that a ring of stones once stood in the central area, defined by a ditch 30–40 ft wide. Moreover, a large round barrow is situated south-west of the site in the same way as Gib Hill is related to Arbor Low.

The Yorkshire group (ten sites) contains some of the largest sites encountered so far. Seven of them are in the 600–800 ft diameter range and of these six are of the relatively unusual Class IIA form, i.e. they have both inner and outer ditches with the bank between. Undoubtedly the most celebrated of the Yorkshire sites are the Thornborough Circles, three large henges built in a line with half-mile gaps between, situated about five miles north of Ripon. Each is about 800 ft in diameter with their double entrances very much in the same place, north-west and south-east. The outer ditches of all three are now filled as a result of regular ploughing. The most

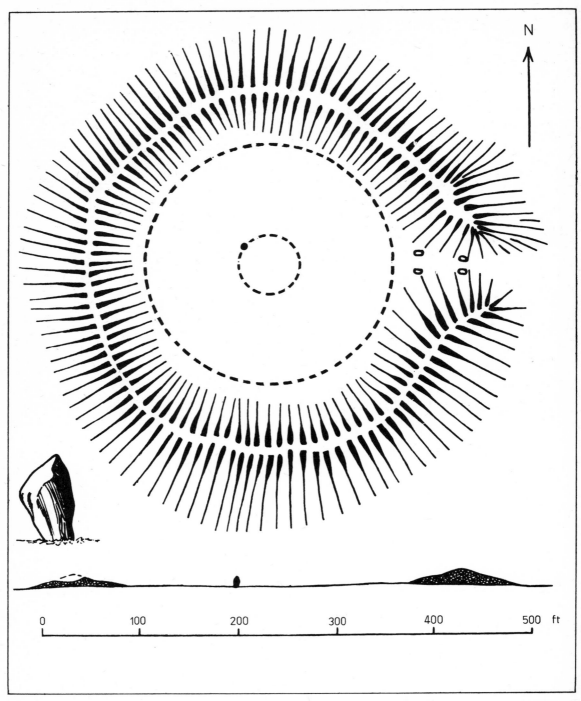

Fig. 38   Plan of the henge monument at Mayburgh, Westmorland.

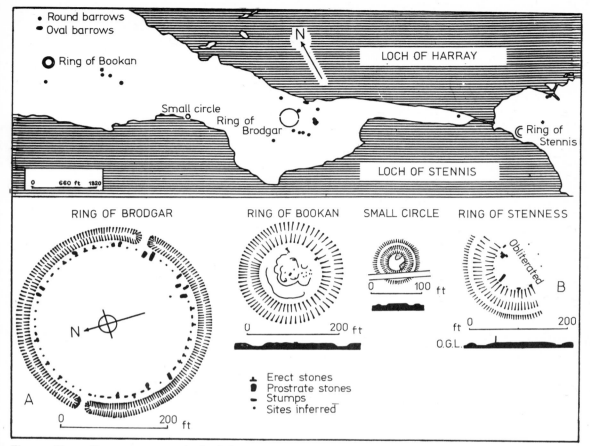

Fig. 39 Plans of henge monuments in the Orkneys:
A, Ring of Brodgar; B, Stenness.

accessible of the three is the centre circle, although the northern one is the better preserved because of its cover of trees. Three other henges (at Cana and Hutton Moor east of Ripon, and at Knottingley, West Riding) are likewise of Class IIA and still of considerable size (570 ft, 570 ft and 600 ft in diameter respectively). Another site in the Ripon region, Nunwick, is somewhat larger (c. 690 ft in diameter) but is of straightforward Class II type. The remaining sites are noticeably smaller: in the West Riding, Castle Dykes near Aysgarth (diameter 185 ft), and Yarnbury (diameter 116 ft), both Class I; and in the East Riding, Rudston (290 × 240 ft),

Class I, and Paddock Hill (diameter 300 ft), Class IA.

The most notable of the Lake District sites are King Arthur's Round Table and Mayburgh, near Penrith, separated by only a quarter of a mile. At King Arthur's Round Table, a Class I henge c. 300 ft in diameter, excavation has shown that there was a central cremation burial covered by some sort of stone structure. Mayburgh is somewhat larger (c. 360 ft in diameter), Class I, and is unusual in that the surrounding bank has no accompanying ditch, either inside or out (Fig. 38). There is a stone 9 ft high near the centre, and it is known that there were originally four, with four more flanking the entrance. Broomrig in Cumberland (165 ft diameter) is of

Class I and has a single stone at the entrance. There is a fourth, doubtful, site, Little Round Table, close to the two other Westmorland sites, with a diameter of c. 300 ft, but the classification and other features are uncertain.

The Scottish henges are widely scattered from Dumfries-shire to the Orkneys and do not constitute a single group. About twenty sites are involved, four of them doubtful. The confirmed henges are more or less evenly divided between Class I and Class II but no geographical separation is observable. Both types occur throughout the whole occupied area. The two Orkney sites (Ring of Brodgar and Stones of Stenness) both have stone settings within (Fig. 39). At the former (sixty stones, 465 ft diameter) there is no surviving evidence of a bank although one may have existed originally (Pl. 24). Stenness is smaller (200 ft diameter) with about twelve surviving stones and a conventional ditch and outer bank. Further south there is a group of four in Ross and Cromarty close to the Moray Firth. They are all relatively small (70–120 ft diameters), three of them (Canonbridge, Contin and Culbokie) being Class I and one (Muir of Ord) Class II. Further south again there is a scatter of five sites in eastern Scotland, one of them doubtful. In Aberdeen, Broomend of Crichie and Clashindarrock are respectively 54 ft and 110 ft in diameter and of Class II and Class I. At Broomend of Crichie there is a circle of six stones, and a central pit was uncovered in excavation. The two other certain henges are Huntingtower, Perthshire (120 ft diameter, Class I), and Balfarg, Fife (280 ft diameter, Class I), with a circle of ten or eleven stones and another two at the entrance. Most of the remaining Scottish sites (seven in number) are between the Forth and the English border. Five of them are of Class II: Cairnpapple, West Lothian, Newbigging (alternative name Weston), Lanarkshire, Normangill, Lanarkshire, Coupland (actually in Northumberland), and Broadlee, Dumfriesshire. Of these only Cairnpapple has an internal stone setting, of twenty-four stones The five sites range in diameter from 110 to 310 ft. The two remaining sites, Rachan

24   Ring of Brodgar henge monument, Orkneys.

Slack, Peeblesshire, and Overhowden, Berwickshire, are at the upper end of the range (280 ft and 310 ft respectively), and are both of Class I. The one remaining Scottish site is far to the west of the remainder, at Ballymeanoch in Argyllshire (Class II, 115 ft diameter). It has a central feature in the form of a cairn which contained two stone cists or box-like recesses.

In Ireland, apart from four outlying sites, henge monuments are confined to the Dublin region. One of the outlying sites, The Giant's Ring, a Class II henge in County Down, near Belfast, is over 700 ft in overall diameter with a bank still standing some 15 ft high. At the centre are the remains of a megalithic tomb in the form of a dolmen. Dun Ruadh, Tyrone, Class I, is smaller (170 ft diameter) and has a circle of seventeen stones. In the west, at Lough Gur, Limerick, the Lios henge (Class I) consists of a 150-ft diameter ring of contiguous stones, up to 9 ft high, backed against an outer earth bank some 30 ft wide. The single entrance on the east is also lined with upright stones. Also in the west, Lisroughan in Galway, a Class I henge, has the more conventional arrangement of bank outside the ditch, and two large stones associated with the entrance.

In the Dublin region the biggest single group (of five sites) is that associated with the Boyne cemetery of megalithic tombs. They are normally referred to by the letters M, N, O, P and Q (originally allocated by Coffey), but Evans has more recently used a different set of letters (A, B, C, D, E respectively). Henges A and B, near the Knowth megalithic tomb, are similar in having both inner and outer banks with the ditch between. Site C (Class I) is ploughed out and was discovered by aerial survey. The space enclosed was about 400 ft in diameter and the bank was outside the ditch. Henges D and E are near Dowth megalithic tomb. D is quite small, but E is a Class II henge some 450 ft in diameter, apparently with no ditch. Apart from the Boyne henges there are half a dozen other sites in the Dublin area:

Micknanstown, Meath, Class I, Mullaghtealin, Class I, Longstone Rath, Kildare, Class II and three sites at the Curragh, Kildare, two of them of Class I, the other Class II.

Apart from those in Wessex the only sites not so far considered are five in eastern England which are most appropriately dealt with here. The two sites at Maxey, Northamptonshire, may be in the same category as those at Dorchester, too small (diameters of 21 ft and 60 ft) to be regarded as true henges. Thornhaugh in the same county is of more normal dimensions (c. 275 ft in diameter) and is Class IIA. Stratford Hills, Suffolk, is smaller (190 ft diameter) and of Class I, while the remaining East Anglian site, at Arminghall, Norfolk, is of similar dimensions (185 ft diameter), but of Class IA, i.e. with the bank between two ditches. The most interesting features at Arminghall, however, were those revealed by excavation, and consisted of a setting of eight massive timber posts within the enclosure, in the plan of a horseshoe (Fig. 40). This quite clearly recalls the horseshoe arrangement and stone uprights at Stonehenge, and Arminghall will be brought into the discussion of the henge monuments in Wessex.

Henge monuments in Wessex and adjacent areas

Between a quarter and one-third of all henge monuments in the British Isles are located in Wessex and the immediately surrounding areas. The latter include six sites in Somerset, all of Class I, four of them, the Priddy Circles, about four miles north of Wells, forming a single compact group extending in a north/south line for over three-quarters of a mile. They are unusual, in henge terms, in having the banks inside the ditches, although the same is true at Stonehenge. The three southern circles are similar in size (c. 600 ft in diameter overall) and equidistant from each other (c. 270 ft). The northern circle is further away (c. 500 yds) and marginally smaller than the others. Excavations in the

113

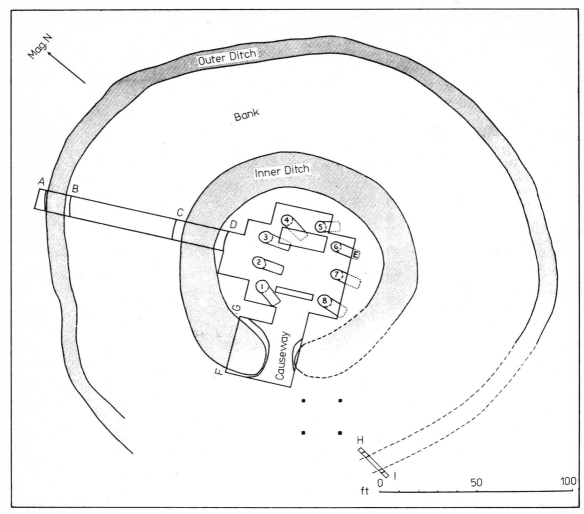

Fig. 40   Plan of the Arminghall henge monument, Norfolk.

southern circle have shown that the bank, some 12 ft wide, was probably faced on both sides with timber, recalling the stone revetting at The Lios, Lough Gur in Ireland, mentioned earlier. The two other Somerset sites, Gorsey Bigbury and Hunter's Lodge, are more conventional in plan, with the bank outside the ditch, and considerably smaller, each around 200 ft in overall diameter.

The northern part of the Wessex group comprises a group of sites in Oxfordshire with just one in the adjacent part of Gloucestershire. The five small circles at Dorchester, Oxfordshire, have been mentioned earlier as probably too small to be regarded as true henge monuments. The same may be true of Hanborough (also Oxfordshire) with an overall diameter of c. 70 ft. Dorchester Big Rings, on the other hand, is very much of henge dimensions, with a diameter of c. 500 ft. It is a Class

IIA structure, with entrances facing north and south. Two other Oxfordshire sites, Westwell and The Devil's Quoits, are of similar size (c. 500 ft diameter) and again of Class II. The latter has within it a circle of seven stones. The Gloucestershire site, Condicote, is smaller (c. 350 ft in diameter) and of Class I, possibly Class IA.

The remaining Wessex sites are concentrated in Dorset and Wiltshire. Among the most interesting of the Dorset sites are the three Knowlton henges (Fig. 25), a linear group like the Priddy and Thornborough groups mentioned earlier. The southern circle (Class I), surrounding Knowlton Farm, is the largest (c. 800 ft in diameter). It is clear that originally there was a berm or flat space between the ditch and the outer bank. The central circle is smaller (c. 350 ft diameter), better preserved, and likewise of Class II. The most fascinating thing about it, however, is the fact that it contains the ruins of a church, apparently in use from the twelfth to the sixteenth centuries. It seems very unlikely that the builders were completely unaware of the religious significance of the site they had chosen. The northern circle (much damaged by ploughing) is smaller than the others (c. 275 ft maximum diameter) and apparently D-shaped rather than circular in plan.

Maumbury Rings, Dorchester, Dorset, although it started life as a Class I henge monument, was subsequently re-used as a Roman amphitheatre and later again as a gun emplacement in the Civil War. The site is about 350 ft in diameter and the bank some 15 ft high, part of this being the Roman addition when the structure was re-used. The henge arrangement was conventional with the bank outside the ditch, although nothing of the latter is now visible. The ditch consisted, in fact, of a ring of forty-four pits virtually edge to edge, many of them being up to 35 ft deep, suggesting that they were dug for ritual rather than practical purposes.

The last group of henge monuments to be considered here are Avebury, Durring-ton Walls, Woodhenge, Marden, Mount Pleasant and Stonehenge. Avebury, Wiltshire, encloses no less than 28½ acres and a considerable portion of the present-day village of Avebury (Figs. 41, 42B & Pl. 25). It has an overall diameter of just under 1,500 ft. The bank is between 75 and 100 ft wide at the base and still stands some 14–18 ft above external ground level. Excavation has shown that the flat-bottomed inner ditch was originally 30 ft deep. There were no less than four original entrances, facing approximately north, south, east and west. The space inside the ditch (some 1,150 ft in diameter) contains the remains of three circles of standing stones. The outer circle was, when complete, some 1,100 feet in diameter and enclosed the two smaller circles. It consisted originally of about 100 stones, at about 35-ft intervals, although only about thirty stones now survive. Most of the stones are between 9 and 19 ft in overall length (i.e. including the portion in the ground). They can be divided into two types, A and B. Type A is a tall, relatively narrow, parallel-sided stone with a broad, flattish base. Type B, on the other hand, is often roughly diamond-shaped with a pointed base. The most widely held theory is that they represent male and female symbols.

Of the two inner circles the southern (c. 340 ft in diameter) now consists of five stones and the identified sockets for four more. The stones and the intervals between them appear to follow the pattern of the outer circle. Assuming a 35-ft interval there would originally have been about thirty stones in the circle. The centre seems to have been occupied by a single, large standing stone (The Obelisk, long since destroyed), which was at least 21 ft long and as much as 7 ft in diameter.

The Northern Circle (four surviving stones 320 ft in diameter) would have originally contained about twenty-seven stones. The main internal feature, at the centre, is known as The Cove, of which two of the three original stones are still in place.

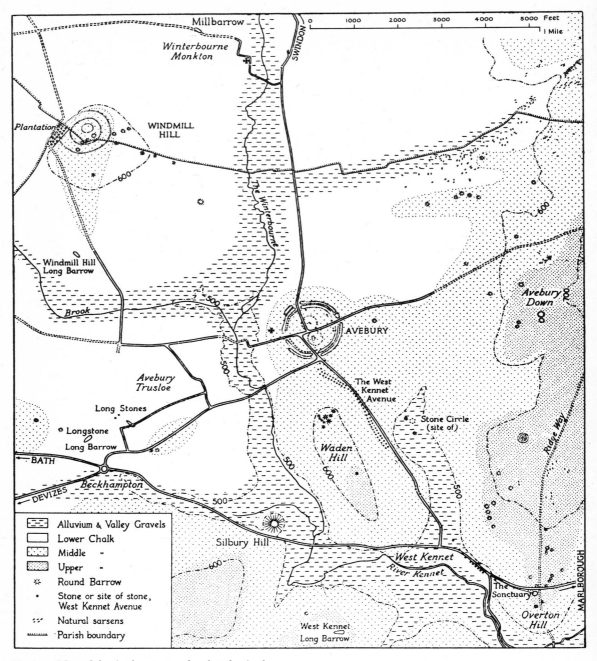

Fig. 41 Map of the Avebury area, showing the Avebury henge monument, the West Kennet Avenue and The Sanctuary.

25   Oblique aerial view of Avebury henge monument, Wiltshire.

The stones formed three sides of a rectangle, with the open side towards the north-east. Stone I, 16 ft high, is of Type A, and so apparently was the now lost stone (III). Stone II, on the other hand, is quite clearly of Type B, with a height of 14 ft and a maximum width of 16 ft. From the southern entrance of Avebury a (restored) avenue of standing stones known as the West Kennet Avenue extends in a generally south-easterly direction for about half a mile (Fig. 41). Originally, however, it was three times this length, linking Avebury with an unusual structure known as The Sanctuary on Overton Hill (below). The stones in the Avenue are set in pairs, about 50 ft apart. Each pair is about 80 ft from the next pair along, and there were

thirty-seven pairs in this northern section. Presumably, therefore, the whole avenue consisted originally of about 110 pairs of standing stones. Each pair, at least in the northern section, consists of one (presumed) male (Type A) and one (presumed) female (Type B) symbol. The remains of The Sanctuary, excavated in 1931, consist of the sockets in the ground for seven concentric rings of stone and timber uprights. The outer ring (A) has a diameter of about 140 ft and originally contained just over forty stones. Within this, ring B (sockets for timber posts) has a diameter of 67 ft. Ring C consisted of sockets for alternate stone and timber uprights. Within this again were progressively smaller rings (D, E, F and G) of sockets for timber posts. These remains, except for the outer ring (A), have usually been interpreted as those of a series

117

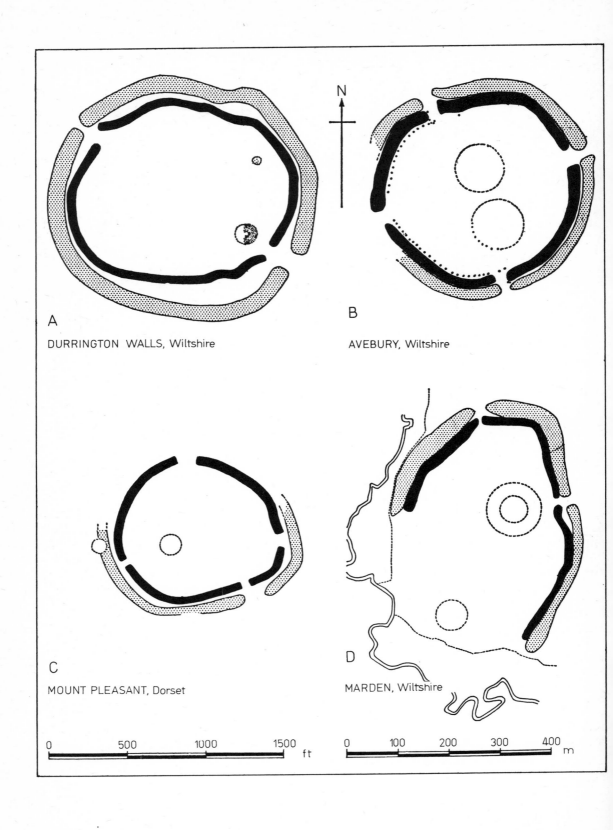

A

DURRINGTON WALLS, Wiltshire

B

AVEBURY, Wiltshire

C

MOUNT PLEASANT, Dorset

D

MARDEN, Wiltshire

N

0   500   1000   1500
ft

0   100   200   300   400
m

of progressively more elaborate circular buildings, but more recently it has been suggested that roofed structures were not involved, the whole monument being a developing series of free-standing timber circles, translated in its final phase into a double-ringed setting of stone uprights.

Durrington Walls, about two miles north-east of Stonehenge (Fig. 48) is even larger than Avebury, although much less well preserved (Fig. 42A). It has an overall diameter of something over 1,600 ft. Ploughing over the centuries has largely obliterated the ditch, and the enclosing bank is also very much eroded. Apart from its great size the interest of Durrington Walls lies in the internal structures discovered during excavations in the years 1966-8. The Southern Circle (130 ft diameter) seems to have involved two major structural phases. Phase 1 consisted of four concentric rings of wooden posts, with diameters of approximately 100, 77, 48 and 7 ft. Although a roofed structure is not ruled out, the relative lightness of the timbers (6-8 in. in diameter) makes an architectural interpretation rather less likely than one involving some pattern of free-standing timber circles.

Phase 2 consisted of six concentric rings of more substantial timber uprights, ranging in diameter from 130 ft down to 35 ft (Fig. 43). The larger timbers make it feasible to suggest a fairly elaborate roofed structure. Apart from the innermost ring (F) the timbers increase in size towards the centre and this has led to the suggestion that there was an outward sloping roof, from ring E to ring A, with an open court in the middle containing a ring (F) of free-standing posts. Two very large post-holes in the outermost ring (A) indicate the existence of an entrance. These architectural interpretations involve a high degree of speculation. It may well be that the original structure was nothing but six concentric free-standing timber circles.

There is some slight evidence of a first phase in the Northern Circle, but the bulk of the evidence relates to Phase 2, which consisted of a ring of posts some 50 ft in diameter with a rectangular setting of four massive posts at the centre (c. 20 × 20 ft). These remains are generally interpreted as those of a circular hut with a conical roof, although again the speculative aspect of all this must be emphasised. About 60 ft in front of the 'hut' was a timber façade, approached by an avenue of timber uprights.

The discovery of both Southern and Northern Circles was the result of excavating only a very limited area of the interior of Durrington Walls. The question which inevitably arises is the number, and type, of other structures which may still be concealed beneath the surface, not only at Durrington but at other henges as well.

Some 200 ft south of Durrington is Woodhenge (Fig. 48), a true henge monument originally involving timber uprights. The plan strikingly recalls the Southern Circle at Durrington and, to a lesser extent, The Sanctuary. The earthwork portion of the site consists of a ditch and outer bank with an overall diameter of c. 270 ft, and a single entrance facing north-east (Fig. 44). Inside, excavation (1926-8) uncovered six concentric rings of post-holes for wooden uprights (now marked by concrete pillars), from 145 down to 39 ft in diameter, completely filling the central space (150 ft in diameter). The best-known reconstruction (by Professor Stuart Piggott) involves a circular roofed structure with a central open court. Other reconstructions have been proposed but it must be emphasised again that there is no proof of roofing. Woodhenge may well have been a setting of free-standing upright posts, in one or more structural phases.

Marden, in the Vale of Pewsey, Wiltshire, is unusual because of its great size (35 acres) and its non-circular plan (Fig. 42D). The overall shape is an irregular oval with the normal ditch and outer bank

Fig. 42 Plans of the four large henge monuments in Wessex: A, Durrington Walls; B, Avebury; C, Mount Pleasant; D, Marden.

119

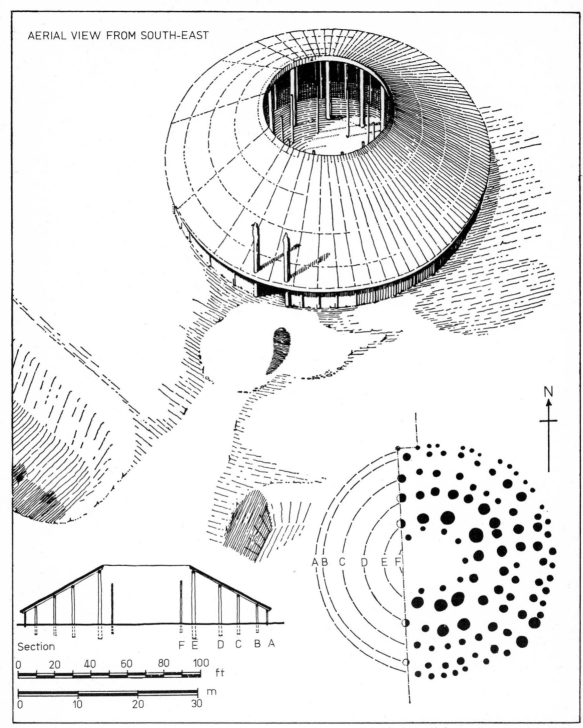

AERIAL VIEW FROM SOUTH-EAST

Section

F E D C B A

A B C D E F

N

0 20 40 60 80 100 ft

0 10 20 30 m

Fig. 43 Plan, section and drawn reconstruction of the Southern Circle at Durrington Walls, Wiltshire.

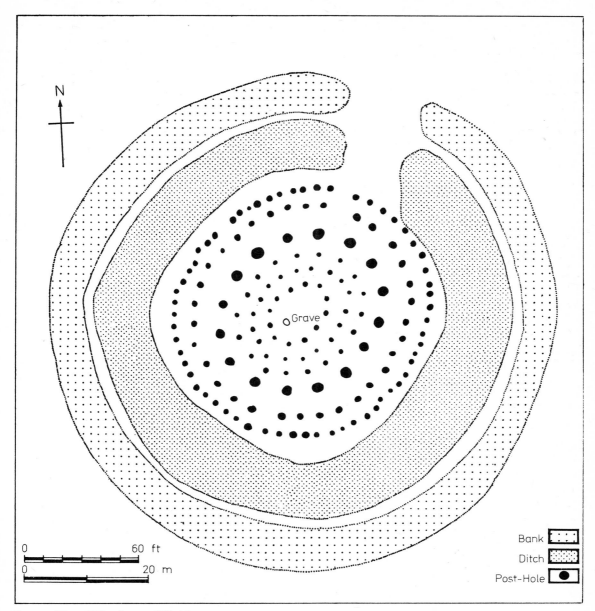

Fig. 44 Plan of Woodhenge, Wiltshire.

arrangement on the north-west, north and east. The southern and western sides, however, were formed not by earthworks but by the River Avon, producing an enclosed space some 1,500 ft long and some 1,100 ft wide. Equally unusual are the entrance arrangements. Two entrances make Marden a Class II henge monument, although the two entrances are not opposite each other, being placed on the northern and eastern sides. The main discovery during the 1969 excavations were the remains of a circular timber structure just inside the north entrance, consisting of a ring of post-holes (twenty-one in number) irregularly spaced around a ring 34 ft in diameter. Additional posts, mostly internal, appeared to form no particular pattern. Whether roofed or not, this was quite clearly a much less complex structure than those described already at Woodhenge, Durrington and The Sanctuary.

The smallest of the four large henges is Mount Pleasant, Dorset (980 × 880 ft internally), which has been virtually

Fig. 45 Plan of the timber structure at Mount Pleasant henge monument, Dorset.

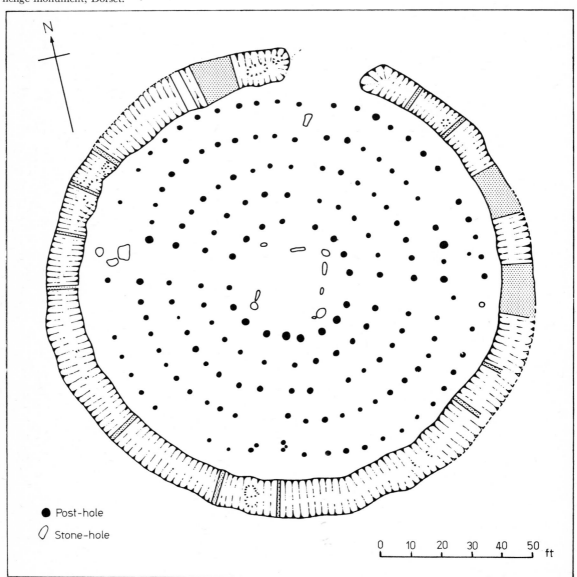

● Post-hole

◖ Stone-hole

0 10 20 30 40 50
ft

obliterated by ploughing (Fig. 42c). Like Avebury it had four entrances, although these were very unevenly spaced. Excavations in 1970 established the existence within of a circular timber structure with a surrounding ditch and bank (200 ft diameter) and a single entrance (Fig. 45). This is, in fact, a small henge monument, very similar to Woodhenge. The similarity is carried further by the timber structures (five concentric rings) which occupy virtually the whole of the interior space (c. 140 ft in diameter). The whole setting is divided into quarters by four corridors or avenues and the overall impression is one of very careful symmetrical planning. Whether these post-holes are the remains of a roofed structure or simply of timber circles are again matters for speculation.

At a later stage the timber structure was replaced by one of stone on a different and simpler plan. A stone 'cove' or rectangular setting of upright stones, some 20 ft square and open to the south, was built at the centre of the enclosure. On the north, west and east were three outlying stones, more or less on the line of the (earlier) outermost timber circle. This replacement of a timber structure by one of stone recalls the sequence at The Sanctuary.

In many ways the most fascinating discovery at Mount Pleasant was the evidence of what appears to have been a very substantial timber stockade or fence surrounding the summit of the hill about 10 ft inside the ditch. Judging by the trench in which it stood this fence was some 16 ft high and built of upright timbers 12–15 in. in diameter standing edge to edge. If it did, indeed, surround the whole of the summit it would have been over half a mile long (some 2,800 ft) and would have required about 2,500 separate lengths of timber. Where excavated, on the west, it blocked the western entrance through the earthworks and was, therefore, presumably not contemporary with it, but both its chronological position and, more importantly, its function, are matters yet to be established.

Stonehenge, the most famous of all henge monuments, will be described first of all in terms of its visible features and then in terms of its structural history. The surrounding earthwork consists of an inner bank, a ditch and a small counterscarp bank with an overall diameter of c. 375 ft. Immediately inside the bank are a series of holes, known as the Aubrey holes, fifty-six in number. Thirty-four excavated examples have been marked on the ground with patches of white chalk. They were originally discovered by the Wiltshire antiquary John Aubrey in the seventeenth century (hence the name), and will be considered again under structural sequence. Other rings of holes (the z and y holes, the Q and R holes) will also be dealt with then.

The innermost of these rings, the z holes, immediately surrounds the stone structures for which Stonehenge is principally renowned, beginning with the Sarsen Circle (Fig. 46). Sarsen is a form of sandstone, the nearest source of which appears to be Marlborough, some twenty miles away, so presumably the stone was transported from there for the construction. The Sarsen Circle consisted of thirty uprights and thirty lintels, of which twenty-five uprights (seventeen standing and eight fallen) and six lintels remain (Fig. 46, 1–30). The dimensions of the average upright are $7 \times 3\frac{1}{2} \times 13\frac{1}{2}$ ft high, plus another 3–5 ft buried in the ground; the average weight was about 26 tons. They formed a circle just over 97 ft in diameter and were placed at $3\frac{1}{2}$-ft intervals. The lintels were, on average, $10\frac{1}{2}$ ft long, $3\frac{1}{2}$ ft wide and $2\frac{3}{4}$ ft high, so that the overall height of the circle was around 16 ft. The lintels were held in position by mortise-and-tenon joints, each upright having two projecting bosses or tenons, fitting into corresponding recesses or mortises on the underside of the lintels. In addition, the lintels were linked to each other, end to end, by vertical tongue-and-groove joints. The most interesting aspect of the lintels, however, is their careful shaping; each one is curved so that they form a continuous, true circle, rather than a series of straight lines (Pl. 26).

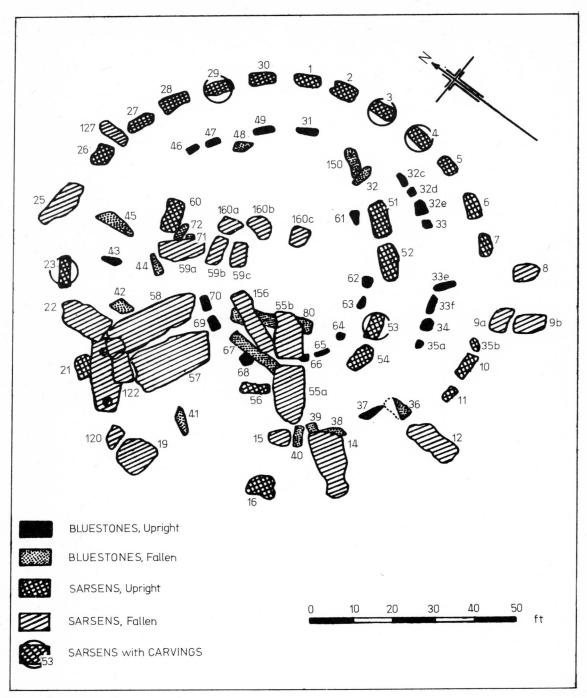

BLUESTONES, Upright

BLUESTONES, Fallen

SARSENS, Upright

SARSENS, Fallen

SARSENS with CARVINGS

Fig. 46   Plan of the stone structures at Stonehenge, Wiltshire.

26 The Sarsen Circle and a trilithon at Stonehenge, Wiltshire.

About 10 ft inside the Sarsen Circle is the Bluestone Circle. Bluestone is simply a popular term for stone (dolerite) which is entirely foreign to central southern England. In 1923 Dr H. H. Thomas of the Geological Survey proved that it came from the Prescelly Mountains in north Pembrokeshire. The implications of this in terms of transportation are enormous. The stones in the circle (75 ft diameter) are much smaller than the Sarsen stones and much less regular in spacing and in shape (Fig. 46, 31–49). Inside the Bluestone Circle is the Sarsen Horseshoe, a U-shaped arrangement of great stone uprights and lintels forming five groups of three stones each, hence the term *trilithons* (Fig. 46, 51–60). The uprights of the trilithons are

larger again than those of the Sarsen Circle, up to 9 × 4 ft and, including the lintel, originally up to 24 ft high. In fact, only the central trilithon is of this height, the others stepping down symmetrically on either side; the second and fourth trilithons are 21½ ft high (with the lintel) and the two outer groups (the first and fifth) are 20 ft high. As in the Sarsen Circle uprights and lintels were linked by mortise-and-tenon joints. The open side of the horseshoe faces north-east, directly towards the entrance (between stones 1 and 30 of the Sarsen Circle) and the Avenue (below).

Inside the Sarsen Horseshoe, and on a very much smaller scale, is the Bluestone Horseshoe which appears to have involved nineteen dolerite uprights set at 5½-ft centres (Fig. 46, 61–72). All appear to have been carefully dressed to a square section

(c. 2 × 2 ft) and ranged in height from 6 to 8 ft, the smaller stones being at the outer ends of the horseshoe. The occasional survival of both mortises and tenons in the Bluestone indicates that at some stage they formed trilithons, and that the present arrangement differs considerably from the original one. This point will be returned to under structural sequence.

Within the Sarsen Horseshoe and some 15 ft in front of the central trilithon is the so-called Altar Stone (Fig. 46). It is some 16 ft long, 3½ ft wide and 1¾ ft thick, and made of a fine-grained sandstone which originates on the shores of Milford Haven in Pembrokeshire. It is the only stone from this particular source at Stonehenge. The term Altar Stone would suggest a horizontal position, much as it is now, but there is, in fact, some evidence that it once stood on end, in a socket now concealed beneath it, on the main axis of the site.

The Slaughter Stone (21 × 7 × 3 ft) lying on the east side of the entrance through the earthwork, was probably one of a pair of uprights which formed part of the entrance to the monument. The corresponding stone on the other side has now gone but its socket (E) has been identified.

The Station Stones are two sarsen blocks placed diametrically opposite each other just inside the bank, on the south-east and the north-west. The former position of two other stones, also diametrically opposite each other, approximately north and south, is marked by the two so-called Barrows. Lines between the two Station Stones and between the two stone-holes within the Barrows intersect, at an angle of forty-five degrees, at the centre of the stone structure and lie symmetrically on either side of the main axis. Lines between each Station Stone and its adjacent Barrow Stone are parallel to the axis. Such a precise layout must be deliberate and must be connected with the overall planning of the monument.

The Heel Stone is a sarsen block some 16 ft high, standing within, but not at the centre of, The Avenue. It marks, but only approximately, the point of sunrise on Midsummer Day to an observer standing at the centre of the monument. Many claims have been made about the purpose of the Heel Stone, most particularly that it marks precisely the point of sunrise on Midsummer Day. It does not, and as far as can be calculated, did not do so when Stonehenge was built. Either the Heel Stone was intended only as an approximate marker or else it had some other purpose.

The Avenue, just over one and a half miles long, was apparently a processional way of linking Stonehenge to the River Avon (Fig. 48). It begins at the earth-work entrance of Stonehenge on the north-east side and consists of two parallel banks, about 40 ft apart, with outer ditches. It runs north-east for about a third of a mile. Beyond this it has been obliterated by cultivation but it apparently then turned to run eastwards for about half a mile and then south-eastwards for the remaining three-quarters of a mile to terminate on the banks of the Avon. It may be connected with the transportation (almost certainly by water) of the Bluestones from Pembroke-shire, the last overland section from the river to the site being marked by a cere-monial avenue, a permanent monument to what was presumably a very important event.

The structural history of Stonehenge still contains some gaps but the broad outlines are now established. Three main building stages are involved, of which the earliest (Stone-henge I) consisted of the surrounding bank and ditch, the Aubrey Holes, the Heel Stone, two stones at the entrance (in holes D and E), and certain timber structures of uncertain type. The earthwork and the ring of Aubrey Holes share the same centre point, presumably because they are con-temporary: this differs from the centre point of the later stone structures. Stones D and E and the timber structures stood symmetrically on the axis passing through this earlier centre point and are therefore likely to be associated with it. The four timber posts in the (later) Avenue may have formed some sort of outer gateway or ceremonial arch. The possibility of some central timber feature has been suggested. This would fall within the area inside the Bluestone Circle, most of which has not yet been excavated.

Stonehenge II involves the Q and R holes, discovered only in 1954, and a setting in them of Bluestones different from the present arrangement. These formed two concentric rings 74 and 86 ft in diameter, with thirty-eight stones in each ring forming thirty-eight radially arranged pairs. At the entrance, two long trenches housed four stones each and the two trenches flanking these three stones each. It is noticeable that the axis of this entrance is the same as that of the sarsen structures of Stonehenge III. It is also the axis on which The Avenue is built and it has been proved to have been built in Stonehenge II rather than III.

Stonehenge III involved the complete removal of the Phase II double Bluestone Ring and the filling up of the Q and R holes to provide a level working surface. The new structure involved eighty-one stones, and eighty-two if an additional Station Stone is allowed on the south-west, as seems likely. The Bluestones in the Q and R holes had also totalled eighty-two and this may indicate continuity with the earlier structure. Stonehenge IIIa then consisted of the five great sarsen trilithons, the Sarsen Circle, with its continuous lintel, the four Station Stones and the Slaughter Stone and its former companion. At this stage, the Bluestones do not seem to have been involved. Stage IIIb involves an arrangement of the Bluestones for which there is no conclusive evidence. The Y and Z holes (sixty in number), which also appear to form part of Phase IIIb, form two rings (c. 130 and 185 ft in diameter) outside the Sarsen Circle. They appear to have been intended for a setting of (undressed) Bluestones, but never, in fact, to have been used as such. There is no sign on any of them that they ever contained upright stones. Associated with this intended plan was an (inferred) setting of

the remaining twenty-two (dressed) Bluestones either within the Sarsen Horseshoe or outside Stonehenge altogether. The former seems the more likely since one or two of the surviving Bluestones show evidence of having once formed a trilithon arrangement, presumably a reflection of the larger sarsen structure. However, once the plan to house sixty undressed Bluestones in the Y and Z holes was abandoned, then presumably the setting of twenty-two dressed Bluestones, wherever it was, was dismantled also, making way for the new and final plan of Stonehenge IIIc. This is fairly straightforward and embraces the arrangement of the Bluestones as we see them now, in the form of the Bluestone Circle and the Bluestone Horseshoe, giving Stonehenge its final shape.

There is no question that the greatest interest in the three recently excavated sites (Durrington, Marden and Mount Pleasant) arises from the structures found within them. At Durrington (Southern Circle, Fig. 43) and Mount Pleasant (Fig. 45) there are remains of concentric rings of timber uprights, closely comparable with structures known for many years at Woodhenge (Fig. 44), immediately outside Durrington, and The Sanctuary, closely associated with Avebury (Fig. 41). In addition to the more complex structures there are simpler circular structures at Marden and Durrington (North Circle). These new discoveries result from the excavation of only small parts of the interiors. The possibility of further structures in these and other henge monuments is now a very real one. It should be stated again that there is no evidence that the structures involved were roofed. The suggestion of a roof is simply part of the attempt to find a rational explanation for a setting of postholes. In a sense the only safe course is to limit any proposed interpretation to those structural members for which there is evidence, i.e. post-holes and the uprights to go in them. In other words, these post-holes are, in the writer's view, the remains of concentric rings of free-standing timber posts. In any case, the posts seem far too numerous simply to support roofs which could have been supported with less, making a ritual function the more likely. The only structural elaboration which could be contemplated is the possible inclusion of timber lintels between the posts. It may well be that Stonehenge, in spite of its elaborate stone structure, has more to do with these newly discovered settings of post-holes than at first sight appears.

In the first structural phase at Stonehenge (I) Professor R. J. C. Atkinson envisaged the possibility of a timber structure at the centre of the enclosure based on the evidence of a large number of post-holes uncovered by Lt-Col. Hawley (1924–8). Whatever form of structure they represented there is no question that in subsequent phases Stonehenge was an unroofed structure of free-standing uprights, with or without lintels. It would seem probable, therefore, that the Phase I structure was also a setting of free-standing uprights, in this case of timber. The stone settings may have a relevance to the various concentric (timber) circles. The removal of all the stones from Stonehenge (Fig. 46) would leave a complex setting of concentric rings not dissimilar in general plan to Durrington, Mount Pleasant, Woodhenge and The Sanctuary. It would certainly not be identical (Stonehenge always seems to have been something special), but there would be a family resemblance which would make it feasible to suggest that the circles were of the same general nature as Stonehenge, i.e. concentric rings of uprights, possibly with lintels between, built of timber rather than stone.

The structural sequence at The Sanctuary provides a further link with Stonehenge. The final stage appears to have been two concentric circles of stone uprights with diameters of c. 50 and 130 ft, perhaps recalling the two double settings at Stonehenge, in the Q and R holes in Phase II, and in the Y and Z holes in Phase IIIb. At The Sanctuary the preceding structures involved five concentric rings of timber posts, representing one or more structural phases. If the structure was, in fact, roofed then the adoption of a double stone circle represents a radical change in plan. It seems much more logical to see the earlier structures also as free-standing timber circles, so that only a change of material was involved in the final phase.

Outside Wessex the Arminghall henge monument (Fig. 40), involves timber uprights which were certainly not part of any roofed structure. They were a horse-shoe-shaped setting of eight very massive posts, the only feasible elaboration being the possible addition of lintels. Although different in many ways from the concentric rings of generally lighter timbers, the Arminghall henge does further support the idea of free-standing circles of timber uprights, similar to those of stone.

It has already been tacitly assumed that henge monuments are sanctuaries or religious monuments, and it is difficult to go much beyond this without entering the realms of pure speculation. They have often been linked to the great cathedrals of medieval times and this is probably not a bad analogy. Certainly in terms of the output required they must be seen as occupying a very important place in the minds of the people who built them, and in the absence of evidence as to any other, practical use, a religious function seems virtually certain. The suggestion that Stonehenge had some sort of astronomical function does not necessarily invalidate the religious concept. The two functions may indeed be closely bound up with each other. The functions of the internal structures, particularly those recently discovered, are equally difficult to perceive, and there are more questions than answers. Are these the only internal structures or would excavation reveal more? If they are the only ones why, at Durrington, for example (Fig. 42A), are they not in the centre of the site? Are the simpler structures (Durrington, North Circle, and Marden) perhaps more domestic in character, the houses of the resident priests? These and many other questions reflect the difficulty, in pre-historic archaeology, of deducing religious beliefs from purely material evidence. It has to be accepted that there is much that we will never know about the use and significance of henge monuments.

There appear to be no prototypes any-where in Europe for henge monuments. They appear to be a purely British pheno-menon. The most recent suggestion is that their beginnings are to be found in the causewayed camps of the Windmill Hill people. As pointed out earlier, causewayed camps are now seen as ritual rather than utilitarian enclosures. They are broadly comparable in size (up to 21 acres in overall area) and Dr Isobel Smith has pointed out that it is doubtful whether two *independent* (my italics) traditions of con-structing non-utilitarian enclosures would have arisen at this time. The available carbon-14 dates also point in the same direction, causewayed camps persisting down to c. 2500 B.C., with some henge monuments extending back as far as the same date. On this basis the more hap-hazard plan of the causewayed camp can be seen as rationalised c. 2500 B.C. into the more regular formula which we recognise as a henge monument, and, for the moment at least, this appears to be the most satis-factory explanation.

It looks then as if the roots of the idea of sacred enclosures must be credited to the Windmill Hill people, even if the enclo-sures at that time took the form of cause-wayed camps. Judging by pottery, the people actually responsible for the develop-ment of the true henge monument were the so-called Secondary Neolithic peoples. In particular, those Secondary Neolithic people who used pottery known variously as Rinyo-Clacton or Grooved ware were responsible for the construction of the very large enclosures of Durrington type, for the circular timber structures within them, and for Woodhenge, Stonehenge I, Maumbury, and possibly The Sanctuary. Durrington is a Class II (double entrance) henge and it has been customary to see these as later

than Class I and associated with the Beaker peoples. At Durrington, however, there is no doubt that the structure is pre-Beaker (Beaker pottery is present, but late on the site) so that henges of both Class I and Class II, and features such as the Aubrey Holes and the deep pits at Maum-bury, would appear to be attributable to the Secondary Neolithic population. Among the Beaker contributions to the repertoire of prehistoric monuments are stone circles, some of which appear in henge monuments and may have replaced earlier timber structures. Presumably Stonehenge II (the double stone circles) belongs to this phase, as does the change from timber to double (stone) circles at The Sanctuary. It has been suggested on more than one occasion that at Avebury the existing stone circles were a replace-ment of earlier timber settings, not so far located.

The sequence outlined so far (Windmill Hill—Secondary Neolithic—Beaker) will comfortably accommodate all phases of henge development, except Stonehenge III. In Wessex the Beaker peoples were succeeded by the Wessex culture, and there is little doubt that it was the Wessex people who were responsible for the final, dramatic elaboration of Stonehenge. They alone would appear to have had the resources to undertake such a formidable task. Their close association with Stone-henge is confirmed by the concentration of Wessex culture burials in the area im-mediately around the site, forming great barrow cemeteries. Whether, as Professor R. J. C. Atkinson has said, these Wessex people alone were responsible for the design and construction of Stonehenge is another and much larger question which cannot be pursued at length here. He suggests influence from the contemporary Minoan/Mycenaean world of the east Mediterranean and this is a very plausible suggestion. The design and the many refinements of Stonehenge indicate a well-established architectural tradition and this suggestion should always be kept in

mind in any consideration of the final
stages of Stonehenge.

In terms of actual years there is little to be
added to the dates given at the beginning of
the chapter (2500–1500 B.C.). In spite of
numerous carbon-14 dates the variations
(plus or minus) make any attempt at
greater precision suspect for the group as a
whole, although they can be a help in
dealing with individual monuments. Nor
need anything be added to the bracket
'Late Neolithic/Early Bronze Age' which
embraces the cultures of the people mentioned above: Secondary Neolithic, Beaker,
Wessex, for henges proper, with an extension back into the Windmill Hill (Primary
Neolithic) culture before 2500 B.C., for the
roots of the idea of circular sanctuaries
which are now presumed to lie in causewayed camps.

6 Barrows and Graves

Shortly after 2000 B.C. there arrived in the British Isles new peoples from the continent, identified by pottery vessels known as beakers (hence the Beaker people), who brought with them a new and distinctive burial tradition which was in marked contrast to the existing Neolithic practice of collective burial in chamber tombs. The new practice brought in by the Beaker people was that of individual burials by inhumation (i.e. as opposed to cremation) under circular covering mounds without chambers, at least in any megalithic sense; for although they lacked the often elaborate internal structures of Neolithic burial monuments they were far from being featureless mounds of material, as will be seen below.

Circular burial mounds or round barrows built by the Beaker and later Bronze Age people are the most numerous and most widely distributed prehistoric monuments in the British Isles. How numerous is very difficult to say, but the original figure must be in the tens of thousands, perhaps somewhere between 10,000 and 50,000, although thousands of these must have been completely destroyed through agriculture and other agencies over the centuries from medieval times onwards. In spite of these very large figures, however, there are two points to take note of. First of all, round barrows are not the only type of Bronze Age burial monument. Some other, less numerous but equally interesting types will be dealt with later in this and the succeeding chapter. Secondly, even this extended range of burial structures by no means accounts for all Bronze Age burials. It is probably true to say that the majority of Bronze Age people were buried far more unceremoniously, in flat graves with no superstructure, so that they are discovered only by accident, in ploughing or construction work, etc. Quite clearly the ratio of flat burials to barrow burials will never be known in its entirety, but one or two samples may give some indication of the overall pattern. In Scotland, out of 142 Food-vessel burials, 127 were flat graves and only fifteen were covered by barrows. The same sort of pattern is true of a sub-group of beakers, known as C-beakers, again in Scotland. Out of a total of 123 C-beaker burials only seventeen certainly and five possibly were beneath covering mounds, the rest being flat graves. On this basis only seven to ten per cent of Bronze Age burials were covered by mounds, the rest being flat graves, so that in looking at the range of Bronze Age burial monuments, one is still looking at only a small, albeit special, part of the overall picture of Bronze Age burial practice.

It is appropriate at this stage to say something about terminology. The word barrow means literally a hill and is, there-

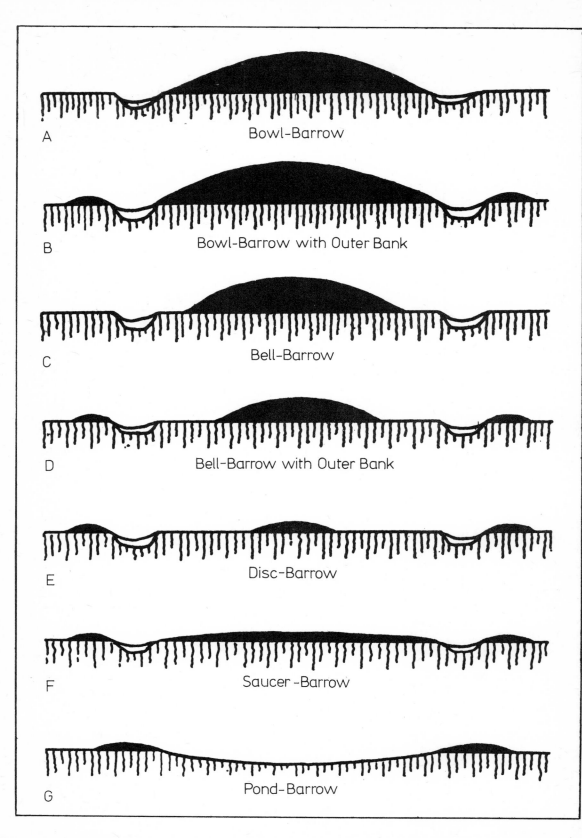

A   Bowl-Barrow

B   Bowl-Barrow with Outer Bank

C   Bell-Barrow

D   Bell-Barrow with Outer Bank

E   Disc-Barrow

F   Saucer-Barrow

G   Pond-Barrow

fore, descriptive of the shape rather than the composition of the mound in question. However, a broad distinction is generally made on the basis of composition, the term *barrow* usually indicating a mound composed of earth, as opposed to one made of stone. For the latter the term *cairn* is the usual designation. Such structures are, for geological reasons, found in the highland regions of the west and north, while the earthen mounds or barrows are appropriate to the lower regions of the south and east. This distinction is not, of course, absolute, either geographically or in terms of composition, since there are mounds which involve both earth and stone, quite apart from those in which the original composition is not apparent from surface examination. By far the most numerous and widely distributed of all Bronze Age mounds are *bowl* barrows, so-called because in appearance they resemble an inverted bowl (Fig. 47A). They vary in size from around 30 ft in diameter to as much as 150 ft in diameter and from 3 or 4 ft to as much as 20 ft in height. In some cases the barrow is surrounded by a ditch, sometimes with a small bank on its outer edge (Fig. 47B). Barrows without ditches are often described as being scraped-up, implying a shallow stripping over a relatively wide area. The presence of a ditch is not always apparent in surface examination, eroded material from the mound often concealing its existence.

The common and widely spread bowl barrow of the lowland zone is the counterpart of the stone cairn of the highland zone. Between them they account for the vast majority of Bronze Age burial mounds in the British Isles. The bowl form virtually exhausts the varieties of stone cairn. Among the earthen barrows, however, are a number of other very clear-cut types, even if these are relatively few in number (c. 500) and largely, but not entirely, confined to the Wessex region of southern England. One of the most distinctive types is the bell barrow, so called from its present bell-like appearance (Fig.

47C). This is achieved by leaving a berm or ledge between the foot of the mound and the edge of the ditch, which is, of course, an essential feature of the type. The result is a low but none the less recognisable bell-like shape, hence the name (Pl. 27). The average berm is c. 12–15 ft wide, with narrower types usually in the region of 8–10 ft. At the other end of the scale there are berms 15–25 ft wide, with the mound correspondingly reduced in size. Beyond the wide-bermed type there is the bell-disc type, intermediate between the true bell barrow and the disc barrow (below) in which the berm is so wide, and the central mound so small, that the bell-like appearance is no longer apparent and it almost qualifies as a disc barrow.

Apart from variations in width, the berm of the bell barrow can be altered in other ways as well. In raised-berm types mound material is spread over the berm as well, creating an artificial berm several feet above ground level. In double-bermed types, the inner berm is artificial, the outer one natural. All of the bell barrows considered so far have consisted of a single mound surrounded by its own berm and circular ditch. In the case of some double bell barrows, where the second mound is quite small, the surrounding ditch is circular, but in all others it is oval (Pl. 27). In the quadruple arrangements the four mounds are always in a straight line. There seem to be no triple bell barrows surrounded by a single ditch. The nearest type consists of two single bell barrows (i.e. each with its own ditch) with an ordinary bowl barrow between, but this looks like a later addition.

Disc barrows consist of a circular, or sometimes oval, ditch, with an outer bank, surrounding a flat, disc-like space (hence the name), with one or more very small mounds, one of which is normally in the centre (Fig. 47E). The henge-like appearance of disc barrows has often been commented on and it may be that they are, in fact, based on the henge monuments (Pl.

Fig. 47 Types of Bronze Age barrow.

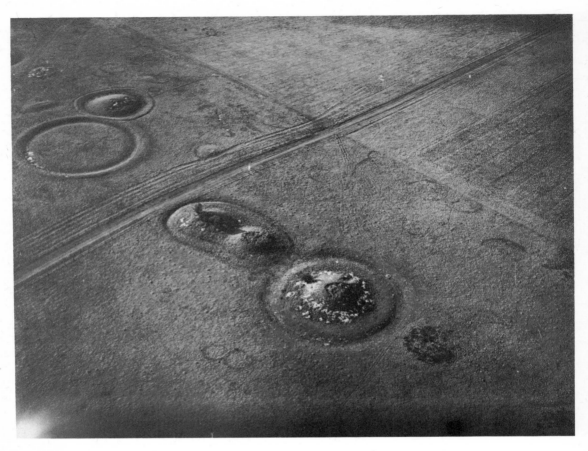

27 Oblique aerial view of part of the Normanton
Down cemetery, near Stonehenge, Wiltshire.

27). Variations on the basic plan include
oval disc barrows with twin mounds at the
centre, and what are known as confluent
barrows, with a figure-of-eight plan, one
circular disc barrow cutting into another.

The two remaining types are rather less
common and are known as saucer barrows
and pond barrows. A saucer barrow is, as
its name implies, relatively low as compared with a bowl barrow, usually only a
couple of feet high although perhaps more
than 60 ft in diameter (Fig. 47F). Like
many of the other Wessex barrows it is
surrounded by a ditch with an outer bank.
Pond barrows are something of a contra-
diction since they do not involve a mound

at all, but rather a shallow, circular pond-
like depression, surrounded by a low bank,
up to 120 ft in diameter, with the burials
in pits dug into the base (Fig. 47G).

Although there are many round barrows
and cairns in valleys and low-lying
positions generally, there are others in
which it is quite clear that a careful
choice of situation has been made. Advan-
tage was taken locally of hill tops, promontories and ridges. Barrows, either
singly or in groups, were so positioned
that they stood out in profile or silhouette
against the sky when viewed from the
valley below, where presumably the
builders had their settlements, although, as
was made clear in Chapter 1, these have
hardly ever been located.

Although there are many isolated single barrows, there are also a considerable number which occur in groups of two or more, sometimes many more, and these are deemed to form barrow cemeteries. Many of the most famous groups are located in the Stonehenge region, a further indication of the sanctity of the region. Barrow cemeteries can be divided into three main types, linear, nuclear and dispersed, although some groups have characteristics of more than one type. Linear cemeteries are perhaps the most striking, and consist, as their name indicates, of a row of barrows forming a straight line, often of considerable length. One of the most clear-cut examples is the Cursus group about half a mile north-west of Stonehenge and just south of the Cursus. It consists of seven barrows

strung out east and west over a distance of about a third of a mile, some of them of considerable size, up to 194 ft in diameter overall (Fig. 48). The Cursus cemetery also embraces another dozen or so barrows a little further to the west, not arranged in linear fashion. The Normanton cemetery (about three dozen barrows south of Stonehenge), consists of a linear group about half a mile long with a non-linear group to the west and a scatter of other barrows to the south (Pl. 27). The Winterbourne-Stoke group, west of Stonehenge, involves two parallel linear arrangements, east and west. The eastern line begins with a long barrow, succeeded by a bowl barrow, then a pond barrow, and then two bell barrows (178 and 164 ft in diameter), with six bowl barrows beyond, the whole group having a length of nearly half a mile. The parallel line to the west is shorter and

Fig. 48 Map of the Stonehenge area showing the principal Bronze Age barrow cemeteries.

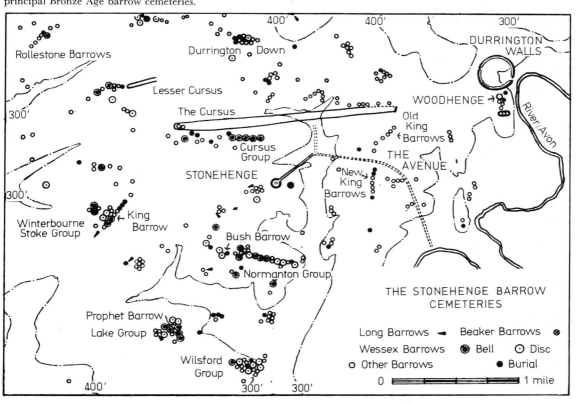

consists mainly of bowl and disc barrows (Fig. 48).

There are many other linear arrangements in Wessex. Linear cemeteries were, however, by no means confined to Wessex. The Braddock cemetery in Cornwall, three miles north-east of Lostwithiel, contains eight bowl barrows forming an east/west line, very much in the Wessex manner. In Somerset, the Ashen Hill group, four miles north of Wells, also contains eight barrows, seven bowl and one (possible) bell, forming another east/west line. The Devil's Jumps cemetery in Sussex, four miles south-west of Midhurst, consists of five very large bell barrows, with the probable remains of a sixth, all in line. In Lincolnshire, the Bully Hills cemetery, three miles south of Louth, consists of seven bowl barrows, while in Norfolk, the Seven Hills group originally contained at least eleven mounds in an east/west line, of which only six survive. In Yorkshire, the barrow group at Wharram Percy in the East Riding contains nine mounds, six of which form an east/west linear cemetery. These are only a few examples of linear cemeteries outside the Wessex area.

In nuclear cemeteries the barrows form a compact group, in some cases apparently around one particular barrow. The Lake cemetery, south-west of Stonehenge, consists of five bell barrows (120–150 ft diameters) three disc barrows (c. 180 ft diameters), and at least a dozen bowl barrows, forming a very compact group, about a quarter of a mile in diameter (Fig. 48). The Wilsford cemetery, a little further to the east, consists of five disc barrows (150–200 ft in diameter), a bell barrow (150 ft in diameter), a pond barrow, a saucer barrow and nine bowl barrows (30–100 ft diameters), forming a compact group of similar size to the Lake cemetery. Many other nuclear groups are recorded in Wessex. Nuclear cemeteries of the size just considered are less common outside Wessex. Nevertheless, any closely placed group of as few as three or four barrows embodies the nuclear principle and can be distinguished from the third type of arrangement, dispersed cemeteries.

A dispersed cemetery is a group of barrows which has quite clearly not been based on any particular plan, either linear or nuclear, and is spread, as the name implies, over a relatively wide area. Nevertheless, it is sufficiently coherent to be recognisable as a cemetery rather than a series of separate barrows. Quite clearly any group with such general characteristics is likely to be fairly common and dispersed cemeteries are the most numerous and widespread of all three types. They account for everything in the way of barrow cemeteries which is not either linear or nuclear.

The present state of Bronze Age barrows does not necessarily represent their original appearance. Change in colour is perhaps the least speculative. On the chalk downlands of southern and eastern England the barrows were composed almost entirely of chalk which, when first dug, is a brilliant white. The dazzling effect of a great mound of white chalk against the dark green of the surrounding grass can well be imagined. The effect with stone-built cairns in the limestone areas would have been only slightly less striking. The same sort of contrast would operate to a lesser degree with mounds composed of sand, clay, gravel, etc. For most barrows the growth of vegetation has eliminated the original contrast, but this aspect should always be kept in mind in trying to recreate their original appearance.

The question of shape is more difficult and more speculative. It may well be that the present rounded form is simply a lower and broader version of the original shape. The crown of the dome is the area most affected; unfortunately it is precisely in this area that information bearing on the original appearance is likely to have existed. This allows for the possibility of one other shape which could have given rise to the present appearance, that of a cone-shaped mound, with a low-pointed top. There is some evidence which might support this view. Some mounds appear to have been surmounted by a single standing stone (or there is some evidence of a timber post rising through the centre of the mound), either of which might be interpreted as the apex of a conical rather than a domed structure.

In some cairns there is a kerb around the base of the mound. There is, however, no certainty that the kerbs were restricted to the height of the stones which survive. It is quite possible that the surviving kerbs, originally surmounted by dry-stone walling, rose much higher than they do now. How high is, of course, a matter of speculation, but something in the region of 3–5 ft seems feasible, giving the mound a basically cylindrical shape. The top could have been domed, conical or quite flat. Barrows made of turf are relatively few in number but present rather special structural problems. They would build up vertically even more easily than dry-stone walling, so that the cylindrical shape mentioned above could well be appropriate.

As mentioned earlier, this consideration of original shape is largely speculative. It does seem unlikely, however, that all barrows were built in exactly the same form. Given the large numbers, widespread distribution, and long duration of Bronze Age barrows, some degree of variation in the finished shape seems more than likely.

The question of basic burial rite (i.e. either inhumation or cremation) has been touched on already with reference to the Beaker people and their barrows. In fact, both rites were practised in the Bronze Age, although not to the same degree at any one time. At the very beginning of the Bronze Age the burial rite of the Beaker people was almost exclusively inhumation, cremation being very rare (Fig. 49). Among the succeeding Food-vessel people of the north cremation became more frequent, while in the Wessex culture of the south cremation progressively replaced inhumation. By Middle Bronze Age times cremation was the dominant rite in the British Isles.

Both of these rites had, in fact, been in vogue in the Neolithic period, with the greater emphasis on inhumation. However, the most striking aspect of Neolithic practice was collective burial and it is in this respect that Bronze Age burials differed from what had gone before. The arrival of the Beaker people marked the beginning of individual or single grave burials beneath circular mounds. In fact, occasional group burials are found, but these are very much the exception. The vast majority of Bronze Age burials were separate interments of single individuals. This is not to say that a barrow contained only a single grave, but where it contained more than one (apart from the rare group burials just mentioned) there were a series of separate burials, deposited at different times, rather than a collective burial in the Neolithic fashion. To distinguish between first and later burials the terms primary and secondary burial are used. The primary burial (or burials in the case of group burial) occupied the central position beneath the mound and was quite clearly the one for which the mound was built. However, it was common practice in the Bronze Age to make use of existing barrows for further burials. This was done by digging a pit into the mound and inserting the new burials, which are thus secondary to the building of the barrow. While there is only one primary burial, there can quite clearly be any number of secondary burials, with no way of distinguishing between earlier and later secondaries. Sometimes, when a secondary burial was added, the mound was increased in size by adding an extra mantle of material over the whole surface, derived, in some cases from an outer ditch. The term satellite is used for those burials (additional to the primary) made on the old ground surface before the barrow was built or in the mound while it was being built, i.e. clearly not inserted after its completion, and therefore not secondary as just defined.

Bronze Age burial mounds are characterised by very great variety in their internal arrangement and no overall analysis has yet been attempted. What follows is no more than a summary of some of the commoner features; it is far from being a comprehensive statement and many more specialised features are inevitably omitted.

A term very commonly encountered in barrow excavation reports is 'old turf line' (O.T.L.), referring to the old ground surface on which the barrow was built which is usually uncovered during excavation (Fig. 50). The old surface was not, in fact, always turf, and the term pre-barrow soil has been suggested as more objective; however, old turf line has achieved such wide currency that it is likely to remain in general use even when not strictly appropriate. There is beneath some barrows evidence of burning on the old ground surface prior to the construction of the mound. Some of this may be the result of burning off the vegetation to clear the site, but in other cases it may have had some ritual significance. Certainly some of the larger conflagrations would appear to have formed part of the ceremonial connected with the cremation of the body or erection of the burial mound. The ground beneath is often burned red and there is a surrounding mass of ash and charcoal, possibly the remains of a funeral pyre. There is also evidence beneath a number of barrows of quite large pits which have been dug and refilled (not necessarily with the same material) before the mound was built. Such pits are quite separate from the actual graves, and since they have no obvious practical purpose they must again be presumed to be connected with the ceremonies attendant on a barrow burial. In certain cases traces of fires have been found in the bottom. Such pits can be up to 10 ft long, 5 ft wide and 4 ft deep. In a number of cases the filling was of turves, in others of material noticeably different from the surroundings of the pit. Concealed ditches are another feature which must have a ceremonial rather than a practical use. They must be distinguished from quarry ditches around the edge of a barrow which have been buried by the erosion or enlargement of the mound. The ditches in question were concealed deliberately when the barrow was built. They are usually circular in plan and steep-sided, with a sloping entrance ramp at one point. Presumably they were intended as the setting for some sort of procession, entering via the ramp, going round the circle, and leaving via the ramp again.

At their simplest Bronze Age barrows consisted of a heap, large or small, of earth, chalk, sand or stones, largely according to the local geology, with no other structural feature. The smallest such barrows could be as little as 10 or 15 ft in diameter and only a few feet high and were little more than the immediate covering of the grave (Fig. 49). They could, on the other hand, be up to the dimensions mentioned earlier in describing barrow cemeteries. In most cases, however, the structure went beyond the simple pattern just mentioned. In earthen mounds the commonest addition is a ditch, which both delimits the barrow area and provides some at least of the mound material. Not infrequently the turf from the ditch, the first material to be dug, was heaped over the grave to form a sort of inner mound, over which the remaining material was heaped. The same sort of inner feature was provided in other ways. In composite barrows (i.e. intermediate in type between earthen mounds and true cairns) the inner part is often a small stone cairn covering the grave, over which is heaped a covering of earth to complete the structure. In other cases there is a clay capping to an inner mound, 5–10 ft across, over the primary burial, and in other cases it is possible to distinguish, in excavation, special attention to the primary burial in the form of mounds of clay or flints.

The main structural addition to the simple cairn of stones was the kerb, mentioned already under original appearance. Such kerbs are often seen as survivals of the megalithic tradition in which a stone kerb was a common feature of chambered burial monuments of the same

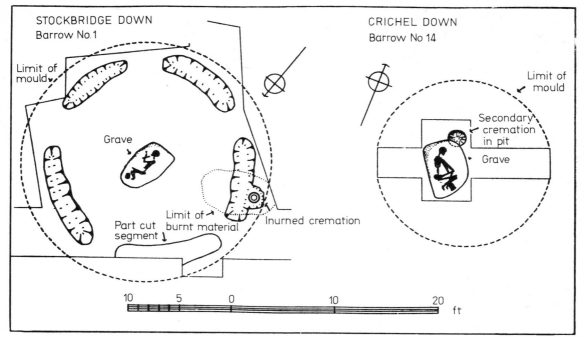

Fig. 49   Plans of two Beaker barrows, with flexed inhumation burials.

generally highland zone in which the stone cairns are found. In fact, kerbs as a structural feature are not confined to cairns. In some earthen mounds there is evidence that turf and other material from the ditch was heaped up on its inner edge to form a kerb which would delimit the remaining mound material. As already indicated, such stone kerbs were not necessarily restricted to their present height. They may well have been higher originally, giving the mound a more drum-like appearance.

Of the two basic burial traditions, inhumation and cremation, inhumation is broadly the earlier in the Bronze Age period. Inhumed bodies were deposited in three forms: contracted, flexed and extended. In contracted burials the knees were drawn up to the chin, while in flexed burials the thighs were approximately at right angles to the body (Fig. 49). In both of these positions the body was normally, but not always, laid on its side. In extended burials the body was normally laid on its back, with the legs out straight. Some bodies show evidence of mutilation, whether for ritual or other reasons. Occasionally a limb has been severed, and in some cases is completely missing from the burial. In other cases, bones rather than complete bodies have been buried, the corpse having been first exposed until all the flesh had rotted away. Some contracted burials show evidence of having been trussed in position before burial. Other bodies appear to have been buried clothed, or wrapped in a shroud, or both, judging by the evidence of remains of wool textiles, buttons and pins.

Inhumation burials were often, but not invariably, in graves, timber coffins or stone cists. In some cases, however, there was no special provision for the burial, the body being simply laid on the old ground surface at the centre of the barrow. This is often the case where the primary burial was of the group variety. Sometimes the ground surface was covered with a layer of cobbles

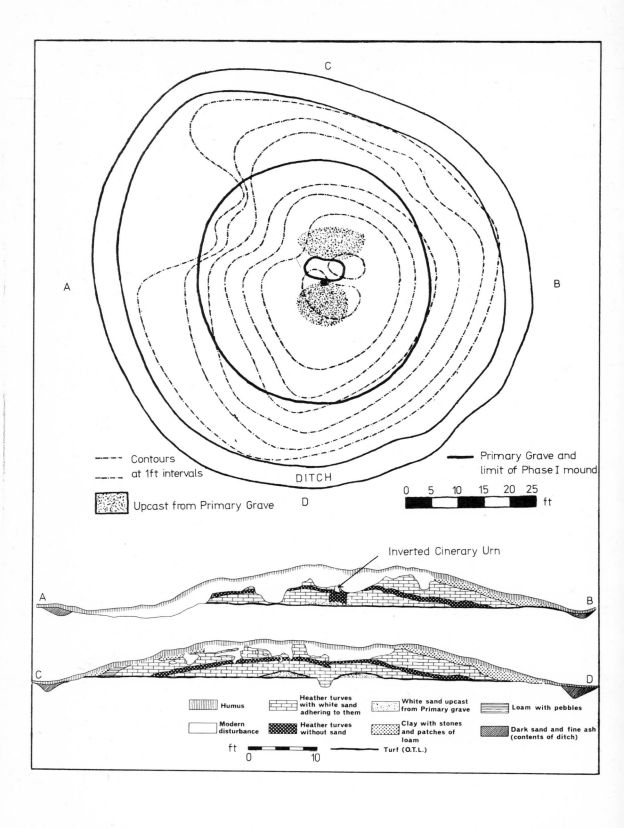

Contours at 1ft intervals

Upcast from Primary Grave

Primary Grave and limit of Phase I mound

0 5 10 15 20 25 ft

DITCH

Inverted Cinerary Urn

Humus

Modern disturbance

Heather turves with white sand adhering to them

Heather turves without sand

White sand upcast from Primary grave

Clay with stones and patches of loam

Loam with pebbles

Dark sand and fine ash (contents of ditch)

ft 0 10

Turf (O.T.L.)

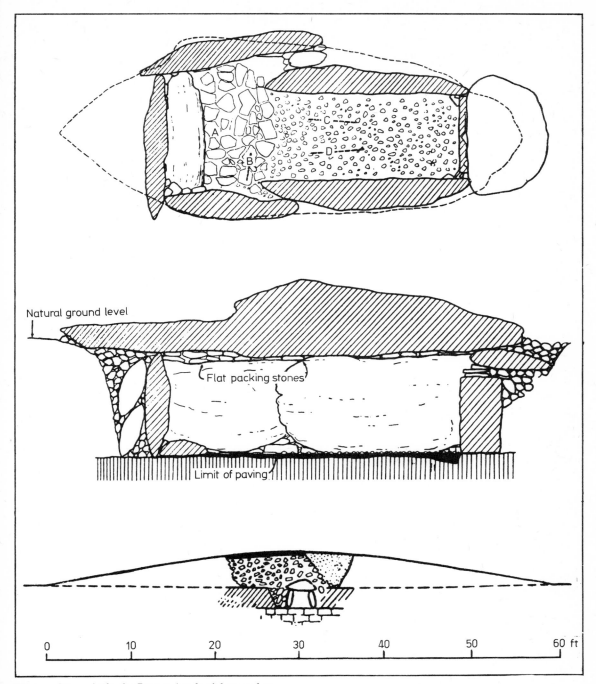

Natural ground level

Flat packing stones

Limit of paving

0   10   20   30   40   50   60 ft

Fig. 51   Stone cist in the Bronze Age burial mound at
Corston Beacon, Pembrokeshire.

Fig. 50   Plan and sections of the Bronze Age burial
mound at Dudsbury, Dorset.

or wooden planks, or moss, straw, reeds, etc., before the body was laid down.

In most cases, however, there was some more elaborate provision for the accommodation of the body. In many cases this took the form of a grave, i.e. a pit, large or small, dug into the old ground surface, (chalk, earth and in some cases rock), in which the contracted, flexed or extended body was deposited (Figs 49, 50). For contracted and flexed burials the grave could be 5–6 ft long, 4–5 ft wide and 2–3 ft deep. For extended burials the length could be up to 7 or 8 ft. Many Beaker burials were in simple graves of the type just described, as were many of the inhumation burials of the Wessex culture people, although the latter also practised cremation on a considerable scale. Over such graves would often be heaped the small inner

mounds mentioned earlier. In some cases the upcast material from the grave can be distinguished in excavation as a mound, or mounds, beside the grave pit (Fig. 50).

One of the commonest alternatives to the excavated grave is the stone *cist*, a box-like structure, in its simplest form consisting of four upright slabs of stone with a fifth on the top, forming a stone coffin (Fig. 51). Such cists are not to be confused with earlier megalithic chambers being in most cases of much smaller dimensions. In some cases the cists are set into the ground forming stone-lined graves, with the capstone flush with the old ground surface (Pl. 28). In other cases the whole cist is set on the old ground surface. There are cists set into the ground which appear never to have been covered with mounds, and these flat graves are, if anything, more numerous than those covered with mounds. Both inhumation and cremation burials are found in cists.

28   Stone cist in the Simonstown barrow, Glamorganshire.

29 Wooden coffin made from a single length of tree trunk.

Quite clearly stone cists are commoner in the stone regions of the British Isles, but there are examples in areas where the stone must have been brought from a distance, suggesting that local availability was not the overriding factor. In a number of cists, the side slabs have been grooved, timber-fashion, to receive the end slab, and look as if they have been based on timber proto-types, in other words, wooden coffins, which form another method of dealing with Bronze Age burials.

Timber coffins take two main forms, one-piece coffins hewn out of a single tree trunk and plank-made or composite coffins. Both inhumations and cremations have been found in both types. In some cases the coffins are placed in graves, in others they have been simply placed on the old ground surface and covered with the mound. The tree trunk coffins are either square-ended or boat-shaped, i.e. the ends have been hewn to a point so that the coffin is very close in appearance to a dug-out

canoe, and it has been suggested that such coffins were in fact symbolic boats, on the lines of the Boat of the Dead in the funerary beliefs of the ancient Near East. The tree trunk, up to 10 ft long and 4 ft in diameter, was transformed into a coffin by hollowing out a recess large enough to contain an extended body where the rite was inhuma-tion; where cremation was practised the recesses were on the whole smaller (Pl. 29). In many cases a coffin lid was formed from the upper segment of the same log. Because of their relatively massive construction tree trunk coffins are more often preserved than their plank-built counterparts. In early accounts these are often referred to as boxes. Probably there was a close relation-ship in size and function between stone cists and plank-built wooden coffins. There were probably made on the lines of present-day packing cases, i.e. of fairly simple construction using roughly hewn planks.

Although the internal features described so far have housed both inhumation and cremations, on the whole the former have tended to predominate. There are, however,

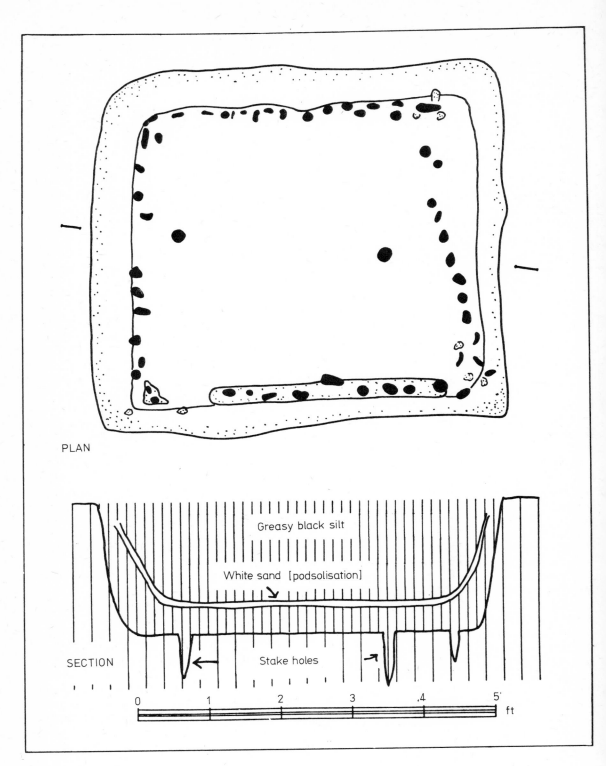

PLAN

Greasy black silt

White sand [podsolisation]

SECTION

Stake holes

0 1 2 3 .4 5
ft

other internal arrangements, which serve the needs of cremation burials. Because the cremated bones of a body are much less bulky than an unburned body the arrangements are on a smaller and simpler scale. Because of the growing popularity of cremation, by Middle Bronze Age times a special, large funerary urn had been developed, 12–15 ins high, large enough to contain the cremated bones of a single body and many cremations were deposited in these (Fig. 50). In some cases, the urn was placed in a small pit in the ground, in others it simply stood on the old ground surface, either upright, sometimes with a stone slab on top, or inverted on a stone slab. Often a cairn of small stones was piled over or around such cremation burials. Not all cremations were necessarily in urns. Cremated remains were often deposited in small recesses or pits as their only container (unurned cremations), and these must be seen as the counterparts of the larger pits or graves for inhumation burials.

Internal features on a somewhat larger scale are represented by what are known as mortuary houses which have been found under a number of barrows in southern Britain. These appear to have been actual timber houses, or rather huts, possibly modelled on the houses of the living, which formed a central feature of the burial mound. In some cases the mortuary house had reached a state of decay before the barrow was heaped over it. In others it appears to have been intact and to have collapsed only at a later stage. This may explain the depression in the tops of some barrows which have not been excavated. A barrow at Beaulieu in Hampshire covered a square mortuary house (c. 5 × 5 ft), set in a square pit 2 ft deep, and outlined by a series of stake-holes (Fig. 52). Two internal stake-holes half way across suggest the possibility of a gabled roof. Another barrow in the same group covered a similar structure with the uprights for the walls set in a continuous bedding trench. In other cases mortuary houses formed tent-like structures up to 8 × 4 ft, with the supporting posts inclined inwards to meet at a ridge-pole. The same principle, of post inclined inwards, was used in some circular mortuary houses, forming a cone-like structure. Presumably all of these structures were modelled on houses of the living, the idea being to provide a symbolic house for the after life, although necessarily reduced in scale in order to fit beneath a domed burial mound.

The remaining internal features of Bronze Age barrows fall into two groups: those with stone settings of various kinds, and those which originally had settings of timber posts. There is rather less information about the stone settings since these are usually found beneath cairns which have been completely excavated less often than earthen barrows. Circular, crescentic and D-shaped enclosures surrounding the central burial and completely covered by the cairn are one type of stone structure and circles of standing stones are another. The latter, and double concentric rings of standing stones, are presumably the stone counterparts of the timber circles to be considered below. Perhaps the most interesting of the internal stone structures are the so-called ring-cairns, since these appear to have existed also as free-standing monuments and may represent the first stage in the construction of some barrows. Ring-cairns will be dealt with as a separate subject later in this chapter, but they can be described for the moment as low circular walls, perhaps 2–3 ft high and 5 ft or more thick, with well-built inner and outer faces, in the manner of the structures associated with the Clava megalithic tombs, which are, in fact, very much part of the same story.

The evidence for timber circles beneath barrows is very much a feature of the post-war period and higher standards of excavation. Because of the lack of method, the very large number of nineteenth-century excavations produced little or no evidence of such features, and although there is some evidence from pre-war excavation, the bulk of the evidence has come from work carried out in the last two or three decades.

Fig. 52 Plan and section of the mortuary house in a Bronze Age barrow at Beaulieu, Hampshire.

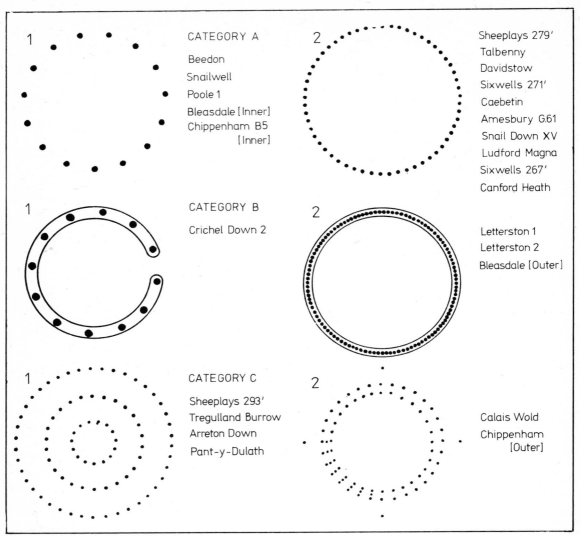

1 CATEGORY A

Beedon
Snailwell
Poole 1
Bleasdale [Inner]
Chippenham B5
[Inner]

2 Sheeplays 279'
Talbenny
Davidstow
Sixwells 271'
Caebetin
Amesbury G.61
Snail Down XV
Ludford Magna
Sixwells 267'
Canford Heath

1 CATEGORY B

Crichel Down 2

2 Letterston 1
Letterston 2
Bleasdale [Outer]

1 CATEGORY C

Sheeplays 293'
Tregulland Burrow
Arreton Down
Pant-y-Dulath

2 Calais Wold
Chippenham
[Outer]

Fig. 53   Plans of timber circles under Bronze Age burial mounds.

Some two dozen Bronze Age barrows are now known to have had timber circles of various kinds incorporated in their structure. In fact, the circles seem to represent an early stage in the history of the monument; in nearly every case known the timbers seem to have been removed before the barrow was actually heaped up over the site. Presumably, therefore, the timber circles had some ritual function associated with the early stages of burial. The exception to this may be some of the larger circles up to 50 ft in diameter, which appear to have been placed around the edge of the barrow, presumably as the main supports of a fence to retain the mound material in position and/or to keep off irreverent trespassers; in which case the posts may have remained in position until they rotted away.

The remaining circles were internal, their

sockets being filled and concealed when the mound was built. These internal circles take two forms, single rings and multiple rings. The single rings consist of a single circular setting, either widely spaced of perhaps ten to twenty posts, or closely-set, with a hundred posts or more, either in separate post-holes, or in post-holes contained within a palisade trench (Fig. 53A, B). The smaller rings resemble hut circles and their posts may indeed have been the main supports for some sort of roofed structure or enclosure used for the earlier stages of the burial ceremonial; they may perhaps be added to the group of barrows which contained mortuary houses. The larger rings, beyond normal hut size, may still have been the supports for some sort of enclosure fences, but they may equally well have been the uprights of a ring of free-standing posts,

possibly with a ritual function, and recalling the upstanding elements in henge monuments. The multiple rings consist of two to four concentric circles of uprights and recall even more strongly the henge tradition (Fig. 53C). They may well be modelled on a smaller scale, on the then still visible uprights (or the structures based on such uprights) of henge monuments, and be an attempt to associate the burial with the great sanctity of such sites. If the henge monument was the temple then the timber circles, and perhaps other structures under barrows as well, were the funerary temples, where ceremonies, perhaps modelled on those in henges, were conducted over the body prior to the erection of the barrow, at which point the timber structures at least were dismantled, leaving only the post-holes and palisade trenches to be discovered by the modern excavator.

Fig. 54 Plans of ring-cairns.

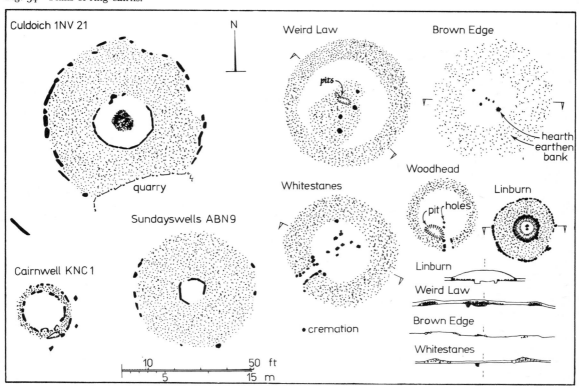

At the beginning of this chapter attention was drawn to the contrast between the Neolithic practice of collective burial and the Bronze Age one of individual burial. In a recent survey of 'Traditions of multiple burial in Later Neolithic and Early Bronze Age England', by F. Petersen, it has been suggested that, rather than being primarily individual graves, Bronze Age burial mounds were cemeteries intended from the beginning to have a series of burials, of which the so-called primary was only one. It is maintained that Bronze Age burial usage was 'a cemetery tradition with the completion of stages in the construction of the barrow constituting events that mark the end of one series of burials and the beginnings of others within a more or less continuous sequence. . . . It should now be apparent that the so-called "primary" burials under many round barrows simply represent the initial interments in monuments intended from the outset to be the site of additional burials as the need arose. The precise rules governing the sequence of events at these sites are of course unknown, but in general terms it is at least conceivable that the normal practice was to defer completing the barrow until the decease and burial of all persons eligible for interment in it had taken place, or at any rate, that the actual or likely incidence of mortality amongst such persons was taken into account when the time came to decide whether or not a particular site was to be "closed down". In cases where several graves containing multiple burials occupied the area later sealed by the barrow, there is seldom any evidence that their respective periods of use were successive rather than simultaneous; and consequently there is nothing against regarding them as groups of "family vaults", the number and sequence of burials in them reflecting the mortality rate of the particular population elements served by the individual grave during whatever stretch of time it remained physically and ritually accessible.'

At the beginning of the chapter it was mentioned that round barrows were not the only type of Bronze Age burial monument. One of the principal alternative forms was the ring-cairn which, as also mentioned earlier, was in some cases incorporated in a round barrow structure, but in other cases appeared to have existed as an independent structure, and it is in this latter form that they will be considered here (Fig. 54). The most clear-cut examples of ring-cairns are those sites associated with the Clava group of megalithic tombs in Scotland. These appear to be of Late Neolithic/Early Bronze Age date and may well provide the origin for the group as a whole. 'Ring-cairns' may be defined as monuments with a genuine bank of cairn material, revetted inside and out, surrounding an open, central area in which burials are deposited. There is as yet no complete or even near-complete inventory of ring-cairns but they certainly exist in noticeable numbers in north-east Scotland and Wales, and probably in many other areas as well, still awaiting discovery and recording.

Closely allied to the ring-cairn is what is known as the kerb-cairn. This is characterised by a ring, or kerb, of massive boulders, up to 20 ft in diameter, with a filling of cairn material to a depth of 2–3 ft in which the burials were deposited. It is, in a sense, the central portion of a ring-cairn, consisting of the inner revetment and the filling over the burials. Again these are represented in eastern Scotland and Wales, but this pattern probably represents the amount of work that has been done in these areas rather than the real distribution pattern. Another circular, non-barrow type is the embanked circle, a low circular bank of stones or earth, perhaps 6–10 ft wide and 2–3 ft high and up to 80–90 ft in diameter, surrounding a flat space containing a series of cremation burials dug into the ground. Other types (cairn circles, embanked stone circles) involve rings of standing stones and as such will be dealt with in the next chapter.

7 Circles and Standing Stones

Stone circles

There are some 900 stone circles in the British Isles, free-standing and otherwise, not including those circles of contiguous stones which are simply the surviving kerbs of destroyed round barrows. They vary in size from as little as 10 ft to nearly 400 ft in diameter, although both extremes are comparatively rare. Stone circles can be divided into three main groups on the basis of size. The first group embraces sites with a diameter between about 25–40 ft. These are on the whole less numerous than the larger sites, except perhaps in Ireland. The second group consists of sites with diameters between 60 and 120 ft. These represent a considerable group in England and Wales. There is something of a concentration at, or very close to, diameters of 80 ft. The third group is relatively small and takes in those sites with the largest diameters, 200 ft and over.

In recent years views on stone circles have been greatly influenced by the work of Alexander Thom. His careful survey of a large number of sites has revealed, among much other information, the fact that many of them are not truly circular but are, nevertheless, carefully laid out, displaying a hitherto unsuspected knowledge of geometry among the builders. He has been able to demonstrate that there were several different types of oval arrangement, each clearly based on sound geometrical principles. One of the commonest types is the flattened circle in which one side is distinctly flatter than the others (Figs 56, 57). There are three ways of drawing such rings (Thom's Types, A, B and D) and they quite clearly represent a deliberate choice on the part of the builders. Egg-shaped rings represent an equally deliberate choice; again there are two ways of laying them out (Thom's Types I and II). The third variation on the oval theme is the ellipse. Examples of all of these will be noted as they occur.

In south-west England there are between thirty and forty stone circles. Outstanding among these is the complex at Stanton Drew, Somerset, about six miles south of Bristol, which consists of three circles and associated features (Fig. 55). The main circle (c. 370 ft diameter) has twenty-seven surviving stones, mostly now fallen. To the east are the remains of a stone avenue about 40 ft wide and 250 ft long. About 150 ft to the north-east the smallest circle (c. 100 ft diameter, eight surviving stones) also has a stone avenue on its eastern side. About 450 ft south of the main circle the third circle (150 ft diameter, ten surviving stones) has no avenue. Some 450 ft to the west a feature known as The Cove, consisting originally of three large standing slabs, is on the same axis as the centres of the main and north-eastern circles and is, therefore, presumably part of the complex. Equally,

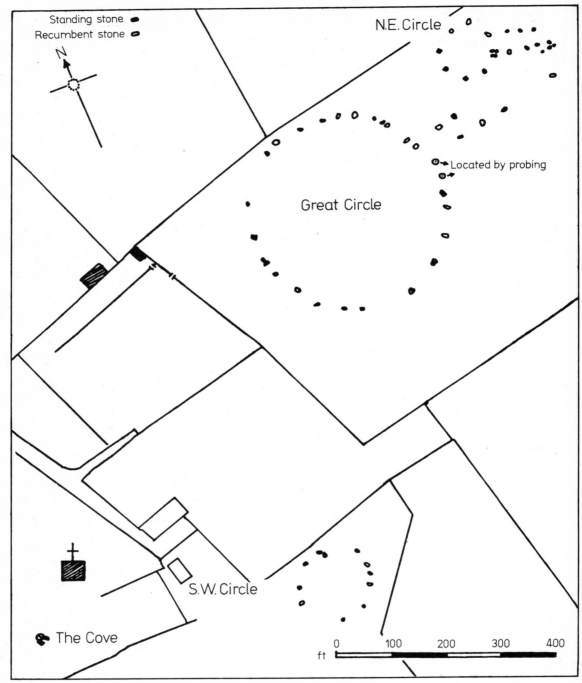

Fig. 55 Plan of the stone circles at Stanton Drew, Somerset.

Legend:
- Standing stone ●
- Recumbent stone ◖
- N.E. Circle
- Great Circle
- S.W. Circle
- The Cove
- ⊙→ Located by probing
- N

ft 0 100 200 300 400

a standing stone some distance to the north-east (Hauteville's Quoit) is on the same axis as the centres of the main and south-west circles, so that the whole Stanton Drew complex consisted of three circles, two avenues, The Cove and Hauteville's Quoit. Stanton Drew was quite clearly an important religious centre and demonstrates why the (presumed) builders, the Beaker people, were able to make such an important structural contribution to existing sanctuaries such as Stonehenge and Avebury.

Another important south-western group is known as The Hurlers, about four miles north-east of Liskeard in Cornwall. It consists of three circles in a line with diameters of 110 ft (thirteen stones), 135 ft (seventeen stones) and 105 ft (nine stones). Originally each circle would have had

about thirty stones. There are the remains of a group of two circles at Tregaseal, north-east of St Just, Cornwall, and there are two other similar groups in Devon, at The Grey Wethers, two and a half miles north of Postbridge (103 ft and 116 ft diameters), and at Merivale on Dartmoor. Many of the remaining sites in the south-west are single circles, ranging in diameter from 25 to about 150 ft. The Scorhill circle (90 ft diameter), six miles west of Moreton-hampstead, Devon, has thirty surviving stones (Pl. 30), and Withypool Hill (119 ft diameter), three miles south-west of Exford, Somerset, has thirty-seven. The smallest south-western circle is the Nine Maidens, one mile south of Porthmeor, with a diameter of only 24 ft and eleven surviving stones, six of them still standing.

At least three south-western sites are now

30   Stone circle at Scorhill, Dartmoor, Devon.

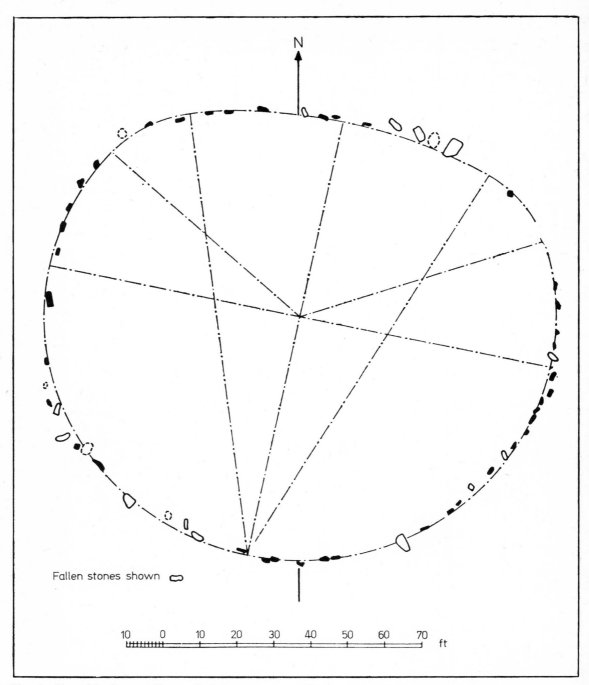

N

Fallen stones shown ⬭

10   0   10   20   30   40   50   60   70
⊔⊔⊔⊔⊔⊔⊔⊔   ft

Fig. 56   Plan of the Stannon (flattened) circle at
Dinnever Hill, Cornwall.

known to have been carefully laid out in non-circular fashion. The Stannon circle, Dinnever Hill, two and a half miles south-east of Camelford, Cornwall, is an example of Thom's Type A flattened circle, being noticeably flattened on the north side (Fig. 56). Rough Tor, also in Cornwall (153 ft diameter) has a pronounced flattening on the north-east (Thom's Type D). Post-bridge in Devon is an example of the true ellipse (34 and 30 ft diameters) with twenty-two surviving stones.

Stone circles are noticeably scarce in Wessex. The only examples appear to be in Dorset and then only in southern and western areas, away from the main concentration of henge monuments. Two of the circles, at Hampton Down near Portesham (sixteen stones), and Winterborne Abbas (nine stones), are quite small, 35 and 25 ft in diameter respectively. The circles at Kingston Russel and Rempstone are larger (c. 80 ft diameter).

Beyond Wessex in the Midlands, East Anglia and south-east England stone circles are rare or non-existent. The Rollright Stones, Oxfordshire, are one of the few examples known. The circle (104 ft in diameter) has fifty to sixty surviving stones, but the gaps indicate that the original number was probably in the region of seventy or eighty. Near by are the King's Stone, a standing stone, and the Whispering Knights, a burial chamber. Two circles in Shropshire are so close to the Welsh border that they will be dealt with in the main group of Welsh sites.

The south-western distribution is continued to the north in Wales, mainly in the counties of Brecknockshire, Radnorshire, Montgomeryshire, Denbighshire and Caernarvonshire, where there are some thirty to fifty stone circles, a high proportion of them between 60 and 100 ft in diameter. One of the few larger sites, Waun Mawr, is in Pembrokeshire, near Nevern; it is some 150 ft in diameter with only four or five surviving stones. There is an even larger circle (c. 175 ft diameter) at Hengwn in Merionethshire, originally composed of

sixty to seventy stones. Immediately outside the circle is a surrounding ditch, and its accompanying bank is between and behind the stones; other examples of associated earthworks in Wales will be encountered later. At the other end of the scale one of the two circles on Mynydd Trecastell, Brecknockshire, is only 27 ft in diameter; the other circle, about 100 ft away, is 80 ft in diameter. Also in Brecon are another two circles, c. 300 ft apart, at Nant Tarw, each c. 70 ft in diameter. Outside the western circle is a massive outlying stone. In Montgomeryshire, Lled Croes yr Ych (81 ft diameter, five surviving stones) has another circle to the west, about 400 ft away (62 ft diameter, eight surviving stones).

In North Wales sites are concentrated in a small number of groups. The Clocaenog Moor group, Denbighshire, consists of six circles, 15–45 ft in diameter, at least one of which has its stones set in a bank, and this seems to be a feature of many of the North Wales sites and appears in two sites of the Gwyffylliog group, also in Denbighshire. Capel Hiraethog I, Gwyffylliog, has an earthen bank 55 ft in diameter with six or seven empty sockets on the outer slope. Capel Hiraethog II (95 ft diameter) also now lacks any upright stones, but the removal of three is recorded. Capel Hiraethog III (50 ft diameter, originally eighteen or twenty stones, now three) surrounds a small mound, c. 15 ft in diameter. There are remains of two other stone circles in the same parish at Y Foel Frech. The main circle at Penmaenmawr, Caernarvonshire, also has associated earthworks. The Druid's circle (c. 90 ft diameter) consists of an earthen bank, with a clearly defined entrance on the west, and nine or ten large stones, up to 6 ft high, quite clearly the remains of a much larger number. There is a similar but smaller site to the south-west (40 ft diameter) and at least two other stone circles in the same general area.

One of the two Shropshire circles, which can be grouped with the Welsh sites, is of the flattened circle variety. Black Marsh,

Hemford, has a maximum diameter of 76 ft with its flattened portion on the western side. It has thirty-eight surviving stones including one at or near the centre. The other site, Mitchells Fold, is of similar dimensions with sixteen stones surviving.

Beyond Wales the distribution is continued in northern England, mostly on the western side from Derbyshire to Cumberland. The Derbyshire circles are mostly small, the exception being Eyam Moor (100 ft diameter) with sixteen stones set within a circular bank of earth. Of the remaining circles the one at Barbrook is

Fig. 57   Plan of Long Meg and her Daughters, Cumberland.

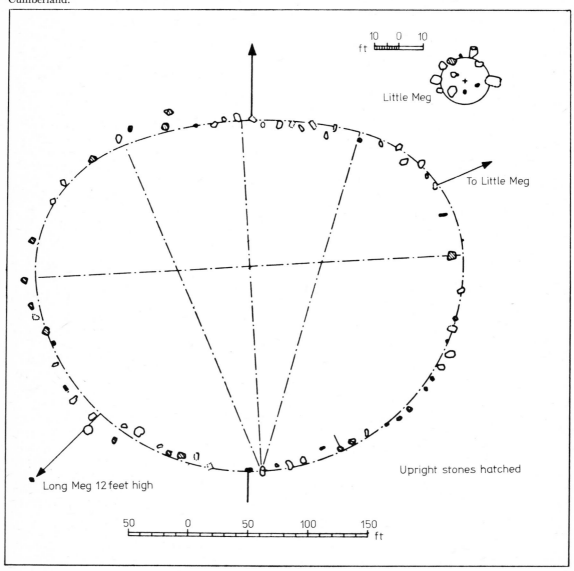

of Thom's flattened variety (48 ft diameter). There are other, smaller circles on Stanton Moor (Nine Ladies), west of Stanton Moor (Doll Tor), on Harthill Moor and on Froggatt Edge.

The Yorkshire sites are likewise of small dimensions, the largest being the Twelve Apostles on Ilkley Moor, with twelve stones in a bank 52 ft in diameter. Blakey Topping near Pickering is of similar dimensions and is one of a number of sites in the eastern part of the county. The other sites are the High Bridestones (two circles) near Whitby and Standing Stones Rigg near Scarborough. Small circles on Ilkley Moor have closely set stones and may be the remains of kerbs rather than true free-standing circles.

In the Lake District (Cumberland and Westmorland) the outstanding site is Long Meg and her Daughters, two miles north of Langwathby, Cumberland. It is distinctly oval in plan (c. 360 × 305 ft) and is, in fact, a flattened circle of Thom's Type B, with the flattening on the north side (Fig. 57). It had fifty-nine stones (originally c. seventy) of which twenty-seven are still standing up to 9 ft in height. These are the daughters. Long Meg is an outlying stone, some 60 ft to the south-west, about 12 ft high. There are traces of a bank surrounding the circle. The Carles, Castle Rigg, is also of the flattened variety (110 ft diameter) and many of the Lake District circles are noticeably larger than those elsewhere in the north: Grey Croft, one mile north of Seascale (80 ft diameter), Swinside, two and a half miles north-east of Broughton (90 ft diameter), and Elva Plain, three and a half miles north-east of Cockermouth (100 ft diameter), all in Cumberland, and two of the Shap circles (80 and 105 ft diameters), and Gamelands, one mile east of Orton (138 ft diameter), in Westmorland. There are the remains of an avenue from the circle one mile south of Shap to Thunder Stone, three-quarters of a mile north-west of Shap. The larger Shap circle surrounds the remains of a burial mound, and so originally did the Little

Meg circle, Cumberland. The circles in the Eskdale Moor complex, Cumberland, also contained burials. The largest circles, of the flattened variety (c. 100 ft diameter) contained five small burial cairns, three other circles (c. 50 ft diameter) each contained one, and the fifth circle (70 ft diameter) contained two. Another complex of five circles (50, 48, 70, 60 and 16 ft diameters) at Lacra, one and a half miles north-west of Millom, Cumberland, also included at least one which originally had a burial mound within. Associated with some of the circles are the remains of stone avenues. The remaining sites in the north of England are three or four sites each in Lancashire and Northumberland.

The distribution in northern England is continued in Lowland Scotland and the southern part of the Highland zone. In the far north (Orkneys, Shetlands, Caithness, Sutherland, Ross and Cromarty) stone circles are few and far between. In Scotland much of the attention devoted to stone circles is focused on a particular type, known as the recumbent stone circles, and these will be considered later.

The various types of oval ring distinguished by Thom are all represented in Scotland. Cambret Moor, Kirkcudbrightshire, is a flattened circle of Type A with a diameter of 55 ft and twenty-eight stones. The ring at Allan Water, Midlothian, is an egg-shaped arrangement of Thom's Type I with a very noticeable difference (10 ft) between the long (53 ft) and short (43 ft) diameters. Borrowston Rig in the same county is also egg-shaped, but of Type II variety with diameters of 153 and 135 ft. Two sites in Inverness, Daviot and Boat of Garten, and one in Aberdeen, Sands of Forvie, have their stones arranged in the form of true ellipses, and are of similar dimensions (48/50 ft, 43/47 ft and 42/45 ft).

The remaining true circles range in size from about 10 to 188 ft in diameter. Kintraw, in Argyllshire, is an example of the smaller type of circle. It is 21 ft in diameter with about ten surviving stones, although the gaps indicate that the original number was probably around twenty; about 12 ft to the north-east is a large standing stone about 12 ft high. Caulside in Kirkcudbrightshire has similar associated features but is on a much larger scale, 81 ft in

diameter with about fifteen surviving stones; again the gaps would appear to indicate an original total of about twice this number.

In the Outer Hebrides and Skye as a whole there are about twenty stone circles. However, the greatest concentration appears

Fig. 58   Plan and oblique view of the stone circle and alignments at Callanish, Outer Hebrides.

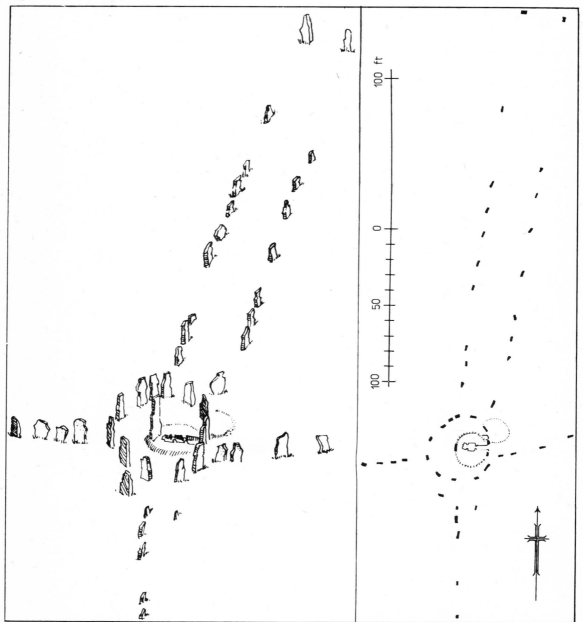

to be in the Isle of Lewis, where there are about a dozen circles, many of them at or near Callanish. The main ring at Callanish (Callanish I) is of Thom's Type A flattened circle (Fig. 58). It has a diameter of some 43 ft and is flattened on the eastern side. The ring encloses the greater part of a round, chambered cairn some 25 ft in diameter. Externally it is accompanied by five separate stone alignments. There are lines of four stones each to east and west and a line of six stones to the south. To the north there are two lines of eight stones each, forming an avenue about 30 ft wide. Within a mile to the east are two other rings (Callanish II and III), the latter a double ring. Callanish IV, about two miles to the south-east, is elliptical (46 × 32 ft) with six surviving stones, one of them at the centre.

The two remaining groups to be considered in Scotland are the stone circles of the Clava group, and the recumbent stone circles. The Clava group in the Inverness region consists of both conventional, megalithic Passage Graves and structures of the ring-cairn type. Both types are surrounded by stone circles. A noticeable feature is the fact that the stones of the circle, and also of the kerb delimiting the internal structure, are graded in height, the tallest stones being normally in the south-west quadrant. This is frequently the position of the entrance of the megalithic tombs within and this may be the origin of the practice. This would suggest that the ring-cairns are later than the megalithic tombs, since they follow the same practice although they have no entrances. Another noticeable feature is the regular number of stones in the free-standing circle. In a large number of cases the number is twelve and this must represent a deliberate choice on the part of the builders. Diameters vary from c. 60 to 100 ft with many around 80 ft.

To the east of the Clava group, in Aberdeenshire and surrounding areas, are the recumbent stone circles. A recumbent stone circle is one which contains one stone lying horizontally on the ground between two of the uprights (Fig. 59). The majority of such circles enclose a ring-cairn so that quite clearly there was some link between them and the Clava group, with which they share a number of significant features: the stones are graded in height in the same way, with the emphasis on the south-west quadrant; the number of stones is frequently twelve; and the diameters are broadly similar. With regard to the recumbent stone, it is suggested that this is derived from the Clava Passage Grave, being the counterpart or survival of the stone lintel over the passage grave entrance. One or two examples will suffice to show the general nature of recumbent stone circles. The site at Midmar Church, Aberdeenshire, had the two tallest stones in the circle (8 ft high) in the south-west quadrant, with the recumbent stone, some 15 ft long, between them. The original number of stones, including the recumbent stone, was probably twelve. Twelve stones were quite certainly involved in the circle (63 ft diameter) at Easter Aquorthies, also in Aberdeenshire. The two flanking stones were 7 and 8 ft high and the recumbent stone was 12 ft long. As in a number of other cases, the recumbent and its flankers were set inside the main line of the circle and there were the remains of some structure inside them, presumably to provide a link with the ring-cairn inside. At Sunhoney, Aberdeenshire, the circle (83 ft diameter) again contained twelve stones including the recumbent which was 17 ft long. The upright stones were 5–8 ft high.

Recumbent stone circles are recorded also in Ireland, principally in Co. Cork. They are very much smaller than the Scottish sites (10–30 ft in diameter) and do not appear to have enclosed ring-cairns. The most noticeable difference, however, is in the position of the recumbent stone. Instead of being between the tallest pair of uprights, the Irish recumbent stones are on the opposite side of the circle. In spite of this local variation the intention, whatever it was, was presumably the same as

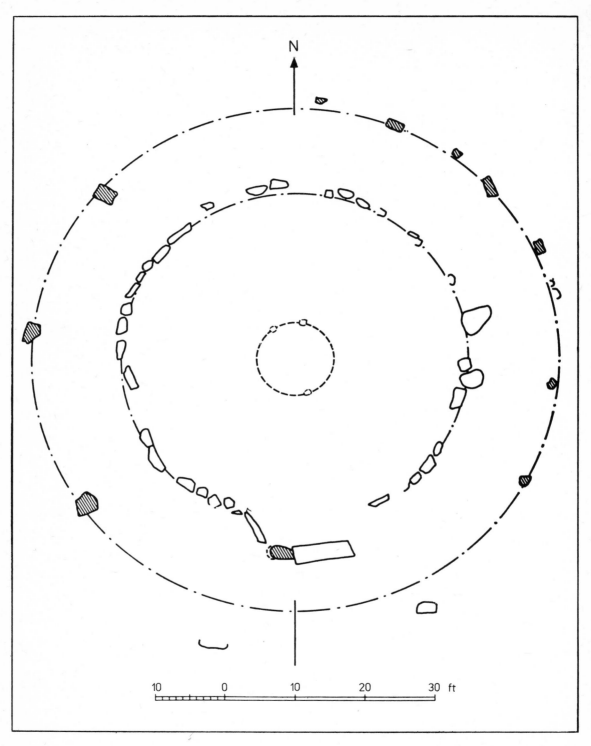

in north-east Scotland. The two groups are a long way apart and since there appears to be a clear line of development for the Scottish sites, the Irish sites are probably derived from them, although just how it is difficult to see.

Outside the Cork area there is another concentration of stone circles (of non-recumbent type) in Co. Tyrone and the adjacent areas of Derry and Fermanagh. The circles tend to be larger, up to 50 ft in diameter, with proportionally more stones, although the latter tend to be small in size, often only a foot or so high, and consequently difficult to see because of the vegetation. Associated with many of these circles are stone alignments or, in some cases, irregular groups of three standing stones. In the Lough Gur region, Co. Limerick, the stone circles include types consisting of a ring of separate boulders instead of upright stones. In the border area of Co. Kildare-Wicklow, on the other hand, a number of stone circles have very large uprights. The stone circle surrounding New Grange, Co. Meath, was mentioned in Chapter 3. A number of other examples are known, both in Meath and Co. Tyrone. Other counties where stone circles are well represented include Louth, Down, Donegal, Galway and Cavan. Many of the known circles in Ireland still await detailed planning and recording, and there are probably many more yet to be discovered.

It has been said on many occasions that if henge monuments are the cathedrals of prehistoric times, then stone circles are the parish churches, and this is a useful if not entirely accurate analogy. If the henges are seen as great religious centres then the idea of smaller, local religious centres built in general imitation of them seems a distinct possibility. Certainly it would be difficult to explain the large number of stone circles which have no other associated feature,

such as a burial mound, in any other way, and the function of local sanctuaries or religious centres for a large number of stone circles can be suggested with some degree of confidence. However, local stone circles cannot strictly speaking be said to imitate henge monuments since, as was pointed out in Chapter 3, stone circles are not an integral part of the henge tradition. They represent a contribution made to a small number of henges by the Beaker people. But it was this element of a limited number of henges which appears to have been seized on as the diagnostic feature of a local sanctuary and built in very large numbers throughout the British Isles, as outlined above.

In addition to the free-standing circles, however, there were others in which quite clearly the sanctuary function was not exclusive. Just as present-day burial is closely bound up with churches, so in prehistoric times there was a desire to be buried in association with a sacred place, as witnessed for example by the great barrow cemeteries grouped around Stonehenge. An even closer association could be achieved by being buried within a sanctuary, or in a burial place built in imitation of a sanctuary, and this may be the explanation of many stone circles, particularly those with associated features inside, such as a burial mound or ring-cairn. But the absence of other features does not necessarily mean that the circle was a sanctuary. Circular areas delimited by banks and housing a number of flat burials are not uncommon, and the circle of standing stones may be simply another method of marking off such an area for the purpose of burial. Without excavation of the interior it is impossible to know, and even if burials are found it is still not possible to be certain that the original purpose of the circle was burial. We will probably never know the precise balance between the sanctuary function and the burial function in stone circles, and perhaps the two functions were never much separated in the minds of the builders anyway.

Fig. 59   Recumbent stone circle and ring-cairn at Aquorthies, Kingausie, Kincardineshire.

31   The Longstone on Shovel Down, Dartmoor, Devon.

Standing stones (Pl. 31)

As far as numbers and distribution are concerned we probably know less about standing stones than we do about almost any other type of prehistoric monument. There is the added difficulty that we cannot be certain that all standing stones are prehistoric. They can be virtually of any period. More so than in any other type of prehistoric monument it is necessary to keep a very open mind on the date and purpose of standing stones. In a sense all one can do is note the physical characteristics of a certain number of examples, keeping in mind the reservations expressed above.

The monolith in Rudstone churchyard near Bridlington in Yorkshire is one of the largest in Britain, some 25 ft high, 6 ft wide and 2¼ ft thick. The type of stone indicates a geological source at least ten miles to the north, so that there must have been some compelling reason for bringing it to its present site. Two standing stones near the Merry Maidens Circle in Cornwall were 13½ and 15 ft high. Another standing stone in Cornwall, at Tresvennack, is 11½ ft high. The Beardown Man, three miles from Two Bridges in Devon, is of similar height, while the Long Stone on Exmoor is 9 ft high. In Ireland another Long Stone, at Punchestown in Co. Kildare, is 23 ft long overall and weighs nine tons. It stands 19½ ft high above the ground. At its foot a small burial cist was found, which, although empty, does suggest a Bronze Age date. The monolith in nearby Longstone Rath is nearly as tall (17½ ft) and it too had a burial cist at its foot containing the cremated remains of two adults, again presumably of Bronze Age date. At New Grange, Co. Meath, two stones each c. 10 ft high, form part of the great complex of prehistoric monuments in the bend of the River Boyne.

Standing stones (*meini hirion*) are fairly common in Wales. Two examples in Brecknockshire at Llwynyfedwen, Llangynidr and Cwrtgollen near Crickhowell, are around 12 ft high and are presumed to be of Bronze Age date, although there is no evidence as to their date or function. However, another large standing stone, Maen Llwyd in Glynllifon Park, Caernarvonshire, did in fact mask the site of a burial which produced burnt bones and remains of an urn which was probably of Bronze Age type, and at least some of the other standing stones in Wales must be of the same type. There is also some evidence from Wales of standing stones set in burial mounds, with at least the upper portion protruding above the surface. The numerous standing stones in Scotland include a number of small groups which are neither alignments nor, apparently, the remains of circles. Three stones at Clachan an Diridh, near Pitlochry, Perthshire, form a triangle (c. 12 × 12 × 18 ft) and another three at Great Bemeray, Isle of Lewis, are of the same shape (18 × 18 × 33 ft).

Stone rows, either single or double, have again been encountered already in association with stone circles. Although only three stones are involved, The Devil's Arrows, near Boroughbridge in Yorkshire, contain some of the largest standing stones in the British Isles. They are between 18 and 22½ ft in height and form a north/south line with intervals of 200 and 370 ft. The Nine Maidens in Cornwall, three miles north-east of St Columb Major, consist, not unexpectedly, of nine stones up to 7 ft high, strung out at irregular intervals in a north-east/south-west line, some 350 ft long. A much longer stone row runs north/south on Butterdon Hill near Ivybridge in Devon. It is over 6,000 ft long with a large burial cairn at the southern end and a large upright stone at the northern end. Stone rows, both single and multiple, are relatively common on Dartmoor (Pl. 32). At Merrivale, about four miles east of Tavistock, there is a whole complex of remains, including two double stone rows running parallel to each other, east and west. The

north row is nearly 600 ft long and has a stone slab across the eastern end as if to indicate clearly the termination of the setting. The south row is longer (c. 850 ft) but it too is terminated in the same way. There are many other rows, of generally similar type, in the Dartmoor region.

In Wales, at Parc-y-Meirw near Fishguard, Pembrokeshire, there is a row of four standing stones (8–11 ft high) spread over a distance of 150 ft. There is a much shorter alignment on Cribarth, Craig-y-nos, Brecknockshire. Seven stones form a line only 45 ft long with an outlier, on the same alignment about 26 ft to the south-west.

In Scotland the alignment at Ballochroy in Kintyre is very short (c. 20 ft) and consists of three stones, 12, 11 and 6 ft high, running north-east/south-west. The alignment at Callanish, Callanish v, is not much longer (c. 40 ft) and involves three stones, each 4 ft high. There are two associated stones, one c. 110 ft to the north, one a similar distance to the south-east. The Eleven Shearers, Roxburghshire, is much longer (c. 400 ft overall) with some

32 Stone row on Stalldon Down, Devon.

twenty-five stones, but is not on a single alignment. It runs east and west for about 300 ft, but towards the east changes direction by about 150 degrees towards the south. One of the most complex systems of stone alignment is found in Mid Clyth in Caithness. Over 150 stones are involved covering an area c. 200 × 150 ft. They are set out in over twenty rows running approximately north and south. In fact, the rows are not parallel, there being a noticeable convergence towards the north, narrowing from the maximum of 200 ft to only c. 115 ft. There is another complex of standing stones in Sutherland, at Learable Hill, where there are four (possibly five) parallel rows running east and west, plus several other alignments immediately to the north.

In recent years functions other than ritual have been suggested for many of the sites under discussion and also for Stonehenge. The work of Alexander Thom has already been mentioned. Apart from their knowledge of geometry he also suggests that the builders made use of a unit of length which he calls the Megalithic Yard, 2.72 ft in length. He further suggests that the builders were preoccupied with obtaining dimensions (diameters and circumferences) in whole numbers rather than fractions of Megalithic Yards. Since, however, in strict geometrical terms, the circumference of a circle is $3\frac{1}{7}$ times the diameter then only certain diameters in whole numbers would produce whole numbers also in their circumferences; for example, a diameter of 14 Megalithic Yards would produce a circumference in whole numbers (44 Megalithic Yards), but a diameter of, say, 13 or 15 MY would not. From this point of view the true circle was unsatisfactory and this may explain the relatively large number of non-circular arrangements, where there is much greater flexibility in adjusting the relationship between the diameters and the perimeters. Why prehistoric man should have been so concerned with such relationships we shall probably never know.

Perhaps the most interesting of Thom's suggestions is that stone circles and alignments were used for astronomical purposes as indicators of the rising and setting points of the sun at the solstices, and probably also for observation of the moon and some of the more prominent stars. What he suggests in essence is that these stone structures acted as both clocks and calendars, the movement of stars indicating times (at night) and the movement of the sun indicating the dates or time of year. Unfortunately space does not allow this fascinating theory to be pursued or even adequately summarised here. Those interested in this aspect of the subject should consult Thom's own *Megalithic Sites in Britain*, published in 1967.

Thom's ideas have not found universal acceptance and must be regarded as a hypothesis awaiting further evidence. There seems no reason to doubt the knowledge of geometry which he claims for the builders of the various kinds of non-circular rings. His surveys have demonstrated more than adequately that these rings were carefully constructed and they can only have been done by people with an understanding of geometry, even if this understanding was of a practical rule-of-thumb kind rather than a deep theoretical knowledge. On the question of the Megalithic Yard there must be greater reservation. That some unit of measurement was in use seems highly probable, but whether it was an agreed standard at precisely 2.72 ft is open to question. It may, again, have been a much more rough-and-ready type of measurement (perhaps the pace of a man of average height) which would still give results broadly similar to those Thom quotes. Certainly, even using the 2.72 Megalithic Yard, there are variations in the figures which give cause to doubt whether anything quite so precise was in use. On the astronomical side Thom has produced some very interesting factual evidence and it is now difficult to rebut entirely a claim for an astronomical function for some of the circles and alignments involved. This is not to say that we must see all stone circles as astronomical observatories. The whole case is far from being conclusively proved and the primary function must still be seen as that of sanctuaries. The two functions may, in fact, have been combined and may eventually have become inseparable. For primitive man the most striking natural phenomena must have been the presence and movement of the sun, moon and stars. These he must have seen as great powers in themselves or the work of some great and mysterious power. In either case it would be natural to try to associate his sacred monuments with them, so that religion and astronomy were not, in fact, alternative functions of these structures, but, in the minds of the builders, the same function. A great deal more work is needed on stone circles, standing stones and stone rows, including much more precise survey than hitherto, before we can begin to make any unequivocal statements about prehistoric man's capabilities in the field of astronomy. One of Thom's final points, with regard to dates, makes use of modern astronomical knowledge of the movements of the more prominent stars which indicates that the various sighting lines formed by stones would have been correct in the centuries between 2000 and 1700 B.C. This is broadly in keeping with traditional dating for the introduction of the stone circle to these islands by the Beaker people, shortly after the beginning of the second millennium B.C.

8 Hillforts and Ramparts

Until fairly recently it would have been in order to entitle this chapter 'Iron Age Hillforts' without further qualification. In the last few years, however, as a result of certain carbon-14 determinations, and for other reasons, doubts have been cast on this traditional view. There is no question of the Iron Age date of many hillforts. What is now being suggested is that some of them belong also to the preceding Late Bronze Age period, i.e. perhaps up to five centuries earlier than has hitherto been envisaged, so that the long-used term Iron Age hillfort may no longer be appropriate.

The story begins in the North Alpine region of Europe (south-west Germany, south-east France) in the years shortly after 1200 B.C. From around that date begins what is known as the North Alpine Urnfield culture which, some five centuries later, c. 700 B.C., was to give birth to the Hallstatt civilisation which marks the beginning of the Iron Age in Europe north of the Alps. It was during the development of the Late Bronze Age Urnfield culture that the structures which we call hillforts first began to appear, possibly around 1000 B.C. There is thus no difficulty, as far as the European evidence is concerned, in invoking a Late Bronze Age date, perhaps as early as 850 B.C., for hillforts on this side of the Channel. These first European essays in large-scale fortification may well have been based on knowledge derived from the east

Mediterranean world either by trade or by mercenary service there of Urnfield warriors.

It was not until about 700 B.C. that iron working began in Europe north of the Alps, coinciding approximately with changes in the Urnfield civilisation which were sufficiently marked to warrant a new name, Hallstatt, which thus stands at the beginning of the Iron Age in the North Alpine region. It is quite clear, however, that iron using was not of itself the distinguishing feature of Hallstatt civilisation. From c. 700 B.C. on rich warrior burials, with four-wheeled carts, and later two-wheeled chariots, found in the area indicate the arrival there of powerful warrior chiefs, ultimately from the steppe region of south Russia, where there was a similar burial tradition among the Scythians. The Hallstatt civilisation is thus composed of three main elements: first, the basic Urnfield population; second, the Scythian addition, possibly in the form of a ruling warrior group; and third, the knowledge of iron working derived probably from the head of the Adriatic. The amalgam of these three produced what we call the Hallstatt civilisation in the years shortly after 700 B.C. It is quite certain from Classical sources that the Hallstatt people were Celts (Gr. *Keltoi*), and almost equally certain that the preceding Urnfield people also were Celts.

Between 700 and 500 B.C. Hallstatt culture expanded to occupy much of central and western Europe, including by the end of the period eastern and south-eastern England. After some two centuries' duration the Hallstatt civilisation gave way to the closely related La Tène civilisation to which it had in a sense served as a prelude. Burials with Hallstatt four-wheeled carts were now replaced by La Tène two-wheeled chariots, and there were many other changes as well, particularly in the decorative arts, as seen on military and luxury equipment. From its centre in the Rhine/Marne area the La Tène civilisation expanded in all directions, eventually embracing by c. 250 B.C. virtually the whole of France, the Low Countries, Switzerland, western and southern Germany, Czechoslovakia and the middle and upper Danube regions, with large-scale raiding beyond, notably into Italy and Greece, where the unwelcome presence of the Celts is recorded historically c. 400 B.C. and 279 B.C. respectively. The European background to the study of hillforts thus embraces some twelve centuries, from c. 1200 B.C. to the Roman conquest, and three successive cultures, Urnfield (1200–700 B.C.), Hallstatt (700–500 B.C.) and La Tène (500 B.C. onwards). During the greater part of this period, from c. 1000 B.C. on, the commonest field monuments in the Celtic world, from Spain to the Balkans and from the Alps to Scotland, were the fortified enclosures known as hillforts, of which there must be at least ten thousand in Europe and the British Isles.

As already indicated, events in Europe were not without their effects here, seen primarily in hillforts, several thousand of which are recorded, mostly in the western regions of England, Scotland and Wales. Unfortunately, the background against which these must be seen is at present uncertain. For many years the Iron Age in Britain has been described in terms of what is known as the ABC system, but recently doubts have been expressed about this, and a number of carbon-14 dates are impossible to reconcile with it anyway. It is clear that some new and different chronological framework is required for the Iron Age in Britain. This is obviously outside the scope of the present survey, but any chronology proposed for hillforts must loom large in any overall Iron Age chronology.

The defensive aspect of hillforts needs to be emphasised. These enclosures are not military establishments like, say, Roman forts or medieval castles. They are defensive in the same way that a town wall is defensive (and some of them may have been just that), with the limited function of keeping enemies out. They were built to meet the needs of separate communities, with no particular reference to neighbouring forts, except perhaps those very close at hand. For the most part they appear to have been independent of each other, and in this independence lay the seeds of their downfall at the hands of the Romans.

The term enclosure is a very apt description of what these structures look like. They are simply areas of natural ground surrounded by stone, earth or earth-and-timber ramparts, usually with ditches in front of them. The ramparts have in most cases collapsed so that what we see now are grass-grown banks of earth, or banks of loose stones, with their accompanying ditches partly filled with the collapsed material. In their present condition ramparts stand 5–10 ft above the interior and 10–20 ft above the ditch bottom, although in some cases the latter dimension may be up to 40 ft. In many cases special attention was paid to the entrances, one of the commoner types being the inturned entrance, in which the ramparts turn inwards at right angles to form a narrow corridor with the gates at the inner end (Figs. 60, II & III, & 61).

Hillforts vary considerably in size. There are a few sites over 200 acres in area, and a few which are only a tiny fraction of this ($\frac{1}{12}$th of an acre). The majority, however, are between 1 and 30 acres in area. In terms of simple dimensions this means a diameter of c. 240 ft for a (roughly circular)

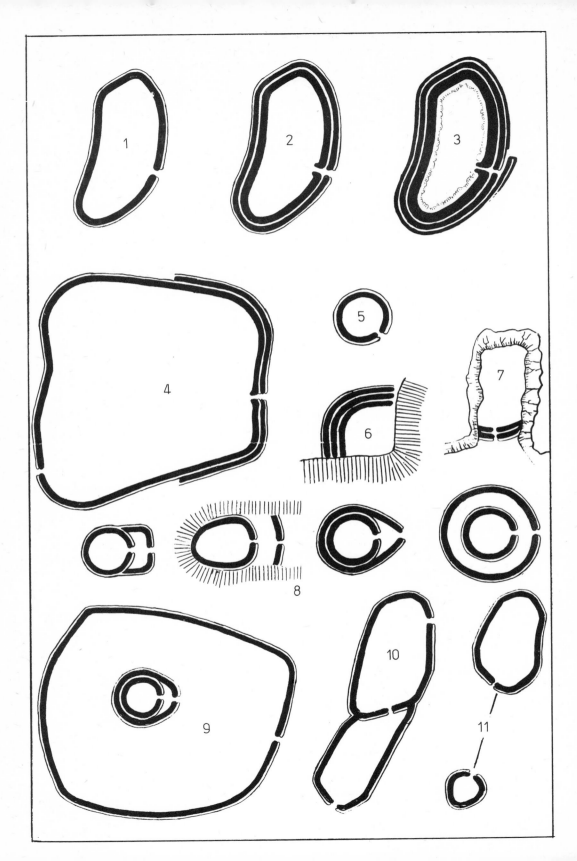

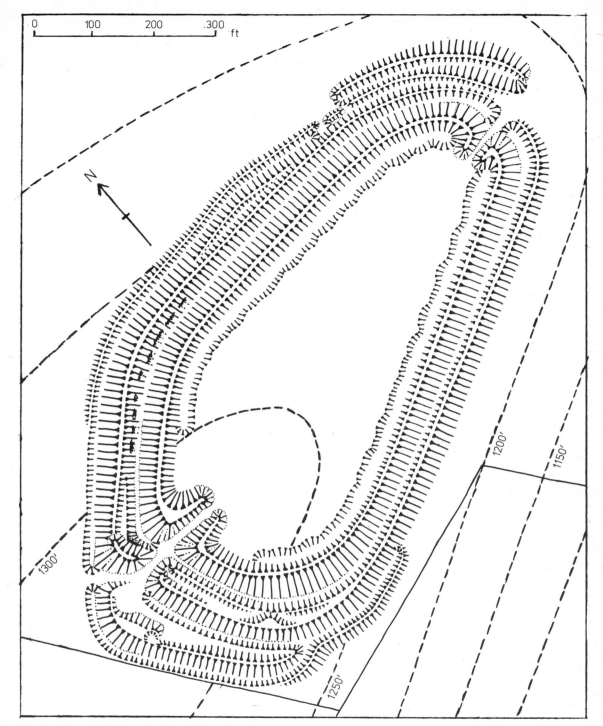

Fig. 61 Plan of the Iron Age fort of Caer Caradoc,
Clun, Shropshire.

167

Fig. 60 Diagrammatic plans of the eleven types of Iron
Age fort.

one-acre fort, 750 ft for a 10-acre fort, 1,100 ft for a 20-acre fort and 1,300 ft for a 30-acre fort.

In terms of defence a *univallate* fort is one which is surrounded by a single rampart, usually with an outer ditch (Fig. 60, 1 & Pl. 33), while a *multivallate* fort is defended by two or more ramparts, with or without ditches (Fig. 60, II, III & Pl. 34). In both cases the defences surround a single enclosure. Sites involving two or more enclosures are referred to as *multiple-enclosure* sites (Figs. 60, VIII, IX & X, 62 & 63).

In terms of siting a contour fort is one which occupies the top of a hill, its defences following, more or less, the lines of the surrounding contours. Promontory forts make use of cliffs or steep slopes on two or three sides with man-made defences only on the remaining, more approachable sides (Pls. 33 & 41). Other types of situation include cliff-edges, ridges and plateaux.

Hillforts in England and Wales

There are some 1,400 hillforts in England and Wales, mostly south and west of a line from the Mersey to the mouth of the

33 The Iron Age promontory fort at Helsby, Cheshire: univallate defences.

34 The Iron Age fort of Eggardon, Dorset: multivallate defences.

Thames, reaching their maximum numbers in the western extremities of Cornwall and Pembrokeshire. Two major traditions can be distinguished, the division between them running approximately from the Conway Valley in North Wales to the Exe in Devon. The 600 or so sites in the Wessex tradition are mostly between 3 and 30 acres in area with either univallate (300 sites) or multivallate (150 sites) defences (Fig. 60, I & II). A special group of about forty multivallate sites with very strong defences and elaborate entrances can be separately distinguished as the Maiden Castle type (Fig. 60, III). The remaining sites are either very large (IV) or of the multiple-enclosure type (X & XI). In the Western tradition (c. 750 sites) the commonest type (c. 500 sites) is a small univallate fort, 1–3 acres in area and often circular in plan (Fig. 60, V). Multivallate forts, of the same size (Fig. 60, VI), are

comparatively few in number (c. eighty sites). Another eighty or so forts are in coastal promontory positions, and are both univallate and multivallate in style (Fig. 60, VII). The remaining sites (c. 100 in number) are forms of multiple-enclosure site peculiar to the Western tradition (Fig. 60, VIII); the two main types are concentric forts, in which the enclosures are placed one inside the other, and annexe forts, in which the enclosures are, broadly speaking, side by side.

In south-eastern England about half of the fifty known hillforts are strung out along the South Downs and are mostly of univallate type, including The Trundle, near Goodwood racecourse, Chanctonbury Ring, The Devil's Dyke and Cissbury, the latter enclosing some 60 acres. The remaining sites in the south-east are in the Weald/North Downs area and on either side of the lower Thames.

Wessex (Dorset, Wiltshire, Hampshire and Berkshire) contains some of the

35   The multivallate Iron Age fort of Badbury Rings, Dorset.

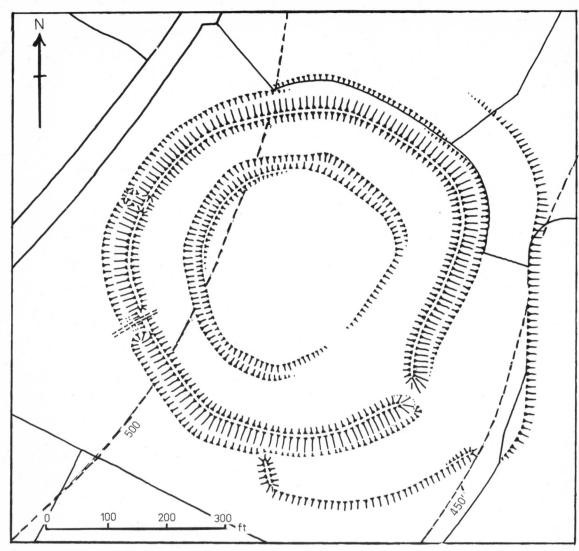

Fig. 62   Plan of the Iron Age concentric fort of
Tregeare Rounds, Cornwall.

largest and most spectacular sites in Britain, including perhaps the most famous of all, Maiden Castle, Dorset. To the east of the Avon the hillforts are mainly of univallate type and include such sites as St Catherine's Hill, near Winchester, Beacon Hill and Walbury in Hampshire, and Old Sarum, Figsbury Rings and Casterley Camp in

Wiltshire. To the west sites are mostly multivallate, many of them of Maiden Castle type, including Eggardon (Pl. 34), Hod Hill, Hambledon Hill and Badbury Rings (Pl. 35) in Dorset, Oldbury, Bratton Castle (Pl. 36), Battlesbury, Yarnbury, Sidbury and Castle Ditches in Wiltshire, and Castle Ditches and Danebury in Hampshire. These sites have two, three and four lines of massive fortifications up to 40 ft high, with especially strong entrances, often in the form of outworks forming barbicans or double entrances, as at Badbury Rings and Bratton Castle. The Wessex region also includes a number of multiple-enclosure sites such as Buzbury Rings and Weatherby Castle in Dorset, and White Sheet Castle and Park Hill Camp in Wiltshire.

The Cotswold region, centred on Gloucestershire, contains about a hundred

hillforts, many of them on the steeper north-west edge of the range facing the river Severn. Few of the multivallate sites are as spectacular as those in Wessex but those worthy of mention include Kimsbury and Uley Bury in Gloucestershire (Pl. 37), and Worlebury and Dolebury in Somerset. Both of the latter are stone-built forts. Multiple-enclosure sites include Bredon Hill in Worcestershire and Haresfield Beacon in Gloucestershire. The Cotswold region also includes a number of very large sites: Nottingham Hill, Gloucestershire

Fig. 63   Plan of the Iron Age fort at Carman, Dumbartonshire.

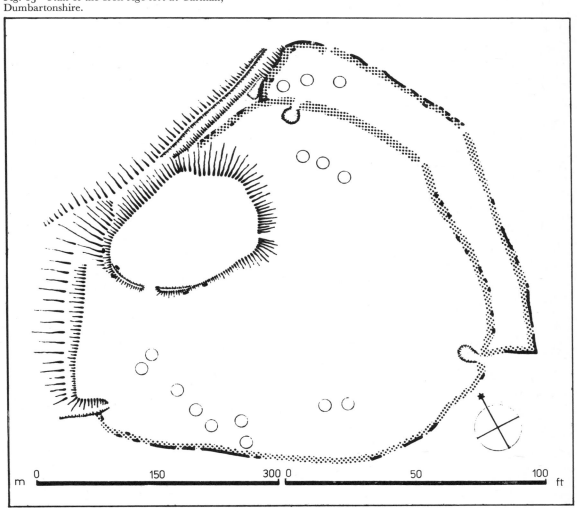

36   The multivallate Iron Age fort of Bratton Castle, Wiltshire.

37   The Iron Age fort of Uley Bury, Gloucestershire.

(130 acres), Bathampton Camp, Somerset (82 acres) and Tedbury, Somerset (72 acres).

The Marcher or Welsh border region stretches from the Severn to the North Wales coast and contains some 250 hillforts. The major group is in southern Shropshire and northern Herefordshire where multivallate sites account for more than half the total. Outstanding among them are Ivington Camp, Wapley Camp and Croft Ambrey in Herefordshire, Burfa Camp, Radnorshire, Fridd Faldwyn, Montgomeryshire, and Norton Camp, Bury Ditches, Caer Caradoc (Clun, Fig. 61), Bury Walls and Old Oswestry, in Shropshire. The latter has no less than seven banks and four or five ditches on its most vulnerable (western) side. There is another small group of multivallate sites in the southern part of the region, the most notable of which is Llanmelin Camp (Pl. 38) and Sudbrook Camp in Monmouthshire, and Symond's Yat and Spital Meend in Gloucestershire. There is also a small group to the north, situated on the Clwydian range in north-east Wales: Moel Hiraddug, Moel y Gaer (Bodfari), Pen-y-

cloddiau, Moel Arthur, Moel y Gaer (Llanbedr), Foel Fenlli, and Moel y Gaer (Rhosesmor). The Marcher region includes also many multiple-enclosure forts such as the Herefordshire Beacon and the Wrekin in Shropshire, Tredegar Camp, Monmouthshire, Coxall Knoll, Herefordshire, and Craigadwy Wynt, Denbighshire.

The last region in the Wessex tradition covers the Chilterns and the Pennines. The main feature of the Chiltern Hills is the distribution of sites along its north-west edge, although the most unusual site in the area, Dike Hills (114 acres, multivallate) is low-lying, in a bend of the Thames near Dorchester, Oxfordshire. Other multivallate sites are Bulstrode Park and Cholesbury in Buckinghamshire and the Aubreys and Ravensburgh Castle in Hertfordshire. The most notable sites in the south Pennines group (c. twenty sites) are Mam Tor, Derbyshire and Almondbury, Yorkshire.

The last two regions constitute the Western tradition of hillfort building. The south-west region (Cornwall, Devon and Somerset) contains about 300 hillforts, the most numerous of which are the small

38 Reconstruction drawing of the inturned entrance at Llanmelin Iron Age fort, Monmouthshire, by Alan Sorrell.

univallate forts, an acre or two in area and often circular in plan. Multivallate sites of the same size and shape are far less numerous, the most notable example being Chun Castle, Cornwall, a stone-built fort in the Land's End district. Outstanding among the coastal promontory sites are Rumps Point, Trevelgue Head (Newquay), Dodman Point, Black Head and Rame Head, all in Cornwall.

The most characteristic form of south-western multiple-enclosure site is the concentric fort: outstanding examples include Tregeare Rounds (Fig. 62), Killibury, Warbstow Bury and Castle-an-Dinas (St Columb) all in Cornwall, and Clovelly Dykes and Milber Down in Devon. The remaining sites have their additional enclosures in the form of annexes, i.e. alongside rather than concentric with the main enclosure. Castle Dore, Cornwall and Denbury Camp, Devon, are two prominent examples.

The last region, south and west Wales, contains some 450 sites. The northern part contains only a scatter of sites, mainly in Caernarvonshire, but these include most of the larger sites in the region, most of them

stone-built with remains of circular huts, such as Conway Mountain, Tre'r Ceiri, Garn Boduan, and Carn Fadrun in Caernarvonshire and Caer y Twr, above Holyhead, Anglesey. In the south, in Cardiganshire, Pembrokeshire, Carmarthenshire and Glamorganshire there are large numbers of small, often circular, univallate sites; there are smaller numbers of multivallate sites, often with the defences occupying two or three times the area of the space enclosed. There are concentric sites and annexe sites, and there are coastal promontory forts, particularly in the Gower peninsula and in Pembrokeshire (Pl. 39). All in all, the pattern of sites is very similar to that in south-west England and emphasises the differences between these two regions on the one hand (the Western tradition), and the five regions of the Wessex tradition on the other. Some of the outstanding sites in the area are Pen Dinas (Pl. 40) near Aberystwyth, Cardiganshire, Carn Ingli, Foel Trigan and Bosherston in Pembrokeshire, Gaer Fawr, Carmarthenshire and the Bulwarks and Summerhouses in Glamorganshire.

Hillforts in Scotland

The great concentration of hillforts in Scotland is below the Clyde/Forth line, with particular emphasis on the south-east in the counties adjacent to the English border. Included with the Scottish hillforts are those of Northumberland which form part of the same distribution pattern. The original number of forts must have been in the region of 1,500, i.e. very much the same sort of figure as for England and Wales. The hillforts involved are on the whole smaller, although no less interesting, than those in southern Britain. In their range of sizes they follow the Western rather than the Wessex tradition, and the same is broadly true of their layout.

There are some 150 hillforts in Dumfriesshire, many of them small circular or oval enclosures, an acre or two in area, with univallate (less frequently multivallate)

39 The Iron Age promontory fort at Linney Head, Pembrokeshire.

defences and simple entrances. Of the remaining sites Castle O'er and Birrenswark are perhaps the most interesting. Castle O'er (850 × 450 ft) about eight miles north-east of Lockerbie, has an inner enclosure (500 × 300 ft), a barbican-type entrance, and an outer line of defence forming a second enclosure. Birrenswark, about five miles north of Annan, is justly famous because of its associated Roman siege works. The 17-acre hillfort appears to have had two ramparts, now somewhat flattened, on the south-eastern side, and five entrances. The Roman structures consist of two temporary camps, immediately below the hill, presumably built when the hillfort was under siege.

North of Dumfries in eastern Lanarkshire and Peeblesshire is a group of well over 100 hillforts, with only a few exceptions quite small (c. 1 acre) in size. The univallate forts are usually circular or near-circular in plan with bank-and-ditch defences. An exception to this rule is Cademuir Hill, two and a half miles south-west of Peebles, which is defended by a 10-ft-thick stone rampart enclosing some 5½ acres. The multivallate forts include

Campswater, near Abington, Lanarkshire, where a small enclosure (200 × 100 ft) is defended by no less than four banks and ditches. Other multivallate forts worthy of note are Black Meldon, Henderland Hill, Ring Knowe, Northshield Rings and Kerrs Knowe, all in Peeblesshire. The multiple-enclosure sites include a number of the concentric type such as Cardrona, with two ramparts, 60–70 ft apart. The largest site in the county, White Meldon (9 acres), has four ramparts; the second largest site, Whiteside Rig, has one large enclosure (1,160 × 330 ft), with a small (c. 100 ft diameter) roughly circular enclosure at one end.

A dozen or so sites in Selkirk form part of a larger group in Roxburghshire. The best known site in the county is Torwoodlee, about two miles north-west of Galashiels, the most interesting feature of which is the later broch (see Chapter 9), placed just inside the western defences. The eighty or so sites in Roxburghshire include many roughly circular or oval sites, an acre or two in area, with either univallate or, less commonly, multivallate defences; some of the latter have three or four banks and ditches, as at Camp Tops and Kip Knowe, near Morebattle, and Little Trowpenny, near Ancrum. There are also a few multiple-enclosure sites such as Castle Hill, Ancrum, and Huntfold Hill, near Hownam. Hownam Law (22 acres) and Eildon Hill (39 acres, the largest in Scotland), both contain large numbers of hut remains, between 150 and 200, and nearly 300, respectively (Fig. 64). Woden Law, with four ramparts on the south and east, is distinguished by Roman siege works consisting of two banks and three ditches, in turn enclosed by other more widely spaced works.

Sites in Berwickshire (c. fifty in number) are mostly small and near-circular in plan with univallate or multivallate defences. There are also a few multiple-enclosure sites such as Cockburn Law (two annexes), and Shannonbank Hill (two concentric enclosures). The outstanding site in Northumberland is Yevering Bell, defended by a stone rampart enclosing some 13 acres, and the remains of 130 huts (Fig. 65). Other notable sites include Hambledon Hill, a three-enclosure site, and Harehaugh,

with multivallate defences (three banks and two ditches), superseding a univallate enclosure. Otherwise the majority of sites are small, roughly circular enclosures with univallate or multivallate defences.

In south-west Scotland sites are less numerous than in the south-east and are located almost entirely on or near the south-facing coasts of Wigtownshire and Kirkcudbrightshire and the west-facing coast of Ayrshire. The hundred or so sites (both univallate and multivallate) are mainly small and often circular in plan, except in promontory situations which are fairly common in the region. There are also a few multiple enclosure sites such as Dungarry and Stroanfreggan, in Kirkcudbrightshire.

The remaining Scottish forts are scattered up the east coast, from the Forth to John o'Groats. Many of them are of the simple, often circular type encountered elsewhere. There are, however, a number of sites of somewhat greater interest. The Chesters, near Drem, East Lothian, has complex defences and well contrived east and west entrances. Traprain Law (32 acres), in the same county, has yielded rich

40 The southern multivallate enclosure at Pen Dinas, Aberystwyth, Cardiganshire, viewed from the northern enclosure.

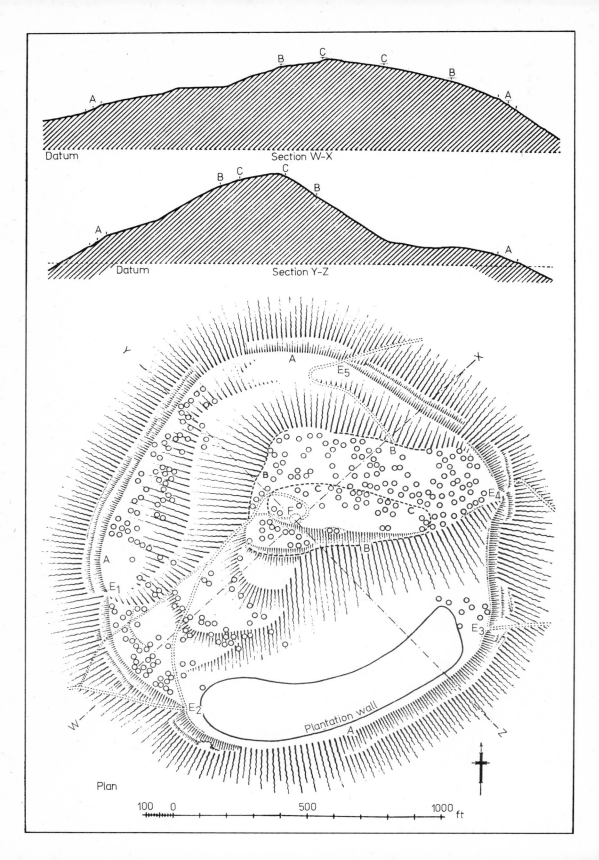

Section W-X

Datum

Section Y-Z

Datum

Plan

E5

E4

E3

E2

E1

Plantation wall

W

X

Y

Z

100   0   500   1000   ft

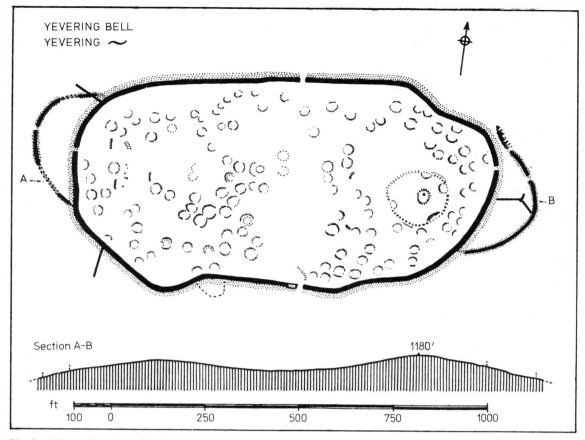

Fig. 65 Plan and section of the Iron Age fort at
Yevering Bell, Northumberland.

finds of metal tools, weapons and ornaments. In Fife, Clatchard Craig (two
enclosures) has, at one point, no less than
seven banks, while Norman's Law (four
enclosures) has stone ramparts 10–16 ft
thick. The two outstanding sites in Angus
are the Brown Caterhun (1,100 × 1,000 ft)
and the White Caterhun (1,500 × 850 ft),
both with complex systems of defences. In
Aberdeen the Barmekin of Echt has two
circular inner walls, three earth ramparts
and five entrances, only two of which
pierce the whole system. Beyond the Moray
Firth there is a scatter of sites in Caithness,
including Buaile Oscar (900 × 450 ft)
defended by a single stone wall.

Hillforts in Ireland

There are, in Ireland, very large numbers
of what are known as 'forts', possibly
between 30,000 and 40,000, but these
include many structures built as late as the
Norman Conquest (1066), and, in some
cases, later still. It is, therefore, impossible
to isolate the range of prehistoric forts.
What can be done is to note the existence
of types similar to those encountered
already on the assumption that they are
broadly similar in function and date.

There are a few hillforts of the contour,
semi-contour or plateau type in Ireland, up
to 20 acres in area and defended by a
single stone rampart or a bank and ditch.
These presumably are the Irish equivalent

Fig. 64 Plan and sections of the Iron Age fort on
Eildon Hill North, Roxburghshire.

of the English univallate forts of the Wessex tradition, and include such sites as Navan, Tara, Dun Ailline and Freestone Hill. At the latter, in Kilkenny, the excavation evidence suggested a date in the fourth century A.D., but at Navan, near Armagh, the finds were of the first century A.D., broadly in keeping with dates elsewhere.

Coastal promontory forts, some 200 in number, are situated mostly in the south and south-west. Their defences consist of one or more ramparts across the neck of the promontory, i.e. very much the same pattern as in south-west England and south-west Wales. It seems feasible to suggest that at least some of these Irish forts are broadly contemporary.

Most of the remaining Irish structures come under the heading of ring-forts. These include many small circular sites (100–200 ft in internal diameter) with either strong multivallate defences, or simpler univallate defences (a bank and ditch or a stone wall). Many of these must be simply Irish versions of the small univallate and multivallate forts which occur in south-west England, Wales and Scotland.

There are thus clear links with the hill-forts in other areas of the British Isles even if the extent of these links cannot as yet be stated in numerical terms.

Original structure

The simplest type of hillfort rampart was the *glacis* or sloping-fronted type, triangular in cross section, with a continuous slope (c. 35–40 degrees) from the bottom of its accompanying ditch to the rampart crest, and this slope or *glacis* (from a French military engineering term) formed the main obstacle to an attacker (Fig. 66A). In most cases its construction required nothing more than the material excavated from the ditch. In terms of both labour and materials the advantages of the type are obvious. Glacis ramparts are from 25 to 45 ft wide and from 7 to 12 ft high, with the rampart crest, in the larger examples,

25–30 ft (measured vertically) above the ditch bottom. Some form of breastwork, a low wall or a fence, behind which defenders could take cover, would seem a not unlikely addition. A considerable number of hill-forts were defended by such simple glacis ramparts. At Sudbrook, Monmouthshire, and Maiden Castle, Dorset, however, there is elaborate stone revetting supporting the backs of very large ramparts, enabling them to stand over 20 ft high above internal ground level and 30–50 ft high above the ditch bottom (Fig. 66B).

The alternative to the glacis rampart is the revetted type in which a vertical rather than a sloping front is presented to the attacker. The simplest type of revetted rampart is a wedge-shaped mass of earth with a vertical outer facing or revetment of timber or stone, carried up to form a breastwork for the defenders (Fig. 67 A, B). Such ramparts were 25–50 ft wide and up to 15 ft high at the front, tailing off to ground level at the rear. Stone revetments take the form of dry-stone walling (Pl. 41), while those of timber are supported by uprights (at intervals varying from 1 or 2 ft to 14 ft), the evidence for which consists of the post-holes or sockets in the old ground surface for the original timbers. The rampart material consists in most cases of the contents of the outer ditch, earth, chalk, gravel, sand, clay, etc. In a number of cases, however, particularly in stony regions, the rampart is composed entirely of stones, with no separately distinguishable revetment. Some such ramparts descend to the rear in a series of steps rather than a gradual slope (Fig. 67c). Another type is the composite rampart made up of a series of walls sandwiched together, each with its own (concealed) revetments.

A more elaborate version of the revetted type is the so-called box rampart in which there are both front and back revetments, 7–14 ft apart, in stone or timber, giving the structure a box-like cross-section (Fig. 67D) At the back there is often a wedge-shaped ramp or buttress of earth which partly masks the revetment. The timber-revetted

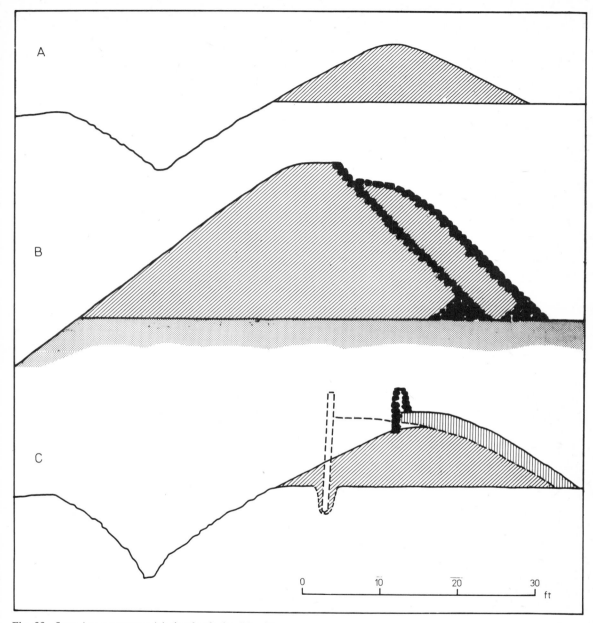

Fig. 66   Iron Age ramparts: (a) simple glacis; (b) with back revetment; (c) hybrid glacis/revetted rampart.

box rampart is often regarded as the classic type of hillfort defence but, in fact, only a dozen or so examples are known in Britain. In some cases there is a combina-tion of stones and timber, the spaces between the wooden uprights being revetted with panels of dry-stone walling.

Timber-laced ramparts represent a rather special type of rampart construction. As used here the term refers specifically to

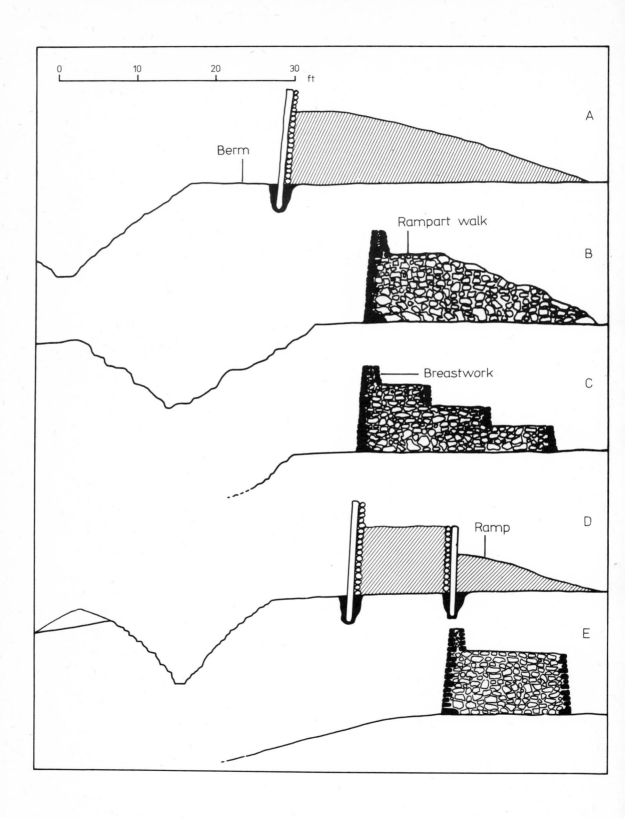

Berm

Rampart walk

Breastwork

Ramp

A

B

C

D

E

0   10   20   30   ft

41 The stone revetment of the wedge-shaped rampart at Carl Wark Iron Age fort, Yorkshire.

stone-built ramparts through which timbers have been 'laced' for strengthening purposes. The technique reached its peak in Gaul during the Roman conquest (58–50 B.C.) where it was described by Julius Caesar under the name *murus Gallicus* (Gallic wall). However, with one possible exception, the British examples do not qualify as true Gallic walls and the term timber-laced is used instead. They appear, in fact, to be an undeveloped, or perhaps a debased, form of the technique as seen in Gaul. Closely associated with timber-laced ramparts is the problem of vitrified forts, in which the stones forming the rampart have fused together as a result of intense heat. Some, perhaps all, of these were originally timber-laced forts in which the timbers had been set alight, the gaps left as they burned away forming flues which would increase the intensity of the fire, causing the stones around them to vitrify and fuse. The majority of timber-laced/vitrified forts are in Scotland, with the emphasis on the east coast region, but there is a scatter of sites in England and Wales as well.

As excavated, many hillfort ditches are 20–30 ft wide and 8–12 ft deep, with a splayed-out V-shape, but both shape and

Fig. 67 Iron Age ramparts: (a) timber-revetted, wedge-shaped; (b) stone-revetted, wedge-shaped; (c) stepped rampart; (d) timber-revetted box rampart; (e) stone-revetted box rampart.

width are probably the result of the erosion of the shoulders. Originally they were almost certainly much narrower, probably only a little wider than they were deep. Rock-cut ditches are inevitably much less regular, but are also less subject to erosion and therefore probably closer to their original shape. The space between the ditch and the front of a revetted rampart (c. 6–15 ft wide) is known as the berm, and appears to have been intended to prevent the undermining of the rampart by erosion of the ditch. Also associated with the ditch in some cases is a bank, usually small, at the head of its outer slope (the counter-scarp), known as the counterscarp bank (10–12 ft wide and 2–3 ft high in most cases).

Ramparts other than the main rampart (i.e. outer ramparts) were in most cases of the glacis type, although not universally so. In stony regions, where no ditches were involved, even outer ramparts were usually of the revetted type.

One rather rare but none the less interesting feature is the *chevaux-de-frise*, an area of closely set stones end-on in the ground which would have acted as a very serious obstacle to anyone trying to rush the more conventional bank-and-ditch defences.

All hillforts are defended by systems made up of one or more of the features just described. The simplest system consists of a rampart by itself. Since a glacis rampart needs a ditch, ramparts standing alone must be of the revetted types, and in fact all the known examples have stone revetments (Fig. 67E). Many of the small hillforts in the highland zone, particularly in Scotland, are defended in this way. Much more frequently, however, the rampart is accompanied by an outer, V-shaped ditch (with or without a counterscarp bank) in which case the rampart can be either glacis or revetted. Between them rampart-alone and rampart-and-ditch systems account for the defences of about two-thirds of all hillforts, that is, all of the univallate forts mentioned earlier, probably numbering over two thousand in all.

The simplest type of multivallate system consists of two (revetted) ramparts with no other features. However, by far the commonest type involves two banks, two ditches and, in some cases, a counterscarp bank. Systems with three, four or even more ramparts also occur, although less frequently than those with only two. Because nearly all multivallate systems are the result of additions to original univallate systems, the arrangements are not always as regular as implied above. For instance, the system may incorporate more than one counterscarp bank, or more than one berm; in other cases the relative positions of bank and ditch may be reversed. Quite clearly the more numerous the features the more varied the possible arrangements.

The defences of multiple-enclosure sites are, in effect, a series of separate systems, according to the number of enclosures, each system of which can be either univallate or multivallate.

The broad principles of entrance design can be gleaned from ground examination. The simplest and commonest type of hillfort entrance is the simple gap (Fig. 62), a straight cut through whatever features are involved in the system: a bank alone, a bank and ditch, or a complete multivallate system. In the latter case the result is a long narrow passage, its length equal to the width of the system. The same result is,

however, achieved in other ways as well. One of these is the gradual thickening of the rampart on either side of the entrance so that the entrance passage is correspondingly lengthened. The more usual way, however, is to turn the ramparts inwards so that they formed a passage (inturned entrances). These can vary from quite short inturns, little more than thickened ends, to inturns defining passages over 100 ft long (Fig. 61). Occasionally inturns are placed obliquely rather than at right angles to the rampart, and in a few cases they are curved. Much more rarely entrance passages are produced by out-turned ramparts or by a combined inturn/out-turn arrangement.

Entrances based on the overlapping principle are another means of producing a narrow entrance passage, in this case parallel to the ramparts. The overlapping arrangements at Hod Hill and Hambledon Hill, Dorset, are outstanding examples contrived in multivallate defences. Even more elaborate is the western entrance at Bury Ditches, Shropshire. The defences on the eastern side of the roadway (bank, ditch and counterscarp bank) are overlapped for about 300 ft by those on the west, consisting of three banks and two ditches.

Outworks is the term used to describe those entrance features which project beyond the main line of the defences. The simplest form of outwork is the single hornwork, either straight or curving, on one side of the entrance, which drastically narrows the angle from which it can be approached (Fig. 61). Twin hornworks, one on each side, form a double or barbican-type entrance and this is the governing principle of most of the remaining examples. There is an excellent example of curving, twin hornworks at Beacon Hill, Hampshire, and a more elaborate version at Danebury in the same county. The barbican principle is best seen in sites such as Badbury Rings, Dorset, and Sidbury and Bratton Castle in Wiltshire, where the entrances are separated by a rectangular box-like enclosure, through which attackers would have to pass to reach the inner gate if they overthrew the outer. Other outworks are semicircular in plan, as at Yarnbury, Wiltshire, and others, again triangular, as at Blackbury Castle, Devon, and an earlier phase of the eastern entrance at Maiden Castle, Dorset.

The bulk of the excavation evidence bearing an original structure relates to two types of entrance, the simple gap and the inturned variety. In the simplest type of entrance in a revetted rampart the revetment is simply carried around the ends of the rampart to form a vertical-sided passage 8–10 ft wide, equal in length to the thickness of the rampart (Fig. 68A). Quite

clearly in a glacis rampart the same procedure cannot be followed, and a special end-revetment has to be provided to make the rampart ends vertical so that timber gates can be inserted (Fig. 68B). In both cases the length of the entrance passage equals, more or less, the thickness of the rampart. One of the simplest ways of lengthening the passage is to extend the end-revetments as free-standing walls, either inwards or outwards, so that approach to the gates is constricted over a much greater distance (Fig. 68A). A further development is to turn the whole rampart inwards as described already so that the extended revetments are reinforced by the solid bulk of a rampart.

Excavation has also produced evidence for other entrance features such as gates,

Fig. 68   Iron Age fort entrances: A, revetted ramparts; B, glacis ramparts.

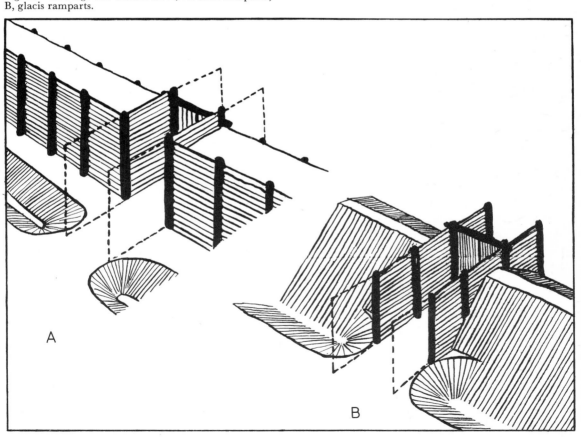

A

B

guard chambers and bridges. The gates, of timber, have not, in fact, survived. What have been uncovered are post-holes for the uprights on which the gates were hung. The gates seem to have been of the double or two-leaved variety, the maximum width for each leaf being about 7 ft, giving a gateway 14 ft wide in all. In some cases there was a third centre post against which the gates closed. Many entrances were, of course, much narrower than this. The gates must have been in the region of 8–12 ft high to be effective barriers and, although there is no evidence as to their construction, it seems highly probable that they were of the ledge-and-brace variety, i.e. with three horizontal and two diagonal timbers on the inside and vertical timbers, nailed on to them, at the front. Even the smallest of such gates must have been fairly heavy and it seems unlikely that they were hinged in the manner of modern gates. Certainly no iron work has ever been found indicating the use of hinges. It seems much more likely that a pivot system was used, the horizontal and diagonal timbers being jointed into an upright post which pivoted in sockets at the top and bottom. In order to provide room for the sockets, and for the pivot posts, the gateposts would need to be cut away down much of their length, and this may explain why such apparently massive timbers were often used for gateposts. Such a system would mean that the whole gate construction could be carried out in timber, although there is some evidence that occasionally iron ferrules or rings were in use to take the wear of regular opening and shutting.

There is clear evidence from a dozen or more sites that guard chambers, usually in pairs, were placed just inside the gates in the thickness of inturned ramparts. Such chambers were normally rectangular in shape (c. 15 × 10 ft), and were presumably open at the front to the entrance roadway. There is evidence from a number of sites of rough paving or cobbling for the road surface in the entrance area and this was presumably to facilitate the movement of traffic, both pedestrian and wheeled.

One other feature for which there is evidence in a number of sites is a bridge across the entrance roadway, either directly above the gate or some little way in front of it. This would link the rampart walks on either side of the entrance and provide an additional, and very advantageous, position for defenders to deal with hostile visitors trying to fight their way into the fort.

There remain two topics to be dealt with, function and chronology. One of the functions traditionally attributed to hillforts is that of temporary refuges in time of danger, and this is a likely interpretation, at least for some hillforts. However, it cannot be accepted as the sole function of the thousands of sites in England, Wales, Scotland and Ireland. Maiden Castle, for example, whatever it had been originally, was, in its final phase, quite certainly a hilltop town, a defended urban and market centre serving the needs of the surrounding countryside. Almost certainly other large hillforts performed the same function, and these may have grown out of the practice of living in defended villages, and this is another likely function of hillforts, that of walled villages. In support of this, there are simple univallate forts which contain groups of from ten to forty huts which presumably represent the permanent living quarters of some of the population. In time, such establishments could have developed to become important urban centres of Maiden Castle type, and this indeed appears to have happened in about twenty sites in southern England in the decades before the Roman conquest.

However, this is certainly not the function of the small, simple, circular sites in south-west England, Wales, Scotland and Ireland. Given the needs of a single farm in terms of farmyard space, many such sites would have served the needs of only a single family and the function of defended or fortified farmsteads is one which must be included in any survey of probable hillfort functions. The multiple-enclosure sites in the same areas may represent some more specialised kind of farming establishment, with more emphasis on livestock than on mixed farming, the different enclosures being to segregate livestock from living areas or, in more complex sites, different kinds of livestock from each other.

Finally, some very large hillforts (50–100 acres) are adjacent to upland pastures areas and it is feasible to suggest that they were, in fact, cattle enclosures. Since a great deal of wealth would have been bound up in livestock, measures against cattle raiding in the form of an enclosure would have seemed a reasonable precaution.

This chapter can be concluded with a brief outline of what, on present evidence, appear to have been the main events in the development of hillforts and their probable dates. As indicated earlier, a number of carbon-14 dates make it impossible to retain the ABC chronology, and a new (long) chronology must be envisaged to embrace all the evidence now available.

The evidence for a long chronology does not depend solely on carbon-14 dates. It has always been conceded that there was a surviving native Late Bronze Age element (perhaps a considerable one) in the early Iron Age cultures in southern Britain, the evidence for which was the similarity in certain artefacts, such as pottery, bronze pins, weaving combs, etc. Some of these were products of the Deverel-Rimbury culture, and while this was still regarded as Late Bronze Age there were no problems. However, the removal of the Deverel-Rimbury culture to the Middle Bronze Age (c. 1200–1000 B.C.) at once opened up a gap which needed to be narrowed in some way. The contexts in which these artefacts appeared were frequently hillforts and the answer must be that hillforts are earlier than visualised hitherto and are not, in fact, Iron Age at all, but Late Bronze Age. There is often, in fact, very little hard evidence that hillforts are Iron Age. The pottery found is called Iron Age simply because it appears in a hillfort; the same type of pottery found elsewhere is then used as evidence for an Iron Age date, but is not, in fact, evidence at all, but a long-held presumption. If the chronological link with the Deverel-Rimbury culture is acknowledged, as it must be, then the beginnings of hillforts need to be placed considerably earlier than the traditional (short chronology) date, and earlier than the Iron Age as a whole. Hillforts may be as early as 1000 B.C., but what is normally envisaged is a late or second Deverel-Rimbury period c. 1000–850 B.C., and it is after this that hillforts are deemed to begin, some 500 years earlier than allowed in the short chronology.

It has been traditional to see the large numbers of hillforts as evidence of a fairly concentrated outburst of activity by a relatively large population. However, large numbers are always explicable in another way, as the work of a smaller population over a much longer period of time, and this, in effect, is what was implied above. The long duration of the hillfort period, however, means that not all hillforts were necessarily in use together. Some forts may have been built, used and abandoned long before others were built, so that perhaps only a matter of hundreds out of the 1,400 or so in England and Wales were in use at any one time. It may be that over several centuries the population of an area successively built and abandoned several hillforts, or perhaps for long periods had no hillforts at all.

The suggestion that hillforts began in the Late Bronze Age does not mean that the Iron Age dating is in any way abandoned. Probably the majority of hillforts still belong to the Iron Age period. What is now widely accepted is that they began to be built at the date suggested (850 B.C.) and went on being built until the Roman conquest of A.D. 43, the advent of iron not being of any particular significance in their development.

The next major event in the hillfort story is the reconstruction or strengthening of many forts in the multivallate style. This again has been moved to an earlier date

(c. 500 B.C.) as a result of certain carbon-14 dates and some recent excavation evidence. Whether the reconstruction was a single event, within a matter of a few years, or a gradual process, spread over decades and possibly centuries, is a matter for speculation, but the writer is inclined to the latter view. If they were all reconstructed around 500 B.C. it is difficult to see how they could have lasted throughout the Iron Age until the next structural phase, c. 100 B.C., a matter of some four centuries, unless they went entirely out of use for the greater part of that period.

By c. 100 B.C. the long and short chronologies come more or less in step with each other. At this stage a number of hillforts (about twenty in Wessex and possibly a similar number elsewhere) were greatly strengthened and transformed into what has been designated the Maiden Castle type, with elaborate entrances and probably a large resident population. These forts were certainly still in use when the Romans arrived and the Roman general Vespasian (later Emperor) records that he captured twenty *oppida* (i.e. hill-forts) in his campaign in southern England. Thus for the hillforts of the Wessex tradi-tion the broad dating pattern is as follows: c. 850 B.C. the beginnings of hillforts, univallate style; c. 500 B.C., the beginnings of the practice of multivallation; c. 100 B.C. the development of the large, Maiden Castle-type forts.

The same sort of chronology must embrace hillforts in the Western tradition. Dates may need to be reduced a little, perhaps to c. 700 B.C. for the earliest forts, but all hillforts in southern Britain must form part of the same broad pattern of events, and happenings and developments in one area are likely to have been very quickly reflected in others. If the long chronology is valid, then it is probably valid for all regions, and certainly provides a more feasible working hypothesis than the current ABC system.

9 Fortifications of the Far North

Iron Age forts of the type described in Chapter 8 are rare, although not entirely absent, in northern and western Scotland. In their place we found two related types of stone-built fortifications known as *duns* and *brochs*. Broadly speaking duns are found in western regions from Wigtownshire in south-west Scotland to the northern end of the Outer Hebrides, with a scatter beyond on the northern mainland, while brochs occur thickly in the Orkneys, Shetlands and Caithness, with a widespread scatter to the south-west among the duns and even to the south among the conventional hillforts. Thus in broad terms the three types of Iron Age fortification occupy three different parts of Scotland: hillforts in the east and south-east; duns in the west and south-west; and brochs in the north, including the Orkneys and Shetlands.

Even in the Iron Age period dates for events in Scotland are difficult to arrive at. Although the bulk of Iron Age sites in the country are the three basic types of fortification just described, there are a few open settlements which indicate that in the earliest part of the Iron Age life was more or less peaceful. These are settlements such as Clickhimin, Jarlshof and Calf of Eday described in Chapter 2, and probably representative of many more yet to be discovered. Allowing that the main Iron Age migration to southern Britain took place c. 500 B.C., the date of these early

Iron Age settlements in the far north can be put somewhere between this date and one date possibly as late as 300 B.C. This presumably peaceful period was followed by one in which it can be safely assumed that all three types of fortification arrived in Scotland, although not necessarily all at the same time. However, it seems fairly certain that at some point in the period all were in existence together, the one generating the other. In broad terms the conventional hillforts of southern and eastern Scotland can be seen as a northward extension of the pattern of similar forts in southern Britain. The duns and brochs of western and northern Scotland are probably best regarded as part of a larger pattern of small stone-built fortifications on either side of the Irish Sea, from Cornwall northwards. Their great numbers in Scotland may have developed in response to a threat from the builders of the hillforts on the southern mainland of Scotland, the Caledonii, who, it will be seen below, later turned their aggressive energies against the Romans. If this is so, then the development of duns could have begun shortly after the initial date of hillforts, perhaps, c. 200–100 B.C. The date of the brochs may have been broadly similar, so that for the last couple of centuries before the Roman penetration of Scotland all three types of fortification were in use more or less at the same time.

Duns

A dun is a small, stone-built, strongly defended fort, often circular or near circular in plan, and up to about 60 ft in internal diameter. The main defensive wall is 10–15 ft thick with a solid rubble core and well built, often neatly coursed inner and outer faces, the latter usually with a noticeable batter (Fig. 67E). In a number of cases the walls appear to have been timber-laced, a technique mentioned earlier in connection with certain hillforts, particularly a group in eastern Scotland. Particular attention was paid to the entrance passage which narrowed in angular fashion to provide door checks for the door which was secured by a bar housed in slots on either side. Access to the top of the rampart was by means of a staircase in the thickness of the wall or by steps projecting from the inner face.

These are the general characteristics of duns. The same characteristics appear in a number of small hillforts and there is, in fact, no hard and fast dividing line between the two. A dun appears to be a specialised form of hillfort, its main distinguishing feature being its small size, usually deemed to be the accommodation for a single family or family group. The conventional hillfort, on the other hand, is usually interpreted as the defensive accommodation for a whole community, large or small, hence the variation in size. Those sites intermediate in size (60–120 ft in internal diameter) are either special duns, perhaps for double or special family groups, or hillforts which have been built on dun principles, unless these characteristics had already developed in hillforts before the dun type (i.e. the very small fort) was evolved.

It is interesting to note that the dominant type of hillfort in western regions of England and Wales is also very small, and often circular in plan, as compared with hillforts to the east. Although not quite so small as duns (they are usually between 100 and 200 ft in diameter) they may well be related to them and may represent in south-west England and Wales what the duns represent in western Scotland. The differences in size may reflect differences in basic economy, arising out of the different geographical environments. Both may well have been intended as the defensive accommodation for a single family group.

The main concentration of duns is on the islands and coastal regions of western Scotland from the southern end of Kintyre to the northern end of Skye; in this region are about 250 out of the 350 known duns. There are another fifteen or so in a group to the south, in Wigtownshire, and another twenty or so thinly scattered through the islands of the Outer Hebrides. Apart from a few on the northern and western coasts of Sutherland the remainder (about thirty or so sites) are in a fairly compact group in Perthshire, midway between the eastern and western coasts, and somewhat isolated from the main distribution.

The sixty or so duns in the Mull of Kintyre have all been surveyed fairly recently (1971) and include a range of examples typical of the group as a whole. A well-preserved example stands on a rocky bluff near the mouth of Borgadel Water. It is almost a true circle in plan, with an overall diameter of 66 ft and an internal diameter of 42 ft, i.e. with walls 12 ft thick, which are preserved up to 6 ft high. The outer face of the wall has a pronounced batter. The entrance is on the western side. It is 4 ft 3 in. wide at the inner end. About half way along it narrows to about 3 ft 6 in. providing checks against which the door closed. Many other duns are similar in size and in many cases vary only slightly from the circular plan. Greater variation is usually the result of particular situations. In promontory situations, as with hillforts, part of the circuit is occupied by natural features, with only an arc or straight stretch of man-made defences. In addition to promontories, a number of sites are located on 'stacks', column-like masses of rock with flat tops with the dun walls following the edge. Dun Fhinn is an excellent example. It is a near rectangle in plan (the shape of the stack), about 45 × 20 ft internally (i.e. smaller than average). Because of the strong situation the surrounding wall is thinner than usual, about 4 ft thick for most of the circuit, and stronger only at the entrance where it is about 9 ft thick. The entrance is of the usual T-shaped plan, about 8 ft wide internally, about 5 ft externally. A number of post-holes, about 4 ft out from the walls, are interpreted as remains of timber buildings built against the inner face of the dun wall, and this point will be returned to later when the relationship of duns and brochs is being discussed.

Two other duns illustrate other aspects of these structures. Dun Kildalloig conformed to the near-circular plan (c. 45 ft internal diameter) with a surrounding wall between 13 and 16 ft in thickness. It has, rather unusually, two entrances, one of which (the eastern) has a guard chamber in the thickness of the wall, opening on to the north side of the entrance passage. There were indications of at least three intra-mural chambers opening on to the central area. The only one of which the dimensions could be established was rectangular (c. 11 × 7 ft) and entered by a narrow passage; it had a paved floor and a hearth. A series of post-holes again suggested the former existence of timber structures against the wall. At Kildonan Bay dun an opening just north of the entrance led to twin staircases in the thickness of the wall which gave access to the top of the dun rampart. A noticeable feature of the wall was an internal revetment, presumably to give greater stability. South of the entrance the internal revetment is replaced by a narrow gallery which divides the wall into two separate parts.

The gallery just described is a fairly simple affair, at ground-floor level. It need not, and probably did not, imply anything other than the normal type of dun rampart. There are, however, more elaborate galleries above ground level in a number of duns (galleried duns), which have been interpreted recently as a link between duns and the second, more elaborate type of fortification to be dealt with here, brochs. Associated with the galleries built in the stone part of the dun are (it is suggested) ranges of timber buildings built against the inside of the dun wall. Post-holes which may have supported such internal ranges were noted in one or two duns above. Much of the suggested evidence derives from the extensive excavations (1953–7) at Clickhimin in the Shetlands (referred to already, in Chapter 2, in terms of its earlier structures), and Clickhimin will be described next.

The Iron Age settlement at Clickhimin described earlier (Chapter 2) was followed by an Iron Age fortification which belongs to the category, mentioned earlier, intermediate in size between duns and conventional hillforts (Fig. 69). It had a dun-type wall, 10–12 ft thick surrounding a roughly pear-shaped area 136 × 125 ft, i.e. large by dun standards but still small by hillfort standards. However, the precise size of the structure is less important than the relationship between the rampart and the domestic structures behind it. Remains of timber structures have been noted already in a number of duns and there is no reason why similar structures should not have existed in both duns and hillforts, both large and small, although probably not to any great extent in the larger forts. However, it is at Clickhimin that the evidence of the close interrelationship between rampart and domestic structure is clearest, and it is this evidence which is deemed to provide the link between duns and brochs.

The internal structures were built against the inner face of the rampart, with the ceiling of the ground-floor rooms level with the rampart walk, which was 6–8 ft above the ground level inside the fort. Their front walls, indicated by post-holes and stone pillars, were 17–18 ft in from the rampart, and extended lengthwise for some 85 ft on the north-east side and for 75 ft on the south-west. For single-storey structures the height of the ordinary dun-

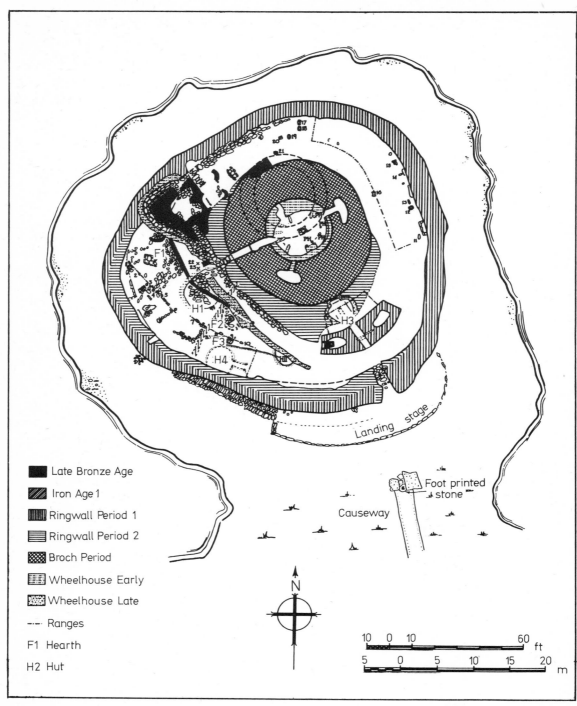

Late Bronze Age

Iron Age 1

Ringwall Period 1

Ringwall Period 2

Broch Period

Wheelhouse Early

Wheelhouse Late

-·- **Ranges**

F1 **Hearth**

H2 **Hut**

Landing stage

Foot printed stone

Causeway

N

10 0 10   60 ft

5   0   5   10   15   20 m

Fig. 69 Plan of the Iron Age fort and broch at Clickhimin, Shetlands.

type rampart is perfectly adequate. For two-storey buildings, however, some addition needs to be made to the rampart to provide a solid surface against which the internal structure can be built. This takes the form of a wall (known as a casement wall) built on the inner edge of the rampart walk and extending upwards to a height sufficient to provide headroom in the internal structures built against it. Door-

Fig. 70   Drawn reconstruction of the Iron Age fort and blockhouse at Clickhimin, Shetlands.

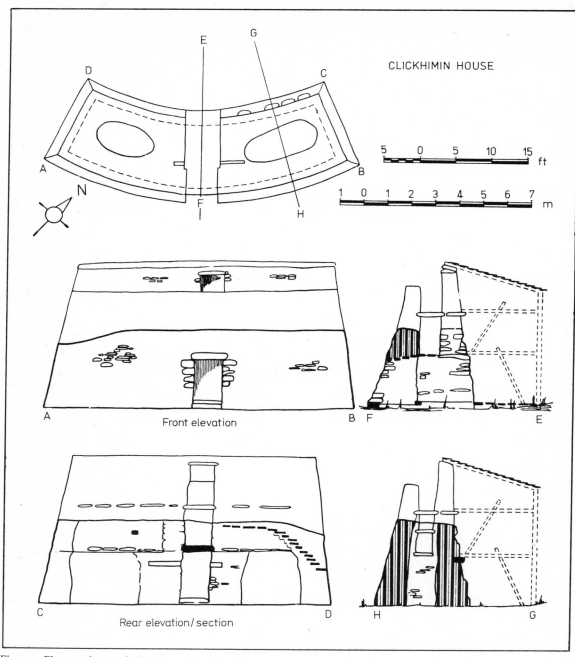

CLICKHIMIN HOUSE

Front elevation

Rear elevation/section

Fig. 71   Plan, sections and elevations of the blockhouse
at Clickhimin, Shetlands.

ways through the casement wall provide access from the upper rooms directly on to the rampart walk. Such upper rooms were probably living quarters, with the lower rooms, opening directly on to the internal space, presumably for the accommodation of livestock and for general agricultural purposes.

One- and two-storey accommodation built against the inner face of the wall in the Clickhimin fashion was probably the rule in many if not most duns (Fig. 70). However, in a limited number of cases there is evidence of even more elaborate internal accommodation, involving a third storey, built against a correspondingly higher casement wall, with the rampart walk now carried above a gallery (hence galleried duns), which provided communication, at first-floor level, between the internal rooms and between them and the rampart walk above by means of a staircase. Although the main encircling wall at Clickhimin is of the simpler type, there is evidence of galleried construction in a somewhat unusual defensive feature known as the blockhouse (Figs. 69, 71). Originally this appears to have been intended to form an integral part of the enclosing wall, acting as both an entrance and an elaborate, three-storey domestic structure. However,

for reasons which can only be guessed at, the enclosing wall was extended, leaving the blockhouse some 10 ft inside the entrance as a free-standing building (Pl. 42). The blockhouse is a curving structure some 42 ft long and, at its widest point, some 14 ft wide. However, it is its elevation which is of the greatest significance in the present context. As with the enclosing wall, a range of timber structures was built against its back wall. These rose to a height of three storeys and were supported by a high casement wall, in front of which was a covered gallery with the rampart walk above. It is structures of this type, found mainly in duns (the galleried duns) which are deemed to provide the prototypes of brochs, although this view is not universally accepted.

Before considering the matter of galleried duns and brochs any further the unusual feature just described at Clickhimin, the blockhouse, calls for some further comment. A few other examples are known. There is a similar blockhouse in a small fort (c. 70 ft in diameter internally) on an island in the Loch of Huxter, on Whalsay, Shetlands. In this case it forms an integral part of the enclosure wall of the fort (c. 5 ft thick), as the Clickhimin blockhouse is presumed to have been originally intended to do. The blockhouse is 41 × 11 ft, and similar in plan to the Clickhimin structure. The

42   The broch and blockhouse at Clickhimin, Shetlands.

blockhouse at the Ness of Burgi near Jarlshof is on a larger scale, over 74 × 21 ft, although its layout is on the same lines as the others. Like Clickhimin it is a free-standing structure, although not for the same reasons. It is in a promontory position with two ditches separated by an outer rampart in front of it. The blockhouse itself forms the entire final line of defence, the rest of the promontory being defended by natural features. There is another, smaller, possible example of a blockhouse on a small island in the Loch of Brindister, south of Clickhimin. These are the only examples of blockhouses known at present, but it is unlikely that they are the only ones built. No doubt future excavation will throw up further examples of the type.

Two of the blockhouses just mentioned, Huxter and Ness of Burgi, appear to have been galleried in the same way as Click-himin, i.e. they appear to have had three-storeyed timber structures against the inner (casement) face of the rampart wall. The height of the casement wall necessary to support such structures is estimated at 18–20 ft and casement walls of this height are recorded in the galleried duns of Dun Ban and Dun Bharabhat in the Hebrides, and these almost certainly involved three-storey timber structures inside. More specific evidence is recorded at Dun Grugaig in Glen Elg, Inverness, where there is a scarcement or ledge to support the second floor, 14 ft up on the casement wall. Allowing for about 6 ft for headroom and 2 ft for the slope of the roof the original casement wall must have been in the region of 22 ft high. How numerous such structures were is difficult to say. Dry-stone buildings are not normally preserved to any great height and in the absence of the upper portions it is difficult to make any statement about the original height of the internal timber structures. Nevertheless, in spite of the relatively smaller number of examples quoted, it is quite clear that some duns did develop to, or were built from the start in, the galleried style, supporting three-storey internal structures.

Brochs

This would appear to represent the maximum development of the dun as such. However, it is suggested, by J. R. C. Hamilton, excavator of Clickhimin, that duns of this stage of development gave rise to the next class of fortification to be dealt with here, the broch (Fig. 72). Brochs and duns, and particularly galleried duns, certainly have many features in common, although this does not prove that one was derived from the other. They could have developed in parallel from some source common to both. Alternatively, the relatively small number of galleried duns could be an attempt to transform some existing duns under the influence of brochs.

A broch is a circular tower some 40–50 ft in overall diameter, rising to a similar height (40–50 ft). The walls are 12–15 ft thick and the interior space 20–25 ft in diameter (Pls. 43, 44). In plan this is simply a compact version of the dun in which the circular plan has been adopted as standard. The entrance follows the same pattern with door checks and sockets for a door bar. It is in the elevation that the main difference between galleried duns and brochs emerges. In fact, up to a height of 20–22 ft (i.e. the roof level of the third storey) the two follow very much the same pattern. As in the galleried duns so in the brochs there are scarcements or ledges indicating two floors above the ground level, and post-holes in the interior indicating the front of the timber range. It is above this level that the fundamental difference between the two is to be found. In broch towers the inner casement wall is carried up for another 20 or 30 ft and is accompanied by an outer casement, forming a double wall with a space in which there was a staircase which wound up to the top of the tower, where there was presumably a platform or rampart walk from which defenders could conduct opera-tions against attackers (Pl. 45). Inevitably the uppermost portions have not been preserved and we cannot be certain of the

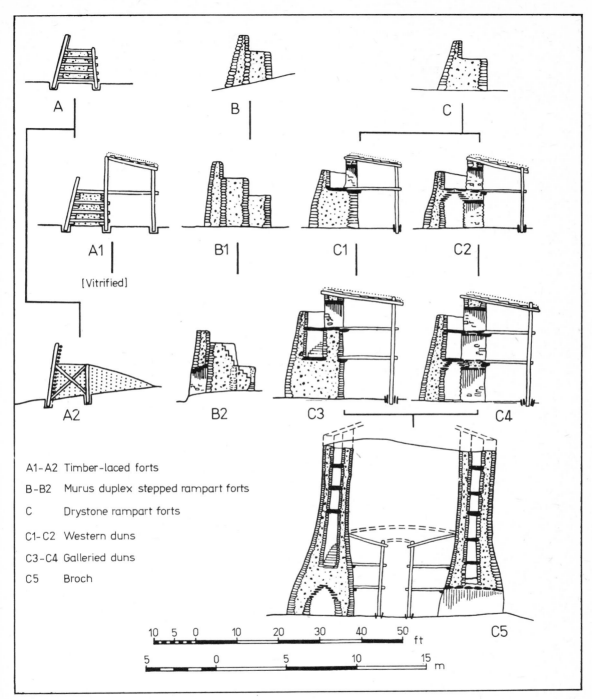

A   B   C

A1

[Vitrified]

B1   C1   C2

A2   B2   C3   C4

A1–A2   Timber-laced forts

B–B2   Murus duplex stepped rampart forts

C   Drystone rampart forts

C1–C2   Western duns

C3–C4   Galleried duns

C5   Broch

| 10 | 5 | 0 | 10 | 20 | 30 | 40 | 50 | ft |

| 5 | | 0 | | 5 | | 10 | | 15 | m |

C5

Fig. 72   Suggested structural relationship between Iron
Age forts, duns and brochs.

43 Reconstruction view of Clickhimin, Shetlands, during the broch period, by Alan Sorrell.

44 General view of the Broch of Mousa, Shetlands.

precise arrangements at the top, but the
staircases make it certain that access to the
top was important; presumably the staircase led on to a rampart walk with a
breastwork at the front, in much the same
way, and of much the same dimensions, as
the ordinary dun. In fact, only a few
brochs have been preserved to a height of
30 or 40 ft and it is not certain that all
brochs were originally of the height
suggested earlier, c. 50 ft. This could be a
maximum height in a range varying
between perhaps 30 and 50 ft. On the other
hand the remarkable uniformity of broch
plans may indicate an equal uniformity in
height.

About 500 brochs are known to exist
within a fairly limited area of Scotland.
The greatest concentrations are in the
Orkney and Shetland Islands and in
Caithness on the northernmost mainland.

In this very compact area are found well
over half of all the recorded brochs, with
around a hundred each in Orkney and
Shetland. The remainder are more widely
scattered, mostly in the western regions of
Scotland, although they occur also far to
the south in the Lowland area, albeit very
widely scattered in small numbers.

Before describing some of the better preserved and well-excavated brochs, some
more general features can be dealt with.
The entrances, of the type described earlier,
are often accompanied by guard chambers,
one or two, which have doorways opening
on to the entrance passage just behind the
door checks. These chambers are contrived
in the thickness of the broch wall and vary
in shape from round, through oval and
sub-rectangular, to some which are angular
in plan. Also in the thickness of the wall at
ground level are galleries (i.e. corridor-like
spaces between the inner and outer case-

45   The Broch of Mousa, Shetlands, interior view.

ments) and separate mural chambers entered from the central space. Basal galleries are not, in fact, very common, being found mostly in the Hebridian region —and even there, not in overwhelming numbers. A number of brochs with basal galleries seem to have collapsed fairly quickly and it may be that the type was structurally weak and quickly abandoned, hence the reason why it is comparatively rare, particularly in the Orkneys, Shetlands and the northern mainland. Mural chambers, contrived in the thickness of the wall, are much commoner and geographically much more widespread. They are circular, oval or elongated oval in shape, 5–7 ft wide and 15–20 ft or more long. The roof is usually corbelled in beehive fashion, i.e. it consists of courses stepped out from each wall until they meet at the apex. Because it is so well preserved,

and so well known, the three mural cells at the Broch of Mousa in Shetland tend to be regarded as the normal pattern, but, in fact, brochs with more than two cells are comparatively rare. From those brochs which have yielded evidence it emerges that about half of all brochs had only a single mural cell. The next commonest arrangement involves two cells and this accounts for another 30 per cent of the total. The remaining brochs have three, four, and in one case only, five mural chambers. From one of the mural chambers, usually to the left of the entrance, rose the staircase which circled upwards, spiral fashion, between the inner and outer casement walls. In a small number of cases there were two staircases. Staircases mostly start at ground-floor level but in half a dozen or so cases, including the Broch of Mousa, they start at first-floor level, i.e. from the level of the first floor of the internal timber range which, probably, had a separate timber stair or ladder from the ground floor. The inner and outer walls of the tower are linked together by bonding slabs which form the floors of a series of superimposed galleries. At Mousa the space between the inner and outer walls seems to have continued to the top of the tower. At other brochs, however, the walls seem to have converged to form a single wall near the top. Presumably the staircase was carried through an ascending passage in the solid wall rather than through an open gallery.

The broch at Clickhimin forms part of the sequence described earlier in Chapter 2. It succeeded the Iron Age fort and preceded the Wheelhouse period (Fig. 69). The Clickhimin tower was 65 ft in overall diameter with walls 17½ ft thick at the base, enclosing a central court 30 ft in diameter. The entrance passage (2 ft 10 in. wide) was on the west side with a doorway about half way along its length but apparently no door checks as in most other brochs and in duns. From the central court narrow doorways led into two, oval mural chambers, one opposite the entrance (13 × 5 ft) and one in the south-west quadrant (12 ft 9 in. × 5 ft 6 in.). Both were corbelled in bee-hive fashion. As at Mousa access to the staircase was at first-floor level via the timber-framed range. The latter was supported by a scarcement or ledge 6 ft high on the court wall and projected 6 ft in front of it, judging by the paving 6 ft wide, delineated by a kerb of upright stones.

As pointed out in Chapter 2 only half of the broch at Jarlshof in Shetland was preserved and that not to any great height (Fig. 18). It was 60 ft in overall diameter with walls c. 17 ft thick and an interior c. 25 ft in diameter, i.e. just a little smaller than Clickhimin. It had an attached roughly D-shaped walled courtyard on its west side, c. 130 × 75 ft. Both courtyard and broch were entered from the west. On either side of the broch entrance were circular guard chambers and opposite the entrance on the other side of the inner court was an oval mural chamber, c. 15 × 5 ft. Presumably the staircase began at the first floor since there is no evidence for it at ground-floor level.

The brochs at Gurness and Midhowe in Orkney have basal galleries of the type described earlier. Gurness is 60 ft in diameter with walls 14 ft thick (Pl. 46). It has the usual type of entrance with guard chambers opening on either side, just behind the door checks. The guard chambers (c. 9 × 6 ft) are not, however, completely enclosed rooms. Their inner ends give direct access to a ground-floor gallery about 3 ft wide which runs the entire circuit of the broch. As pointed out earlier, basal galleries appear to have turned out to be structurally weak and Gurness is an example which collapsed fairly soon after it was built. The broch at Midhowe is of similar dimensions, and likewise had twin guard chambers in the entrance passage (Pl. 47). In this case, however, only one chamber was connected to the basal gallery, which circled most of the broch, but stopped about 5–10 ft from the other chamber. There was also an entrance to the gallery from the central court on the right-hand side.

46   The Broch of Gurness.

47 The Broch of Midhowe.

In spite of their elaborate architecture, broch towers seem to have had a relatively short life. By c. A.D. 80–100 the need for the type of strong defence they represented seems to have passed away. This date coincides approximately with the Roman penetration of Scotland. This penetration was never consolidated into permanent occupation and the frontier settled down further south, on the line of Hadrian's Wall. The result of this seems to have been to turn the attention of the Scottish tribes (the Caledonii) to the south, to the richer Roman province, and away from the peoples of the far north and west (the broch builders). It was the enmity and aggression of the Caledonii, it is suggested, which caused the occupants of the Orkneys, Shetlands, Caithness and the Hebrides to indulge in the building of broch towers for their defence. Equally, it is suggested, it was the diversion of this aggressiveness to the south, against the Roman province, which allowed the peoples of the remoter regions to resume more peaceful modes of living and less elaborate types of domestic architecture. Many brochs are surrounded by settlements of various kinds which grew up when the broch towers were deemed no longer necessary. In some cases the subsequent structures took the form of circular aisled houses or wheelhouses (as described at Jarlshof and Clickhimin), or more irregular agglomerations of rooms and passages (as at Gurness and Lingro). The fact that the brochs are succeeded by fairly conventional domestic architecture on the same site is perhaps an indication of their nature. They may, in fact, have more of the nature of fortified houses (on perhaps a fairly large scale) rather than fortifications in any military sense. The accommodation which could be arranged inside by timber ranges indicates an extended family group, perhaps, of twenty or twenty-five people, in three generations. The finds indicate the ranges of activities appropriate to any normal settlement site: farming, fishing, food gathering, etc. These activities were in being before the brochs appeared, and continued after they were abandoned. The broch tower was, in a sense, an incident, a device made necessary by particular conditions, presumably generated by the hostile tribes of the south and east. When those particular conditions ceased to exist then so did the broch towers which they had brought into being and they fell into ruins, to provide abundant quarries of stone for much future building of a more peaceful nature.

Bibliography

CHAPTER 1   MAN THE BUILDER

Brailsford, J. W., *Later Prehistoric Antiquities of the British Isles*, London, 1953.

Clark, R. R., *East Anglia*, London, 1960.

Cunliffe, B. W., *Iron Age Communities in Britain*, London, 1974.

Evans, E. E., *Prehistoric and Early Christian Ireland*, London, 1966.

Feachem, R. W., *The North Britons*, London, 1965.

Foster, I., and Daniel, G. E., *Prehistoric and Early Wales*, London, 1965.

Fox, A., *South West England*, London, 1964.

Grinsell, L. V., *The Archaeology of Wessex*, London, 1958.

Harding, D. W., *The Iron Age of Lowland Britain*, London, 1974.

Jessup, R. F., *The South East*, London, 1970.

O'Riordain, S. P., *Antiquities of the Irish Countryside*, London, 1953.

Piggott, S., *The Neolithic Cultures of the British Isles*, Cambridge, 1954, reprinted 1970.

Piggott, S. (Ed.), *The Prehistoric Peoples of Scotland*, London, 1962.

Stone, J. F. S., *Wessex*, London, 1958.

Thomas, N., *Guide to Prehistoric England*, London, 1960.

Thomas, S., *Pre-Roman Britain*, London, 1965.

Wainwright, F. T. (Ed.), *The Northern Isles*, London, 1962.

CHAPTER 2   ANCIENT HOUSES AND SETTLEMENTS

Ap Simon, A. M., and Greenfield, E., The Excavation of the Bronze Age and Iron Age settlement at Trevisker Round, St Eval, Cornwall, *Proceedings of the Prehistoric Society*, Vol. 38, 1972, pp. 302–81.

Bersu, G. Excavations at Little Woodbury, Wiltshire, *Proceedings of the Prehistoric Society*, Vol. 6, 1940, pp. 30–111.

Bersu, G., and Griffiths, W. E., Concentric Circles at Llwyn-du Bach, Pen-y-Groes, Caernarvonshire, *Archaeologia Cambrensis*, Vol. 100, 1949, pp. 173–206.

Bulleid, A., and Gray, H. St G., *The Glastonbury Lake Village*, Vol. 1, Taunton, 1911.

Burstow, G. P., and Holleyman, G. A., The Late Bronze Age Settlement on Itford Hill, Sussex, *Proceedings of the Prehistoric Society*, Vol. 23, 1957, pp. 167–212.

Calder, C. S. T., Neolithic Structures in Shetland in *The Northern Isles* (Ed. F. T. Wainwright), London, 1962.

Childe, V. G., *Skara Brae, A Pictish Village in Orkney*, London, 1931.

Clark, J. G. D., and Fell, C. I., The Early Iron Age site at Micklemoor Hill, West Harling, Norfolk, and its pottery, *Proceedings of the Prehistoric Society*, Vol. 19, 1953, pp. 1–40.

Cunliffe, B. W., *Iron Age Communities in Britain*, London, 1974, Chapters 11 and 12.

Fox, A., Excavations at Kestor, *Transactions of the Devonshire Association*, Vol. 86, 1954.

Fox, A., Celtic Fields and Farms on Dartmoor, *Proceedings of the Prehistoric Society*, Vol. 20, 1954, pp. 87–102.

Fox, A., Excavations on Dean Moor, 1954–6, *Transactions of the Devonshire Association*, Vol. 89, 1957, pp. 18–77.

Fox, A., *South West England*, London, 1964.

Frere, S. S. (Ed.), *Problems of the Iron Age in Southern Britain*, pp. 17–28 (Some Smaller Settlements).

Gray, H. St. G., and Bulleid, A., *The Meare Lake Village*, Vol. 1, 1948, Vol. 11, 1953, Taunton.

Hamilton, J. R. C., *Excavations at Jarlshof, Shetland*, Edinburgh, 1956.

Hamilton, J. R. C., *Excavations at Clickhimin, Shetland*, Edinburgh, 1968.

Harding, D. W., *The Iron Age in Lowland Britain*, London, 1974, Chapters 2 and 3.

Hemp, W. J., and Gresham, C. A., Hut-circles in North-west Wales, *Antiquity*, Vol. 18, 1944, pp. 183–96.

Hencken, H. O., An excavation . . . at Chysauster, Cornwall, 1931, *Archaeologia*, Vol. 83, 1933, pp. 237–84.

Holleyman, G. A., and Curwen, E. C., Late Bronze Age Lynchet Settlements on Plumpton Plain, Sussex, *Proceedings of the Prehistoric Society*, Vol. 1, 1935, pp. 16–38.

Jobey, G., A Field Survey in Northumberland in *The Iron Age in Northern Britain* (Ed. A. L. F. Rivet), Edinburgh, 1966, Chapter 5.

Lethbridge, T. C., Excavations at Kilpheder, South Uist, and the problem of Brochs and Wheelhouses, *Proceedings of the Prehistoric Society*, Vol. 18, 1952, pp. 176–93.

McInnes, I. J., Settlements in Later Neolithic Britain in *Economy and Settlement in Neolithic and Early Bronze Age Britain and Europe* (Ed. D. D. A. Simpson), Leicester, 1971, pp. 113–30.

O'Riordain, S. P., Lough Gur Excavations: Neolithic and Bronze Age Houses on Knockadoon, *Proceedings of the Royal Irish Academy*, Vol. 56, Section C, 1954, pp. 297–459.

Perry, B. T., Iron Age Enclosures and Settlements on the Hampshire Chalklands, *The Archaeological Journal*, Vol. 126, 1969, pp. 29–43.

Pettit, P., *Prehistoric Dartmoor*, Newton Abbot, 1974, Chapters 3 and 4.

Radford, C. A. R., Prehistoric Settlements on Dartmoor and the Cornish Moors, *Proceedings of the Prehistoric Society*, Vol. 18, 1952, pp. 55–84.

Simpson, D. D. A., Beaker Houses and Settlements in Britain in *Economy and Settlement in Neolithic and Early Bronze Age Britain and Europe* (Ed. D. D. A. Simpson), Leicester, 1971, pp. 131–52.

Smith, C. A., A Morphological Analysis of Late Prehistoric and Romano-British Settlements in North-West Wales, *Proceedings of the Prehistoric Society*, Vol. 40, 1974, pp. 157–69.

Stone, J. F. S., The Deverel-Rimbury Settlement on Thorny Down, Winterbourne Gunner, S. Wilts., *Proceedings of the Prehistoric Society*, Vol. 7, 1941, pp. 114–33.

Wainwright, G. J., Excavation of a Durotrigian Farmstead near Tollard Royal in Cranbourne Chase, Southern England, *Proceedings of the Prehistoric Society*, Vol. 34, 1968, pp. 102–47.

Wainwright, G. J., The Excavation of a Neolithic Settlement on Broome Heath, Ditchingham, Norfolk, *Proceedings of the Prehistoric Society*, Vol. 38, 1972, pp. 1–97.

CHAPTER 3   THE WINDMILL HILL PEOPLE

Ashbee, P., *The Earthen Long Barrow in Britain*, London, 1970.

Atkinson, R. J. C., The Dorset Cursus, *Antiquity*, Vol. 29, 1955, pp. 4–9.

Grinsell, L. V., *The Archaeology of Wessex*, London, 1958, Chapters II and III.

Keiller, A., *Windmill Hill and Avebury*, Oxford, 1965.

Piggott, S., *The Neolithic Cultures of the British Isles*, Cambridge, 1954, reprinted 1970.

Smith, I. F., Causewayed Enclosures in *Economy and Settlement in Neolithic and Early Bronze Age Britain and Europe* (Ed. D. D. A. Simpson), Leicester, 1971.

Stone, J. F. S., *Wessex*, London, 1958.

CHAPTER 4   MEGALITHIC TOMBS

Corcoran, J. X. W. P., The Carlingford Culture, *Proceedings of the Prehistoric Society*, Vol. 26, 1960, pp. 98–148.

Corcoran, J. X. W. P., The Cotswold-Severn Group in *Megalithic Enquiries in The West of Britain* (Ed. T. G. E. Powell), Liverpool, 1969, Chapters 2 and 3.

Crawford, O. G. S., *The Long Barrows of the Cotswolds*, Gloucester, 1925.

Daniel, G. E., *The Prehistoric Chamber Tombs of England and Wales*, Cambridge, 1950.

Daniel, G. E., *The Megalith Builders of Western Europe*, London, 1958.

De Valera, R., and O'Nuallain, S., *Survey of the Megalithic Tombs of Ireland*, Vol. I, *County Clare*, Dublin, 1961.

De Valera, R., and O'Nuallain, S., *Survey of the Megalithic Tombs of Ireland*, Vol. II, *County Mayo*, Dublin, 1964.

Evans, E. E., *Prehistoric and Early Christian Ireland*, London, 1966.

Grimes, W. F., The Megalithic Monuments of Wales, *Proceedings of the Prehistoric Society*, Vol. 2, 1936, pp. 106–39.

Grimes, W. F., The Long Cairns of the Brecknockshire Black Mountains, *Archaeologia Cambrensis*, Vol. 91, 1936, pp. 259–82.

Henshall, A. S., *The Chambered Tombs of Scotland*, Vol. I, Edinburgh, 1963.

Henshall, A. S., *The Chambered Tombs of Scotland*, Vol. II, Edinburgh, 1972.

Lynch, F. M., The Megalithic Tombs of North Wales in *Megalithic Enquiries in the West of Britain* (Ed. T. G. E. Powell), Liverpool, 1969, Chapters 4 and 5.

O'Riordain, S. P., *Antiquities of the Irish Countryside*, London, 1953, pp. 56–74.

O'Riordain, S. P., *New Grange and the Bend of the Boyne*, London, 1964.

Piggott, S., *The Neolithic Cultures of the British Isles*, Cambridge, 1954, reprinted 1970.

Piggott, S., *The West Kennet Long Barrow Excavations 1955-6*, London, 1962.

Powell, T. G. E., (Ed.), *Megalithic Enquiries in the West of Britain*, Liverpool, 1969.

Scott, J. G., The Clyde Cairns of Scotland in *Megalithic Enquiries in the West of Britain* (Ed. T. G. E. Powell), Liverpool, 1969, Chapter 6.

CHAPTER 5   CEREMONIAL SITES

Atkinson, R. J. C., *Stonehenge*, London, 1956.

Atkinson, R. J. C., *et al.*, *Excavations at Dorchester, Oxon.*, Oxford, 1951.

Burl, H. A. W., Henges: Internal features and regional groups, *The Archaeological Journal*, Vol. 126, 1969, pp. 1–28.

Clark, J. G. D., The Timber Monument at Arminghall and its affinities, *Proceedings of the Prehistoric Society*, Vol. 2, 1936, pp. 1–51.

Grinsell, L. V., *The Archaeology of Wessex*, London, 1958, Chapter V.

Houlder, C. H., The henge monuments at Llandegai, *Antiquity*, Vol. 42, 1968, pp. 216–21.

Smith, I. S., *Windmill Hill and Avebury: Excavations by Alexander Keiller*, Oxford, 1965.

Stone, J. F. S., *Wessex*, London, 1958.

Thom, A., *Megalithic Sites in Britain*, Oxford, 1967.

Thomas, N., *Guide to Prehistoric England*, London, 1960.

Tratman, E. K., The Priddy Circles, Mendip, Somerset, henge monuments, *Proceedings of the University of Bristol Spelaeological Society*, Vol. II, pp. 97–125.

Wainwright, G. J., Mount Pleasant, *Current Archaeology*, No. 23, 1970, pp. 320–5.

Wainwright, G. J., A review of henge monuments in the light of recent research, *Proceedings of the Prehistoric Society*, Vol. 35, 1970, pp. 112–33.

Wainwright, G. J., The excavation of a Late Neolithic Enclosure at Marden, Wiltshire, *Antiquaries Journal*, Vol. 51, 1971, pp. 177–239.

Wainwright, G. J., and Longworth, I. H., *Durrington Walls: Excavations 1966–68* London, 1971.

CHAPTER 6   BARROWS AND GRAVES

Ashbee, P., *The Bronze Age Round Barrow in Britain*, London, 1960.

Fox, C., *Life and Death in the Bronze Age*, London, 1959.

Grimes, W. F., *The Prehistory of Wales*, Cardiff, 1951, Chapter III.

Grinsell, L. V., The Bronze Age Round Barrows of Wessex, *Proceedings of the Prehistoric Society*, Vol. 7, 1941, pp. 73–113.

Grinsell, L. V., *The Ancient Burial Mounds of England*, London, 1953.

Grinsell, L. V., *The Archaeology of Exmoor*, Newton Abbot, 1970, Chapter 5.

O'Riordain, S. P., *Antiquities of the Irish Countryside*, London, 1953, pp. 75–80.

Piggott, S., The Early Bronze Age in Wessex, *Proceedings of the Prehistoric Society*, Vol. 4, 1939, pp. 53–106.

Pettit, P., *Prehistoric Dartmoor*, Newton Abbot, 1974, Chapters 5 and 6.

Thomas, N., *Guide to Prehistoric England*, London, 1960.

CHAPTER 7   CIRCLES AND STANDING STONES

Burl, H. A. W., Stone Circles and Ring-Cairns, *Scottish Archaeological Forum*, Vol. 4, 1972, pp. 31–47.

Evans, E. E., *Prehistoric and Early Christian Ireland*, London, 1966.

Grimes, W. F., The Stone Circles and Related Monuments of Wales in *Culture and Environment* (Eds. Foster and Alcock), London, 1963, pp. 93–152.

Grinsell, L. V., *The Archaeology of Exmoor*,
Newton Abbot, 1970, Chapter 4.
O'Riordain, S. P., *Antiquities of the Irish
Countryside*, London, 1953, pp. 81–94.
Pettit, P., *Prehistoric Dartmoor*, Newton Abbot,
1974, Chapter 7.
Thomas, N., *Guide to Prehistoric England*,
London, 1960.

CHAPTER 8   HILLFORTS AND RAMPARTS

Alcock, L., Hillforts in Wales and the Marches,
Antiquity, Vol. 39, 1965, pp. 184–95.
Cotton, M. A., British camps with timber-
laced ramparts, *The Archaeological Journal*,
Vol. III, 1954, pp. 26–105.
Cunliffe, B. W., *Iron Age Communities in Britain*,
London, 1974, Chapter 13.
Evans, E. E., *Prehistoric and Early Christian
Ireland*, London, 1966.
Feachem, R. W., The Hillforts of Northern
Britain in *The Iron Age in Northern
Britain* (Ed. A. L. F. Rivet), Edinburgh,
1966, Chapter 4.
Forde-Johnston, J., *Hillforts of the Iron Age in
England and Wales*, Liverpool, 1976.
Fox, A., South Western Hillforts in *Problems
of the Iron Age in Southern Britain* (Ed. S. S.
Frere), London, 1958, pp. 35-60.
Grinsell, L. V., *The Archaeology of Wessex*,
London, 1958, Chapter 10, Hillforts.
Harding, D. W., *The Iron Age in Lowland
Britain*, London, 1974, Chapter 4,
Fortifications and warfare.
Harding, D. W. (Ed.), *Hillforts, A Survey
of Research in Britain and Ireland*, 1976.
Hogg, A. H. A., Early Iron Age Wales in
Prehistoric and Early Wales (Eds. Foster and
Daniel), London, 1965, Chapter 5.
Hogg, A. H. A., *Hill-Forts of Britain*, London,
1975.
Jesson, M., and Hill, D. H., *The Iron Age and its
Hillforts*, Southampton, 1971.
Jobey, G., A Field Survey in Northumberland
in *The Iron Age in Northern Britain* (Ed.
A. L. F. Rivet), Edinburgh, 1966,
Chapter 5.
O'Riordain, S. P., *Antiquities of the Irish
Countryside*, London, 1953, pp. 1–26.
Thomas, N., *Guide to Prehistoric England*,
London, 1960.
Wheeler, R. E. M., *Maiden Castle, Dorset*,
London, 1943.

CHAPTER 9   FORTIFICATIONS OF THE FAR
NORTH

Graham, A., Some Observations on the Brochs,
*Proceedings of the Society of Antiquaries of
Scotland*, Vol. 81, 1947, pp. 48–99.
Hamilton, J. R. C., *Excavations at Jarlshof,
Shetland*, Edinburgh, 1956.
Hamilton, J. R. C., Brochs and Broch-
Builders in *The Northern Isles* (Ed.
F. T. Wainwright), London, 1962,
Chapter VI.
Hamilton, J. R. C., Forts, Brochs and Wheel-
houses in Northern Scotland in *The Iron
Age in Northern Britain* (Ed. A. L. F. Rivet),
Edinburgh, 1966, Chapter 6.
Hamilton, J. R. C., *Excavations at Clickhimin,
Shetland*, Edinburgh, 1968.

Index

Abingdon, Berks., causewayed enclosure, 64
Allan Water, Midlothian, stone circle, 155
Almondbury, Yorks., hillfort, 172
Arbor Low, Derbys., henge monument, 107, fig. 37, pl. 23
Arminghall, Norfolk, henge monument, 113, fig. 40, 128
Ashen Hill, Som., linear cemetery, 136
Aubreys, Herts., hillfort, 172
Avebury, Wilts., henge monument, 106, fig. 22, 115, fig. 41, 117, fig. 42, 129
Badbury Rings, Dorset, hillfort, 170, pl. 35, 171, 182
Balfarg, Fife, henge monument, 112
Ballochroy, Kintyre, stone row, 161
Ballymeanoch, Argylls., henge monument, 113
Barbrook, Derbys., stone circle, 154–5
Barclodiad y Gawres, Ang., megalithic tomb, 84, fig. 27
Bargrennan group, Scotland, megalithic tombs, 87
Barkhale, Sussex, causewayed enclosure, 64
Barmekin of Echt, Aberdeen, hillfort, 177
Bathampton Camp, Som., hillfort, 172
Battlesbury, Wilts., hillfort, 170
Beacon Hill, Hants., hillfort, 170, 182
Beacon Hill, Yorks., Bronze Age house, 36
Beardown Man, Devon, standing stone, 160
Beaulieu, Hants., Bronze Age barrow, 145, fig. 52
Belle Tout, Sussex, Bronze Age house, 36, 38
Benie Hoose, Shetlands, Neolithic house, 35, fig. 10
Birrenswark, Dumfriess., hillfort, 174
Black Head, Corn., promontory fort, 173
Black Meldon, Peebles, hillfort, 174
Blackbury Castle, Devon, hillfort, 183
Blackhammer, Orkneys, megalithic tomb, 94
Blakey Topping, Yorks., stone circle, 155
Blissmoor, Devon, Bronze Age settlement, 43
Boat of Garten, Inverness, stone circle, 155
Bodrifty, Corn., Iron Age settlement, 51
Borgadel Water, Kintyre, dun, 188
Borrowston Rig, Midlothian, stone circle, 155
Bosherston, Pembs., hillfort, 173
Boyne cemetery, henge monuments, 113; megalithic tombs, 17, 94–6, pls. 19–20, fig. 32
Braddock, Corn., linear cemetery, 136
Bratton Castle, Wilts., hillfort, 170, pl. 36, 171, 182
Bredon Hill, Worcs., hillfort, 171
Bridestones, Ches., megalithic tomb, 86
Brindister Loch, Shetlands, blockhouse, 194
Broadlee, Dumfriess., henge monument, 112
Broome Heath, Norfolk, Neolithic settlement, 32
Broomend of Crichie, Aberdeen, henge monument, 112
Broomrig, Cumb., henge monument, 111–12
Brown Caterhun, Angus, hillfort, 177
Bryn Celli Ddu, Ang., megalithic tomb, 84, pl. 14, fig. 27
Buaile Oscar, Caithness, hillfort, 177
Bull Ring, Derbys., henge monument, 109
Bully Hills, Lincs., linear cemetery, 136
Bulstrode Park, Bucks., hillfort, 172
Bulwarks, Glam., hillfort, 173
Burfa Camp, Radnor., hillfort, 172
Burton, Pembs., megalithic tomb, 83–4
Bury Ditches, Shrops., hillfort, 172, 182
Bury Walls, Shrops., hillfort, 172
Butterdon Hill, Devon, stone row, 161
Buzbury Rings, Dorset, hillfort, 171
Cademuir Hill, Peebles, hillfort, 174
Caer Caradoc (Clun), Shrops., hillfort, 172, fig. 61

Caer y Twr, Ang., hillfort, 173
Cairnpapple, West Lothian, henge monument, 112
Calf of Eday, Orkneys, Iron Age settlement, 57, 187
Callanish, Lewis, stone circles, 157, fig. 58; stone row, 161
Cambret Moor, Kirkcudb., stone circle, 155
Camp Tops, Roxburgh., hillfort, 174
Campswater, Lanarks., hillfort, 174
Camster Long, Caithness, megalithic tomb, 93–4, fig. 30
Camster Round, Caithness, megalithic tomb, 93, fig. 30
Cana, Yorks., henge monument, 111
Canonbridge, Ross & Crom., henge monument, 112
Capel Garmon, Denb., megalithic tomb, 84
Capel Hiraethog Denb., stone circles, 153
Cardrona, Peebles, hillfort, 174
Carl Wark, Yorks., hillfort, pl. 41
Carles, The, Cumb., stone circle, 155
Carman, Dumbartons., hillfort, fig. 63
Carn Brea, Corn., Neolithic huts, 31
Carn Fadrun, Caerns., Iron Age settlement, 56; hillfort, 173
Carn Ingli, Pembs., Iron Age settlement, 56; hillfort, 173
Carrigillihy, Co. Cork, Bronze Age house, 38, pl. 7
Carrowkeel, Co. Sligo, megalithic tombs, 96, fig. 33
Carrowmore, Co. Sligo, megalithic tombs, 96, fig. 33
Casterley Camp, Wilts., hillfort, 170
Castilly, Corn., henge monument, 107
Castle Bucket, Pembs., henge monument, 107
Castle Ditches, Hants., hillfort, 170
Castle Ditches, Wilts., hillfort, 170
Castle Dore, Corn., hillfort, 173
Castle Dykes, Yorks., henge monument, 111
Castle Hill, Roxburgh., hillfort, 175
Castle O'er, Dumfriess., hillfort, 174
Castle-an-Dinas, Corn., hillfort, 173
Castlewich, Corn., henge monument, 107
Caulside, Kirkcudb., stone circle, 156
Chanctonbury Ring, Sussex, hillfort, 169
Chesters, The, East Lothian, hillfort, 175–7
Cholesbury, Bucks., hillfort, 172
Chun Castle, Corn., hillfort, 173
Chysauster, Corn., Iron Age settlement, 54–5, fig. 17, pl. 11
Cissbury, Sussex, hillfort, 169
Clachan an Diridh, Perths., standing stones, 160
Clashindarrock, Aberdeen, henge monument, 112
Clatchard Craig, Fife, hillfort, 177
Clava group, Scotland, megalithic tombs, 88; ring-cairns, 157
Clegyr Boia, Pembs., Neolithic house, 29
Clettraval, Hebrides, Iron Age settlement, 58–9, fig. 19
Clickhimin, Shetlands, Bronze Age settlement, 44–5; Iron Age settlement, 57, 60, 187, 189–93, 200; broch, 198–9
Clocaenog Moor, Denb., stone circles, 153
Clovelly Dykes, Devon, hillfort, 173
Clyde group, Scotland, megalithic tombs, 87–8, fig. 29, 103
Cockburn Law, Berwicks,. hillfort, 175
Colsterworth, Lincs., Iron Age settlement, 49
Combe Hill, Sussex, causewayed enclosure, 62, 64
Condicote, Glos., henge monument, 115
Coney Island, Armagh, Bronze Age houses, 38
Contin, Ross & Crom., henge monument, 112
Conway Mountain, Caerns., hillfort, 173

Corston Beacon, Pembs., Bronze Age barrow, fig. 51
Cotswold-Severn group, megalithic tombs, 17, 82, 86–7, fig. 28, 88, 94, 101, 103
Coupland, Northumb., henge monument, 112
Court Cairn group, Ireland, megalithic tombs, 97, fig. 34
Coxall Knoll, Here., hillfort, 172
Craigadwy Wynt, Denb., hillfort, 172
Cribarth, Brecon., stone row, 161
Crichel Down, Dorset, Bronze Age barrow, fig. 49
Crickley Hill, Glos., causewayed enclosure, 61, 64; Iron Age house, 60
Croft Ambrey, Here., hillfort, 172; Iron Age house, 60
Culbokie, Ross & Crom., henge monument, 112
Curragh, Co. Kildare, henge monuments, 113
Cursus, Wilts., linear cemetery, 135, fig. 48
Cuween, Orkneys, megalithic tomb, 93
Cwrtgollen, Brecon, standing stone, 160
Dan y Coed, Pembs., henge monument, 107
Danebury, Hants., hillfort, 170, 182; Iron Age house, 60
Daviot, Inverness, stone circle, 155
Dean Moor, Devon, Bronze Age settlement, 41
Denbury, Devon, hillfort, 173
Devil's Arrows, Yorks., stone row, 161
Devil's Dyke, Sussex, hillfort, 169
Devil's Jumps, Sussex, linear cemetery, 136
Devil's Quoits, Oxon., henge monument, 115
Dike Hills, Oxon., hillfort, 172
Dinnever Hill, Corn., stone circle, 153, fig. 56
Dodman Point, Corn., promontory fort, 173
Dolebury, Som., hillfort, 171
Doll Tor, Derbys., stone circle, 155
Dolmen group, megalithic tombs, 98, fig. 35, pl. 21
Dorchester, Oxon., mortuary enclosure, 69; cursus, 78; henge monuments, 105, 113, 114
Dorchester Big Rings, Oxon., henge monument, 114–15
Dorset Cursus, Dorset, 76–8, fig. 25
Downpatrick, Co. Down, Bronze Age house, 36
Dowth, Co. Meath, megalithic tomb, 94–5
Draughton, Northants., Iron Age settlement, 49
Dudsbury, Dorset, Bronze Age barrow, fig. 50
Dun Ailline, Co. Kildare, hillfort, 178
Dun Ban, Hebrides, galleried dun, 194
Dun Bharabhat, Hebrides, galleried dun, 194
Dun Fhinn, Kintyre, dun, 188–9
Dun Grugaig, Inverness, galleried dun, 194
Dun Killdalloig, Kintyre, dun, 189
Dun Ruadh, Co. Tyrone, henge monument, 113
Dungarry, Kirkcudb., hillfort, 175
Durrington Walls, Wilts., henge monument, 105, 115, fig. 42, 119, fig. 43, 122, 127, 128, 129
Dyffryn Ardudwy, Merion., megalithic tomb, 84
East Heslerton, Yorks., long barrow, 72, fig. 22
Easter Aquorthies, Aberdeens., recumbent stone circle, 157
Easton Down, Wilts., Neolithic house, 31; possible Bronze Age house, 36–7
Eaton Heath, Norfolk, Neolithic house, 31
Eggardon, Dorset, hillfort, 170, pl. 34
Eildon Hill North, Roxburgh, Iron Age settlement, 56; hillfort, 175, fig. 64
Eldon's Seat, Dorset, Iron Age settlement, 49
Eleven Shearers, Roxburgh, stone row, 161–2
Elva Plain, Cumb., stone circle, 155
Eskdale Moor, Cumb., stone circle, 155
Eyam Moor, Derbys., stone circle, 154

Ffynnon-Brodyr, Carm., henge monument, 107
Figsbury Rings, Wilts., hillfort, 170
Five Wells, Derbys., megalithic tomb, 84–6

Foale's Arrishes, Devon, Bronze Age settlement, 43
Foel Fenlli, Denb., hillfort, 172
Foel Trigarn, Pembs., hillfort, 173
Fourknocks, Co. Meath, megalithic cemetery, 96
Freestone Hill, Co. Kilkenny, hillfort, 178
Fridd Faldwyn, Montgom., hillfort, 172; Iron Age house, 60
Froggatt, Edge, Derbys., stone circle, 155
Fussell's Lodge, Wilts., long barrow, 69–71, figs. 23, 24; 72, 73, 74, 75
Gaer Fawr, Carm., hillfort, 173
Gairdie, The, Shetlands, Neolithic house, 36, fig. 11
Gamelands, Westmorl., stone circle, 155
Garn Boduan, Caerns., Iron Age settlement, 56; hillfort, 173
Giant's Hills, Lincs., long barrow, 72, fig. 22
Giant's Ring, Co. Down, henge monument, 113
Gib Hill, Derbys., burial mound, 109
Glastonbury, Som., Iron Age settlement, 51–3, fig. 16
Glencrutchery, Man, Neolithic house, 30
Gorsey Bigbury, Som., henge monument, 114
Great Bemeray, Lewis, standing stones, 160
Great Woodbury, Wilts., Iron Age settlement, 47
Green Low, Derbys., megalithic tomb, 84–6
Grey Croft, Cumb., stone circle, 155
Grey Wethers, Corn., stone circle, 151
Grime's Graves, Norfolk, flint mines, 78–80, fig. 26, pl. 13
Grimspound, Devon, Bronze Age settlement, 41
Gruting School, Shetlands, Neolithic house, 36, fig. 11
Gurness, Orkneys, broch, 60, 199–200, pl. 46
Gwithian, Corn., Bronze Age house, 37
Haldon, Devon, Neolithic house, 29
Hambledon Hill, Berwicks., hillfort, 175
Hambledon Hill, Dorset, causewayed enclosure, 62, 64; Iron Age settlement, 51; hillfort, 170, 182
Hampton Down, Dorset, stone circle, 153
Hanborough, Oxon., possible henge monument, 114
Hanging Grimston, Yorks., long barrow, 73
Har Tor, Devon, Bronze Age settlement, 41
Harehaugh, Berwicks., hillfort, 175
Haresfield Beacon, Glos., hillfort, 171
Harthill Moor, Derbys., stone circle, 155
Heathrow, London, Iron Age settlement, 49, pl. 10
Hebridean group, megalithic tombs, 87, 88
Heddington, Wilts., long barrow, 73
Helsby, Ches., hillfort, pl. 33
Hembury, Devon, causewayed enclosure, 64
Hemford, Shrops., stone circle, 153–4
Henderland Hill, Peebles, hillfort, 174
Hengwm, Merion., stone circle, 153
Herefordshire Beacon, Here., hillfort, 172
Heston Brake, Mon., megalithic tomb, 86
Hetty Pegler's Tump, Glos., megalithic tomb, 86
High Bridestones, Yorks., stone circles, 155
High Peak, Devon, causewayed enclosure, 64
Hod Hill, Dorset, Iron Age settlement, 51; hillfort, 170, 182
Holm of Papa Westray, Orkneys, megalithic tomb, 94
Howmae, Orkneys, Iron Age settlement, 57
Hownam Law, Roxburgh, hillfort, 175
Hunter's Lodge, Som., henge monument, 114
Huntfold Hill, Roxburgh, hillfort, 175
Huntingtower, Perths., henge monument, 112
Hurlers, The, Corn., stone circle, 151
Hutton Moor, Yorks., henge monument, 111
Ilkley Moor, Yorks., possible stone circles, 155
Itford Hill, Sussex, Bronze Age settlement, 40
Ivington Camp, Here., hillfort, 172

Jarlshof, Shetlands, Bronze Age settlement, 43–4, fig. 14;
    Iron Age settlement, 56–7, fig. 18, 57–8, 60, 187, 200;
    broch, 199
Kemp Howe, Yorks., Neolithic house, 31
Kerrs Knowe, Peebles, hillfort, 174
Kestor, Devon, Bronze Age settlement, 43; Iron Age
    settlement, 51
Kildonan Bay, Kintyre, dun, 189
Killibury, Corn., hillfort, 173
Kilpheder, Hebrides, Iron Age settlement, 59
Kimsbury, Glos., hillfort, 171
King Arthur's Round Table, Westmorl., henge
    monument, 111
Kingston Russel, Dorset, stone circle, 153
Kintraw, Argylls., stone circle, 155–6
Kip Knowe, Roxburgh, hillfort, 174
Knap Hill, Wilts., causewayed enclosure, 64
Knottingley, Yorks., henge monument, 111
Knowlton Circles, Dorset, henge monuments, 115
Knowth, Co. Meath, megalithic tomb, 95, pls. 19, 20
Lacra, Cumb., stone circles, 155
Lake, Wilts., nuclear cemetery, 136
Langstone Moor, Devon, Bronze Age settlement, 41
Learable Hill, Sutherland, stone rows, 162
Legis Tor, Devon, Neolithic house, 31; Bronze Age
    settlement, 41
Lingro, Orkneys, broch and settlement, 60, 200
Linney Head, Pembs., promontory fort, pl. 39
Lios, Lough Gur, Co. Limerick, henge monument, 113,
    114
Lisroughan, Co. Galway, henge monument, 113
Little Meg, Cumb., stone circle, 155
Little Round Table, Westmorl., possible henge
    monument, 112
Little Trowpenny, Roxburgh, hillfort, 174–5
Little Woodbury, Wilts., Iron Age settlement, 45–7, 50,
    fig. 15
Llandegai, Caerns., henge monuments, 107
Llanmelin, Mon., hillfort, 172, pl. 38
Lled Croes yr Ych, Montgom., stone circle, 153
Llwynfedwen, Brecon, standing stone, 160
Long Bredy, Dorset, bank barrow, pl. 12
Long Meg and Her Daughters, Cumb., stone circle,
    155, fig. 57
Long Stone, Devon, standing stone, 160, pl. 31
Long Stone, Co. Kildare, standing stone, 160
Longbridge Deverill, Wilts., Iron Age settlement, 48
Longhouse, Pembs., megalithic tomb, 83–4
Longstone Rath, Co. Kildare, standing stone, 160;
    henge monument, 113
Lough Gur, Co. Limerick, Neolithic and Bronze Age
    houses, 29, 30–1, 36, fig. 8
Loughcrew, Co. Meath, megalithic cemetery, 96, fig. 33
Maen Llwyd, Caerns., standing stone, 160
Maes Howe group, Orkneys, megalithic tombs, 88,
    90–3, 103, pls. 16, 17, fig. 31
Maiden Bower, Beds., causewayed enclosure, 64
Maiden Castle, Dorset, causewayed enclosure, 62, 64;
    hillfort, 169, 170, 178, 183, 184; long barrow, 68, 76
Mam Tor, Derbys., hillfort, 172
Marden, Wilts., henge monument, 105, 115, 119–22,
    127, fig. 42
Maumbury Rings, Dorset, henge monument, 115, 129
Maxey, Northants., henge monuments, 113
Mayburgh, Westmorl., henge monument, 111, fig. 38
Meare, Som., Iron Age settlement, 53–4
Medway group, Kent, megalithic tombs, 82–3
Meini-Gwyr, Carm., henge monument, 107
Merivale, Devon, stone circles, 151; stone rows, 161

Merry Maidens, Corn., stone circle and standing
    stones, 160
Micknanstown, Co. Meath, henge monument, 113
Mid Clyth, Caithness, stone rows, 162
Midhowe, Orkneys, broch, 199–200, pl. 47; megalithic
    tomb, 94, pl. 18, fig. 31
Midmar Church, Aberdeens., recumbent stone circle, 157
Milber Down, Devon, hillfort, 173
Mininglow, Derbys., megalithic tomb, 84–6
Mitchell's Fold, Shrops., stone circle, 154
Moel Arthur, Denb., hillfort, 172
Moel Hiraddug, Flints., hillfort, 172
Moel Trigarn, Pembs., Iron Age settlement, 56
Moel y Gaer (Bodfari), Flint., hillfort, 172
Moel y Gaer (Llanbedr), Denb., hillfort, 172
Moel y Gaer (Rhosesmor), Flints., hillfort, 172;
    Iron Age house, 60
Mount Pleasant, Glam., Neolithic house, 29, fig. 8
Mount Pleasant, Dorset, henge monument, 106, 115,
    122–3, 127, 128, figs. 42, 45
Mousa, Shetlands, broch, 198–9, pls. 44–5
Muir of Ord, Ross & Crom., henge monument, 112
Mullaghtealin, Co. Dublin, henge monument, 113
Mynydd Trecastell, Brecon, stone circles, 153
Nant Tarw, Brecon, stone circles, 153
Navan, Co. Armagh, hillfort, 178
Ness of Burgi, Shetlands, blockhouse, 194
New Grange, Co. Meath, megalithic tomb, 94, 103,
    fig. 32; standing stones, 160
Newbigging, Lanarks., henge monument, 112
Nine Ladies, Derbys., stone circle, 155
Nine Maidens, Corn., stone circle, 151; stone row, 161
Normangill, Lanarks., henge monument, 112
Norman's Law, Fife, hillfort, 177
Normanton Down, Wilts., mortuary enclosure, 69;
    linear cemetery, 135, fig. 48
Northshield Rings, Peebles, hillfort, 174
Northton, Hebrides, Bronze Age house, 36, fig. 12
Norton Camp, Shrops., hillfort, 172
Notgrove, Glos., megalithic tomb, 86
Nottingham Hill, Glos., hillfort, 171–2
Nunwick, Yorks., henge monument, 111
Nutbane, Hants., long barrow, 73, 74
Nympsfield, Glos., megalithic tomb, 86
Oldbury, Wilts., hillfort, 170
Old Oswestry, Shrops., hillfort, 172
Old Sarum, Wilts., hillfort, 170
Orkney-Cromarty group, megalithic tombs, 17, 88, 93–4,
    104, fig. 30
Overhowden, Berwicks., henge monument, 113
Paddock Hill, Yorks., henge monument, 113
Parc le Breos Cwm, Glam., megalithic tomb, 86
Parc-y-Meirw, Pembs., stone row, 161
Park Hill Camp, Wilts., hillfort, 171
Pen Dinas, Cards., hillfort, 173, pl. 40
Penmaen Burrows, Glam., megalithic tomb, 86
Penmaenmawr, Caerns., stone circles, 153
Penwith group, Corn., megalithic tombs, 83
Pen-y-Cloddiau, Flints. and Denb., hillfort, 172
Penygroes, Caerns., Iron Age settlement, 55–6
Pimperne Down, Dorset, Iron Age settlement, 48, pl. 9
Plumpton Plain, Sussex, Bronze Age settlement, 40–1
Postbridge, Devon, stone circle, 153
Priddy Circles, Som., henge monuments, 113–14, 115
Quanterness, Orkneys, megalithic tomb, 93
Quoyness, Orkneys, megalithic tomb, 93
Rachan Slack, Peebles, henge monument, 112–13
Rame Head, Corn., promontory fort, 173
Ravensburgh Castle, Herts., hillfort, 172

Recumbent Stone Circles, Aberdeens., 157–9
Rempstone, Dorset, stone circle, 153
Rider's Rings, Devon, Bronze Age settlement, 41, pl. 8
Ring Knowe, Peebles, hillfort, 174
Ring of Brodgar, Orkneys, henge monument, 112, pl. 24, fig. 39
Rinyo, Orkneys, Neolithic settlement, 34–5
Rippon Tor, Devon, Bronze Age settlement, 43
Robin Hood's Ball, Wilts., causewayed enclosure, 64
Rollright Stones, Oxon., stone circle, 153
Ronaldsway, Man, Neolithic house, 29–30, fig. 8
Rotherley, Wilts., Iron Age settlement, 49
Rough Tor, Corn., stone circle, 153
Rudston, Yorks., henge monument, 111; standing stone, 160
Rumps Point, Corn., promontory fort, 173
Rybury, Wilts., causewayed enclosure, 62, 64
St Catherine's Hill, Hants., hillfort, 170
Sanctuary, The, Wilts., ceremonial site, 117, 122, 127, 128, 129, fig. 41
Sands of Forvie, Aberdeens., stone circle, 155
Scilly Islands group, megalithic tombs, 83
Scilly-Tramore group, megalithic tombs, 98
Scorhill, Devon, stone circle, 151, fig. 30
Seven Hills, Norfolk, linear cemetery, 136
Shannonbank Hill, Berwicks., hillfort, 175
Shap, Westmorland, stone circles, 155
Shearplace Hill, Dorset, Bronze Age settlement, 38–9
Shetland group, megalithic tombs, 87, 88
Sidbury, Wilts., hillfort, 170, 182
Simonstown, Glam., Bronze Age barrow, pl. 28
Skara Brae, Orkneys, Neolithic settlement, 32–4, pls. 5, 6, fig. 9
Spital Meend, Glos., hillfort, 172
Staines, Middlesex, causewayed enclosure, 64
Stalldon Down, Devon, stone row, pl. 32
Standing Stones Rigg, Yorks., stone circle, 155
Standon Down, Devon, Bronze Age settlement, 41
Stanton Drew, Som., stone circles, 149–50, fig. 55
Stanton Moor, Derbys., stone circle, 155
Stanydale, Shetlands, Neolithic house, 36, fig. 11
Staple Howe, Yorks., Iron Age settlement, 49
Stipple Stones, Corn., henge monument, 107
Stockbridge Down, Hants., Bronze Age barrow, fig. 49
Stonehenge, Wilts., barrow cemeteries, 135–6, fig. 48; cursuses, 76; henge monument, 105, 107, 113, 115, 123–7, 128, 129, pl. 26, fig. 46
Stones of Stenness, Orkneys, henge monument, 112, fig. 39
Stoney Littleton, Som., megalithic tomb, 86
Stratford Hills, Suffolk, henge monument, 113
Stroanfreggan, Kirkcudb., hillfort, 175
Sudbrook, Mon., hillfort, 172, 178
Summerhouses, Glam., hillfort, 173
Sunhoney, Aberdeens., recumbent stone circle, 157
Swarkeston, Derbys., possible Bronze Age house, 38
Swinside, Cumb., stone circle, 155
Symond's Yat, Glos., hillfort, 172
Tara, Co. Meath, hillfort, 178
Tedbury, Som., hillfort, 172
Thickthorn Down, Dorset, long barrow, 74
Thornborough Circles, Yorks., henge monuments, 109–111, 115
Thornhaugh, Northants., henge monument, 113
Thorny Down, Wilts., Bronze Age settlement, 40
Tinkinswood, Glam., megalithic tomb, 86
Tollard Royal, Wilts., Iron Age settlement, 48–9

Torwoodlee, Selkirks., hillfort, 174
Tramore group, Co. Kilkenny, megalithic tombs, 94
Traprain Law, East Lothian, hillfort, 175
Tredegar Camp, Mon., hillfort, 172
Tregaseal, Corn., stone circles, 151
Tregeare Rounds, Corn., hillfort, 173, fig. 62
Tre'r Ceiri, Caerns., Iron Age settlement, 56; hillfort, 173
Tresvennack, Corn., standing stone, 160
Trevelgue Head, Corn., promontory fort, 173
Trevisker, Corn., Iron Age settlement, 51
Trundle, The, Sussex, causewayed enclosure, 62–3, 64, 65; hillfort, 169
Twelve Apostles, Yorks., stone circle, 155
Tyddyn Bleiddyn, Denb., megalithic tomb, 84
Uleybury, Glos., hillfort, 171, pl. 37
Unstan, Orkneys, megalithic tomb, 94
Vinces Farm, Essex, Iron Age settlement, 49
Vinquoy, Orkneys, megalithic tomb, 93
Walbury, Hants., hillfort, 170
Wapley Camp, Here., hillfort, 172
Warbstow Bury, Corn., hillfort, 173
Waulud's Bank, Beds., possible henge monument, 105
Waun Mawr, Pembs., stone circle, 153
Wayland's Smithy, Berks., long barrow, 71, 73, 86
Weatherby Castle, Dorset, hillfort, 171
Wedge-shaped group, Ireland, megalithic tombs, 97–8, figs. 35, 36
West Brandon, Co. Durham, Iron Age settlement, 48
West Harling, Norfolk, Iron Age settlement, 49
West Kennet, Wilts., megalithic tomb, 86, pl. 15
West Kennet Avenue, Wilts., 117
West Plean, Stirlings., Iron Age settlement, 48
Western Oke, Devon, Bronze Age settlement, 41
Westwell, Oxon., henge monument, 115
Whalsay, Shetlands, dun, 193
Wharram Percy, Yorks., linear cemetery, 136
White Caterhun, Angus, hillfort, 177
White Meldon, Peebles, hillfort, 174
White Sheet Castle, Wilts., hillfort, 171
White Sheet Hill, Wilts., causewayed enclosure, 64
Whitehawk, Sussex, causewayed enclosure, 62, 63, 64
Whiteside Rig, Peebles, hillfort, 174
Wideford Hill, Orkneys, megalithic tomb, 93
Willerby Wold, Yorks., long barrow, 72, fig. 22
Willington, Notts., possible Bronze Age houses, 38
Wilsford, Wilts., nuclear cemetery, 136
Wiltrow, Shetlands, Bronze Age settlement, 45
Windmill Hill, Wilts., causewayed enclosure, 15, 16, 17, 29, 61, 62, 64, 65, 67, 75, 129, 130
Winterborne Abbas, Dorset, stone circle, 153
Winterbourne Stoke, Wilts., linear cemeteries, 135–6, fig. 48
Withypool Hill, Som., stone circle, 151
Woden Law, Roxburgh., hillfort, 175
Woodcutts, Iron Age settlement, 49
Woodhead, Cumb., possible Bronze Age house, 37–8
Woodhenge, Wilts., henge monument, 115, 119, 122, 127, 128, 129, fig. 44
Wor Barrow, Dorset, long barrow, 69, 71
Worlebury, Som., hillfort, 171
Wrekin, Shrops., hillfort, 172
Y Foel Frech, Denb., stone circles, 153
Yarnbury, Wilts., hillfort, 170, 183
Yarnbury, Yorks., henge monument, 111
Yarrows, Caithness, megalithic tomb, 93–4
Yevering Bell, Northumb., Iron Age settlement, 56; hillfort, 175, fig. 65

ADIRONDACK COMMUNITY COLLEGE
GN805.F67 1976
Forde-Johnston, James L. Prehistoric Bri

3 3341 00014152 2

GN
805
.F67
1976

Forde-Johnston,
James L.

Prehistoric Brit-
ain and Ireland

35693

OCT 16 78	DATE DUE		
NOV 5 '90			
DEC 12 '95			
MAY 06 '96			
APR 2 5 2002			
MAY 16 2002			
MAR 31 2003			

Adirondack Community College Library